REASONING INTO REALITY

REASONING
INTO
REALITY

A System-Cybernetics Model
and Therapeutic Interpretation
of Buddhist Middle Path Analysis

PETER FENNER

Deakin University

WISDOM PUBLICATIONS · BOSTON

WISDOM PUBLICATIONS
361 NEWBURY STREET
BOSTON, MASSACHUSETTS 02115 USA

Library of Congress Cataloging-in-Publication Data

Fenner, Peter G. 1949–
    Reasoning into reality: a system-cybernetics model and therapeutic inter-
pretation of Buddhist middle path analysis / Peter Fenner.
        p.   cm.
    ISBN 0-86171-060-6
    1. Mādhyamika (Buddhism)   2. Psychotherapy—Religious aspects—
Mādhyamika (Buddhism) 3. System analysis. 4. Cybernetics.
I. Title.
BQ7460.F46   1995   94–9957
294.3'42'011—dc20   CIP

            00   99   98   97   96

                6   5   4   3   2

Designed by: LJ·SAWLit'

Printed in the United States of America.

CONTENTS

CHAPTER TWO

ANALYTICAL MEDITATION

CHAPTER THREE

A SIMULATION MODEL OF MIDDLE PATH ANALYSIS

LIST OF FIGURES

PUBLISHER'S ACKNOWLEDGMENT

THE PUBLISHER ACKNOWLEDGES the kind help of the Hershey Family Foundation in sponsoring the production of this book.

ACKNOWLEDGMENTS

THIS STUDY HAS BENEFITED from the expertise and counsel of many people in Australia, India, Nepal, and the United States. In particular, I wish to thank the late Lama Thubten Yeshe, Lama Thubten Zopa Rinpoche, Geshe Thubten Loden, and Professor Geshe Lhundup Sopa for their teachings on the Middle Path *(Mādhyamika)*. Professor Ludvik Bass helped with the development of the computer model that supports the systems interpretation of the Middle Path, and Dr. Richard Hutch encouraged the overall enterprise. Dr. Manfred von Thun provided some helpful comments on the simulation model. Colin Dean helped editorially and by preparing the index. Finally, I would like to thank the editorial staff of Wisdom Publications for facilitating the transition from manuscript to book.

PREFACE

THIS STUDY HAS BEEN QUITE LONG in its germination. The original idea for developing a computer model of Middle Path (*Mādhyamika*) analysis arose when I was completing a five-week solo meditation retreat at the Tushita Retreat Centre in the hills above Dharamsala in Northern India. I was conducting practical, experiential research to support my doctoral research on the Middle Path and was inspired to speculate about possible cognitive changes that could occur when Middle Path methods of insight (*vipaśyanā*) meditation were used over a long term and in a rigorous and disciplined manner.

When I returned to Australia, I soon realized that my speculations could be aided by a graphic model since I was talking about very elevated states of consciousness that were difficult to describe in natural language. I further discovered that the development of a "graphic model" of the cognitive changes that may occur for advanced Middle Path meditators first needed the development of a "simulation model," i.e., a model that actually simulated and traced the changes I was talking about. This in turn required the development of a system-cybernetics interpretation of traditional Middle Path methods of meditation.

The development of the simulation model was aided by the input of Professor Ludvig Bass of the Department of Mathematics, University of Queensland. Professor Bass's professional expertise lies in the mathematical modeling of human organ functions. He also has a deep interest in the Christian mystic, Nicholas of Cusa, and in Eastern philosophies. (His interest in Eastern mysticism arose during a period of post-doctoral research with the eminent Austrian physicist, Erwin Schrodinger.) These interests have led Professor Bass to produce his own speculative research on mysticism, paradox, and neural brain changes.

My interest in the development of a therapeutic interpretation of Middle Path analysis arose when, in 1987, I began offering practical workshops in Buddhist psychology to help professionals in Australia and Hawaii. The first workshops were titled "Therapeutic Applications of Buddhist Psychology." They presented general Buddhist techniques of insight, compassion, and visualization meditation in a form that could readily be adapted for use in a clinical setting. For example, the exercises in these workshops were usually done in pairs with partners providing feedback and correction to each other in a variety of ways. The "meditative way of being" was thus cultivated in the context of a relationship with another person rather than privately, as is the case in traditional Buddhist meditation.

Within these workshops I also included instruction and exercises in Middle Path methods for developing an experience of openness (*śūnyatā*). Participating professionals consistently found these useful and asked how Middle Path methods of analysis could be used with their clients. It is in response to these needs that I have begun to develop a framework for using Middle Path methods of paradoxical analysis in a Western urban therapeutic setting.

INTRODUCTION

THE MIDDLE PATH (*Mādhyamika*) is a Buddhist tradition of applied philosophical psychology that has been developed over 1700 years of disciplined research. This research was conducted by thousands of highly trained scholar-practitioners in the Buddhist universities and training colleges in Northern India and Sino-Tibet.[1] Such research has been based on well defined and rigorously implemented procedures of self-reflective analysis. It has also been scrutinized through the institution of peer debate. This intensity of research has produced a highly tuned and extremely powerful set of cognitive techniques designed to access a freer and more open way of being in the world. According to Middle Pathers, the techniques and procedures that they have developed have made a radically more satisfying and dynamic way of living available to generations of Indian and Asian practitioners. This claim is to be taken seriously if for no other reason than the fact that the Middle Path tradition has been acknowledged for centuries in the Indo-Asian cultures as perhaps the pinnacle of Indo-Asian intellectual efforts—an assessment that is now being echoed in the West.

The aim of this study is to present the Middle Path tradition in a form that is intelligible and relevant to a professional Western readership. More specifically, we wish to present the Middle Path methods of philosophical and psychological analysis in a form that displays their *essential and unique structure*. At the same time we want this account to create possibilities for the application of Middle Path methods of analysis *in practical domains,* since at root we are dealing with a system designed for the betterment of human life.

The task of producing an intelligible and relevant interpretation of Middle Path analysis is achieved in this study by translating traditional Buddhist Middle Path thought into the contemporary language of psychology and system-cybernetics theory. In doing this the tradition becomes accessible to a much wider professional audience. It is our claim that this study presents the Middle Path in a form that is now intelligible and relevant to the disciplines of philosophy, psychology, psychotherapy, and information processing.

In preparing this study we have chosen a system-cybernetics framework for two reasons: (1) it provides a sound and recognized basis for the interdisciplinary intentions of this study and (2) it allows us to develop a computer-based simulation of Middle Path analysis. The requirement that we produce a computer model has forced us to be rigorous and precise in our description of Middle Path procedures. It has also had the benefit of ensuring that the interpretation we are presenting has genuinely left its original and uniquely Indo-Tibetan cultural moorings behind.

At heart the traditional Middle Path is an applied philosophical psychology. Hence a genuine reinterpretation also needs to capture the preeminently and overriding practical and existential intentions of Middle Path analysis.

While pockets of a contemplative and religious application may develop in Western Buddhist institutes, we anticipate that a quasi-monastic setting will not provide a primary context for future applications of Middle Path techniques.

In 1984 the Dalai Lama suggested that the Middle Path understanding of openness (*śūnyatā*) could have a place in

Western psychotherapeutic practice.[2] There are strong prima facie grounds that psychotherapy will become a major area for Middle Path techniques since Middle Path analysis constitutes an active and cognitive form of intervention that already has parallels with some existing forms of therapy such as Rational Emotive Therapy and Reality Therapy.

While we anticipate that the development of a fully fledged therapeutic application will require the work of a team consisting of Tibetan and Western Middle Path practitioners and professional counselors and therapists, in this study we will outline some extensions and variations to Middle Path analysis that could be applied in urban clinical settings.

The study is developed in four chapters. The first relatively short chapter provides an explanation of the principles that undergird a "system-cybernetics" interpretation of traditional Middle Path literature. This chapter also provides some background on the use and value of computer models in describing cognitive systems.

The second chapter describes the assumptions, principles, and procedures of Middle Path analysis. It is an adaptation of work that appeared in *The Ontology of the Middle Way*.[3] I have included it in this monograph since the model in Chapter Three refers directly to my analysis of Middle Path analytical meditation. The first sections lay out the logical structure of the analytical methods used by Middle Path practitioners. The middle sections outline some traditional formats of Middle Path analysis and then develop a template that serves to describe the essence of all Middle Path analyses. The final sections make some observations about the relationship between Middle Path analysis and the Buddhist experience of openness.

The third chapter develops an exploratory model of advanced

Middle Path analysis. This model is based on a computer simulation of the cognitive changes that most likely occur when Middle Path analysis is used in the hands of experienced practitioners. The model provides us with a benchmark, a core account of Middle Path analysis to which we can recurrently refer when extending Middle Path analysis into the much more fluid and ill-defined contexts that occur in clinical settings.

The final chapter offers a practical extension to the previous chapters by outlining how Middle Path analysis can be applied in the areas of counseling and psychotherapy. This chapter examines the main differences between monastic and clinical settings and examines the implications this will have on future Western applications of Middle Path techniques. This chapter also provides a set of analytical templates that are suggestive of how Middle Path analysis will look in a contemporary Western setting.

ABBREVIATIONS

AK   *Abhidharmakośa* [*Collection on Phenomenology*] of Vasubandhu

BCA   *Bodhicaryāvatāra* [*Introduction to the Evolved Lifestyle*] of Śāntideva

ISP   *Introduction to Systems Philosophy* by Ervin Laszlo

JIABS Journal of the International Association of Buddhist Studies

JIP   Journal of Indian Philosophy

MA   *Madhyamakāvatāra* [*Introduction to the Middle Path*] of Candrakīrti

MABh *Madhyamakāvatāra-bhāṣya* [*Commentary on* Introduction to the Middle Path] of Candrakīrti

MK   *Mūlamadhyamakakārikā* [*Principal Stanzas on the Middle Path*] of Nāgārjuna

PEW   *Philosophy East and West*

PP   *Prasannapadā* [*Clear Words*] of Candrakīrti.

SSE   *System, Structure and Experience* by Ervin Laszlo

SSW   *Systems View of the World* by Ervin Laszlo.

[For full details see Bibliography]

1

SYSTEMIC MODELING
AND THE MIDDLE PATH

Perspectivism and Contextualization

THE THEORETICAL BASIS and support for the system-cybernetics modeling of a descriptive literature, such as Buddhist meditational texts on the Middle Path (*Mādhyamika*), lies with the hypotheses of perspectivism and contextualization. Perspectivism is the view that objects of comprehension may be known and described from more than one point of view. Contextualization is the view that the vantage points that are adopted, in the comprehension and description of phenomena, are conditioned by cultural and presuppositional factors.

Cognitive Structures and Natural Systems

These hypotheses, in turn, are based on (1) the further hypothesis that experience and knowledge are structured by cognitive categories, and (2) an assumption that descriptions have referents. This first hypothesis is recognizably part of the Kantian thesis, namely, that experience is necessarily categorical. In this view, all experience presupposes, and is structured by, "categories of the intellect." Empirical knowledge is therefore necessarily mediated by fundamental categories such as time, space, shape, etc. The assumption is that descriptions make reference to "natural systems." In the case of texts, this is to say no more than that they have an extra-textual referent, or in other words, that they describe something other than themselves. That "something else" is a natural system. In the case of meditation texts, they describe psychological transformations. Our definition of a natural system is: any phenomenon or collection of phenomena that displays a discernible pattern of constancy and/or change.[4] Such a definition is very general and yet includes the essential point that different textual contexts, i.e., different descriptions, may be describing different things and processes.[5] As to the constituents of natural systems, they may, in our definition, be real or ideational.[6] The difference between these may be defined in terms of location. Real systems we understand to be located in space and to have an extramental reality, i.e., are *ens reale*. Ideational systems, as systems of thought, conation, and volition have a mental reality, and thus have an ideational reality, i.e., are *ens rationis*. Meditational texts usually describe cognitive systems.[7]

PERSPECTIVISM

Given that textual materials describe natural systems, and that such natural systems are known through cognitive categories, perspectivism holds that natural systems can be *known, ordered,* and *interpreted* in a number and perhaps any number of ways. As Laszlo writes with reference to models: "If we assume that reality is merely mapped by the models and not determined by them, it follows that the models give so many perspectives of what may be a common core of events."[8] Applying this to textual descriptions it means that meditational transformations can be known, organized, and described around different structural and systemic categories and relationships. Perspectivism, then, at this point parts company with the Kantian thesis and holds that instantiations of cognitive categories exist contingently and not necessarily. In other words, it holds that categories of order, relationship, etc., are "empirically evolved"[9] rather than *a priori* givens. In sum, the view of perspectivism is that the perceptions of pattern, intelligibility, coherency, and even consistency are relative, not absolute, and that any one body of data can be cognized and described through different conceptual schemes. For the most part, this is the view of contemporary philosophy and science.

CONTEXTUALISM

Contextualism we may see as a corollary to perspectivism. It is the view that cognitive categories are conditioned by some number of factors, and that isomorphies exist between cognitive categories and conditioning factors. This last point is to say that a non-random relationship is seen to obtain between the occurrences of at least certain categories and influences.[10] The conditions and influences at work in the formation of cognitive categories have, in the last fifty years or so, become the subject of theoretical and empirical research. The major influences are sociological and intellectual, and can be grouped under the categories, cultural, linguistic, and epistemological. The thesis that culture influences cognitive processing has been initiated with research by the structural anthropologist Levi-Strauss, and more recently carried into the field of religion by the sociologist Peter Berger. Their thesis is that social, cultural, mythic, and religious belief structures and practices partake in the formation of worldviews (Weltanschauungen) and that different beliefs, structures, etc., give rise to different worldviews. The case for linguistic conditioning has been made by Benjamin Whorf, Ludwig Wittgenstein, Noam Chomsky, and others.[11] The generic thesis here is that language structures and linguistic patterns are influential in determining cognitive and perceptual processes. As Whorf writes: "We cut up and organize the spread and flow of

3

events as we do largely because, through our mother tongue we are parties of an agreement to do so not because nature itself is segmented in exactly that way for all to see."[12] Epistemology as a theory of valid cognition is similarly contextually determined. This is to say that there is no one "means for obtaining and validating knowledge" but many, and that the "*perceived* means of justification and validation" can depend on a multitude of factors such as prevalent philosophical theories and religions, cultural, and scientific influences. Thus, to the extent that different epistemologies and their coordinate instruments—such as the empirical, rational, hypothetico-deductive, nominal, intuitional, testimonial, etc.—locate different ontologies, one has the situation that cognitions undergirded by different epistemologies can come to realize different ontologies with respect to the one subject matter. Philosophical sanction for this view was first framed with Whitehead's "objective relativism," and now gains support from theorizing that has accompanied the growth of scientific knowledge. Of mention are the theories of Popper, Laszlo, and Feyerabend.[13]

The contextualization of cognition, then, is the mediation and interpretation of apprehension and understanding by cultural, linguistic, and philosophical factors. What it means, with respect to any area of understanding, is that it will be known, interpreted, and described differently by different cultures, and different language and philosophical communities. Hence, different individuals and communities can and do create different mappings, descriptions, and explanations of the one phenomenon. The relevancy, meaning, and utility of any mapping within a community depends on its conforming with that community's presuppositions, language, etc.

RECONSTRUCTION

Reconstruction, then, is the transposing of a map from one context into another. Where the contexts bridge different language communities, this involves translation in the ordinary sense. Where the philosophical, scientific, religious, and cultural milieus differ, this involves a re-interpretation and re-description, such that a new expression accords, in terms of relevancy and comprehension, with the expressive *genres*, and presuppositions obtaining in the context being constructed into.[14] In the case of re-contextualizing Indian meditational texts and placing their content into a contemporary Western intellectual milieu, reconstruction primarily involves translation in the sense of bridging various intellectual, descriptive, theoretical, and practical paradigms, the principal ones of which we will highlight shortly. To the extent that these paradigms rely on various types of specialized languages, viz., the theological, philosophical, logical, scientific, etc., the process of reconstruction can be viewed as translation in an extended sense.

The languages, or if one prefers, paradigms or milieus into which translations can be made, are theoretically limited only by the number of extant languages and their contexts. Pragmatic considerations, though, such as the usefulness of making a reconstruction, the currency of the context into which a reconstruction is made, and the degree to which paradigm incommensurabilities can be bridged, will in practice reduce the number to some subset of possible languages.

Though there are good reasons for using the system-cybernetics approach we are employing here, there are no theoretical reasons precluding reconstructing around some other genre of description and explanation. In fact one need not look outside of the Middle Path and Perfect Insight (*Prajñā-pāramitā*) systems to find alternative reconstructions. Once we view meditational texts as describing a "natural system," we see not only that they give a contextualized description of religio-philosophical understanding, but that they are already a reconstruction insofar as they are embedded within and have evolved out of a tradition of Perfect Insight exposition. There we see a tradition that begins with the Perfect Insight Sūtras, which are characterized by a pre-formal, imaginal, and repetitive literary style that is typically character-ized by the use of non-cognitive language. The first clear recon-struction of the sutric exposition is by Nāgārjuna. In his texts one sees the Perfect Insight Sūtras transformed into the Mādhyamika; a rigorously philosophical literature that is characterized through-out by trenchant argumentation and syntactical precision. The impetus for Nāgārjuna's reconstruction was a felt need to estab-lish the *validity* of the Perfect Insight worldview. Five hundred years after Nāgārjuna, Candrakīrti in the *Introduction to the Middle Path* (*Madhyamakāvatāra*) typifies yet another contextual-ization of the Perfect Insight, by writing in a genre that is condi-tioned by the educational practices of the Buddhist monastic uni-versities, and which takes full cognizance of the Indian philo-sophical climate. Śāntideva also continues this genre in the *Introduction to the Evolved Lifestyle* (*Bodhicaryāvatāra*). Thus, in the *Introduction to the Middle Path* and the *Introduction to the Evolved Lifestyle* we have texts that are sometimes doxastic, often styled in the form of a debate (*vigraha, rtsod pa*),[15] and which place the Middle Path in the context of Hindu philosophies (*darśana*) and rival Buddhist systems. These characteristics make texts like the above precursors to the later development of tenets (*siddhānta, grub mtha*) literature: a *genre* of meta-systemic texts in which one finds doxological descriptions of the Middle Path.[16] That literature also brings to a climax a trend evident in the chronology of these various reconstructions, in which non-cognitive discourse is progressively replaced by cognitive discourse.[17]

In summary, the sanction for reconstructing Middle Path analysis within a theory of "general systems theory" and system-cybernetics principles derives from our assumptions (1) that Middle Path texts, such as those we have already referred to, intend reference to a "natural system" which is best defined as the perfection of insight (*prajñā*) through the cognition of openness (*śūnyatā*) and (2) that its descriptions and explanations of the Middle Path have been conditioned by various social, though mainly intellectual and practical factors.[18]

Such assumptions, and precedents for reconstruction, can also be found in the expositional traditions of the Middle Path itself. In the past the Middle Path has been reshaped a number of times because of changing intellectual and practical circumstances. A "system-cybernetics description" is yet another contextualization, and one that gives another perspective on the perfection of insight. As such, systemic reconstruction is in sympathy with both traditional and contemporary concerns.

SYSTEMS EXPLANATIONS AND SIMULATION MODELING

The first suggestion to utilize systems thought in religious studies was by Frederick Streng in an article titled "Religious Studies: Processes of Transformation"[19] published in 1974. That paper refers to the work of Bertalenffy and Laszlo, and implicitly states a case for placing the field of religious phenomena into a systems and structuralist orientation. According to Streng, the academic study of religion is best accomplished by interpreting and organizing ". . . religious data in such a way as to expose the dynamics of religion as different processes of ultimate transformation."[20] This reconstrual of the data involves an appreciation of perspectivism[21] and "...development of theoretical constructs based on the interaction of elements in a process of change."[22] Streng also suggests a focus on the perception of the "inner structures of human consciousness."[23]

The entry of system principles into Buddhology is with a paper by Joanna Macy entitled "Systems philosophy as a hermeneutic for Buddhist teaching."[24] Her paper made certain preliminary observations about the feasibility of a symbiotic relationship between Western philosophy and Buddhism, and is significant for its application of Laszlo's cybernetic models to "...the concept and practice of mindfulness in the Theravadin tradition, and those of projection in the Mahāyāna."[25] More recently Macy has contributed a major book length study under the title *Mutual Causality in Buddhism and General Systems Theory: The Dharma of Natural Systems.*[26] The application of systemic devices in the elucidation and interpretation of specific Buddhist texts has yet to be attempted in a sustained way, though Herbert Guenther[27] has drawn on the thought of Erich Jantsch in a supportive role in order to contemporize his translations and studies of the Buddhist Complete Fulfillment (*rDzogs chen*) tradition.

The focus on diachronic systems and structures of consciousness, as suggested by Streng, makes a direct inroad into computational simulations and more particularly into the possibility of modeling and scrutinizing systems of thought conditioning and transformation. As transformational systems are both more radical and more clearly specified in the Eastern rather than Western religions, modeling is much more suited to the former. The Eastern psycho-philosophical systems claim to move consciousnesses from bound states into a variety of liberated states of consciousness and do this in part via the application of various psycho-physiological devices most of which are fairly well articulated.

Computer models, then, may enable us to validate such systems of consciousness transformation and to perceive the eduction of liberated mind-states from their germinal state. In other words, they may permit us to develop an etiology and/or confirm existing etiologies which (claim to) account for the arising, existence, and characteristics of spiritually liberated and enlightened mind-states.

BUDDHISM AND SYSTEMS MODELING

Buddhism is singularly clear in delineating determinants for the hypostatization and transformation of consciousness states. In Buddhism, "The mind is at all times clear-light (*prabhāsvara*) in nature (though) spoiled by accidental faults."[28] The experience or realization of its diaphanous nature is concomitant with liberation and is achieved by a removal of all affective and cognitive staining. The philosopher Nāgārjuna (150–250 A.D.) writes: "There is *mokṣa* (release or liberation) from the destruction of *karmic* defilements which are but conceptualization. These arise from mere conceptual play (*prapañca*) which are in turn banished in *śūnyatā* (or openness)."[29]

Within this system, states of consciousness within mental continua (*citta-saṁtāna*) are determined by the dynamic interplay between the primary influences of habituating and de-habituating forces. The former are accounted for by the Buddhist theory of action (*karma*) and its residues (*vāsanā, saṁskāra*), while the latter are specified within Buddhist principles of meditational practice, and most directly in the techniques and mechanics of analytical insight (*vipaśyanā*). These influences, we will see, function in opposition to each other insofar as action and its residues tend to bind or hypostatize movement within a stream of consciousness where insight by penetrating and breaking down reifying structures is seen as unbinding streams of consciousness;

in other words, as liberating them. This dehabituation and hence freeing of consciousness from its cognitive, perceptual, and emotional limitations is viewed within the soteriological context as a process of consciousness purification (*vyavadāna*)—a process which is facilitated by and in fact dependent upon the initiation and employment of contemplative exercises which consist largely in the structural manipulation of thought-forms.

Further adding to the amenability—though not necessarily ease—of modeling Buddhist thought transformation, is the claim that the above influences, when fully documented, will supply a non-residual explanation of all consciousness states (*citta*), mental phenomena (*caitta*), and transformations. This is to say that its understanding of consciousness states, as embedded in causal nexi, and transformed dialectically and as detailed in *karma-vasanic* principles and the mechanics of analytical insight respectively, gives, in theory at least, a complete and particular account of consciousness determinants. This is in distinction, for example, to theistic religions and transformational paths which introduce indeterminacy by the inherently inexplicable influence of grace. Hence in terms of explanatory criteria and independently of the credibility of any given explanation of mind-states, it is desirable to model and test explanations in which all factors claim to be accounted for and specified—in other words, in which the stochastics are minimized or eliminated altogether. To argue for anything other than this ideal runs counter to the philosophical-empirical method.

THE VALUE OF A SYSTEMS MODEL

The value and uses of reconstruction and especially systemic modeling are many. They arise from the bases which make reconstruction and modeling possible and legitimate. To recall, these are the principles of perspectivism and contextuality. They specify that cognition is a dynamic relationship between a cognized and *conditioned* cognizer. The interaction of knower and known is conditioned by a multiplicity of factors which include language, culture, religion, and philosophy. The end-product of this conditioning is that different cultures, groups of intellectuals, and language communities, etc., confront the world from different perspectives and so come to perceive, know, and describe it differently. Each intellectual milieu constitutes a paradigm of comprehension and expression. As paradigms they exhibit an internal coherency and meaning but manifest incommensurabilities of meaning and expression between each other. In the case of differing cultural paradigms—using the term in its broadest sense—one has cross-cultural incommensurabilities.

The function and value, then, of reconstruction is to transpose ideas from one cultural paradigm into another and so serve to bridge incommensurabilities. Where a transposition is skillfully executed into a contemporary conceptual milieu and expressive *genre*, the results are additionally valuable in terms of relevancy and comprehensibility. When, for example, systems constructs are used the advantages that accrue include the bridging of inter-disciplinary incommensurabilities and the bringing of a perceived precision, perspicuity, and coherency to a set of ideas that may otherwise be relatively opaque and ambiguous.

These leading values will be briefly discussed under the headings: (1) Translation and commensurability, (2) Explanation and description, and (3) Experimentation and validation.

TRANSLATION AND COMMENSURABILITY

The first major area of use for systems models is in the task of facilitating milieu and paradigm translations, and presenting information related to contemplative disciplines in a form that

11

permits a cross-disciplinary commensurability. These two facets draw on the relevancy and neutrality of systems representations respectively.

For the most part, contemplative literatures are culturally distanced from contemporary milieus of understanding and explanation. Much of the literature is relatively archaic, hence temporally removed from the twentieth century, and in the case of Eastern literature it is also geographically distanced. Added together these mean that most of the traditional texts purporting to describe meditative and spiritual techniques and methods, and goals and attainments derive from language, literary, expressive, and conceptual milieus that are different—and often radically so—from their contemporary Western counterparts.

At this point we may just mention some of the main differences in the expression of ideas. By and large the contemplative traditions tend to give discrete-state descriptions of yogic processes. That is to say they give finite, or fixed-state descriptions, oftentimes in forms that resemble doxologies.[30] That same predilection for lists is not shared by Western intellectual disciplines. In preference to describing transformations by some number of profiles, Western disciplines tend to locate "rules," "laws," or "principles" that govern and determine transformations. Instantiated descriptions or profiles of processes, if and when required, are extracted by the insertion of the appropriate information into the functions that describe systematic changes. In other words, contemporary Western disciplines colligate rather than instantiate collections of data. This results in continuous change or linear-flow descriptions rather than discrete-change ones.

This emphasis on continuous-change description has produced impressive expressive tools such as flowcharts and digraphics. From a scientific viewpoint such panoptic devices

12

can produce a more economical description than cataloging phenomena, and also have a heuristic value in the development of explanatory hypotheses. The extentional and linear-flow descriptions are respectively evidenced in Buddhist path-structure literature and systemic models. Related to these traits is a tendency for Eastern philosophical literatures to give atomistic or elemental interpretations of phenomena[31] and for Western disciplines to give "molar" interpretations in which the behavior of phenomena as a whole are described.[32]

Besides the need for appropriate concept translation, traditional and contemporary milieus differ with respect to foci of attention. This is to say they vary not only in regard to *how* data is explained and presented, but in *what* is to be explained. They have different practical and theoretical needs and requirements, such that what is needful of an explanation within the ambit of Western scholasticism need not require an explanation within a traditional Asian philosophical context, and *vice versa*. A major difference in this regard would be the focus of Western disciplines on causal accounts for the stability and change of systems, and a focus on such phenomena within systems as limiting cases and change-over points.

These foregoing points signify and in fact are symptomatic of different practical and theoretical needs and requirements on behalf of the authors and readership of traditional religio-philosophical texts and contemporary intellectual disciplines. The differences in part arise from a traditional emphasis on description and a contemporary one on explanation. They result in different foci of attention and hence change not only *how* data is explained, but *what* is explained. A clear example of this is a traditional interest in the constituents of systems and a contemporary focus on relationships. Other areas where contemporary

13

descriptions differ from traditional Indian ones are the location of necessary and sufficient conditions, the specification of hypothetical and not only empirical limits to the behavior of systems, and an attempt to causally account for the stability and change within systems. In terms of reconstruction and modeling these differences mean that a traditional description and its systemic counterpart will find, locate, and describe different aspects, distinctions, and relationships.

At the same time that simulation modeling assists in the re- and new-specification of traditional literatures, it serves the very valuable task of presenting an important body of knowledge in a form that facilitates its cross-disciplinary comprehensibility and assimilation. The explanatory and expressive devices it uses, such as mentioned above, are genuinely interdisciplinary, and theory- and topic-neutral. These devices have a cathartic effect on reductive and specialized languages. As such they act to overcome incommensurabilities between disciplines and paradigms of explanation, and in so doing can make a significant literature that would otherwise be relatively impenetrable, open and available to disciplines such as psychology, philosophy, and Western religious traditions. In other words, systemic and structuralist devices act as a bridge between disciplines, by creating a metalanguage and doctrinally or subject-neutral mode of description. With respect to religious literature such expressive devices make it possible to de-theologize, or in other words, secularize religious concepts. In so doing "...the study of religion can be interlaced with studies of non-religious data."[33] Systemic thinking additionally facilitates the cross-cultural study of religion[34] allowing religions to fully express their various contents without being reduced to one or another basic or "only" model of religious life, doctrine, experience, etc.

14

EXPLANATION AND DESCRIPTION

The second and very important usage of modeling lies in its ability to succinctly, unambiguously, and informatively describe the cognitive, affective, and volitional systems encountered in contemplative disciplines. In this regard, symbolic representations as may be produced computationally can be more informative in certain areas than natural language descriptions. This is because natural language syntax and grammar is restricted in its ability to give unambiguous descriptions of continuous change systems and recursive processes. Computational models, and the symbolic representations they produce, can, on the other hand, describe behaving systems. Hence, with respect to transformational systems, where natural language descriptions are necessarily only partial, symbolic models can map *all* variations and modifications. As yogic paths are systems in transformation, symbolic models are well equipped to describe these paths. Other areas where representative models are heuristically informative is in the description of so-called second-order models, where some number of systems are viewed as sub-systems which are interrelated in such ways as to produce a high-level system. Such second-order construction permits one to perceive the relationships and dynamic processes occurring *within* one integral or overriding system. The type of model presented in Chapter Three is just such a second-order model. The ability of representative models to capture the stochastics of processes and the balance between the indeterminateness and determinateness of systems we have mentioned previously.

In summary, non-verbalizable conceptualizations are particularly relevant to contemplative systems, characterized as they are by both path structures and a reputed linguistic ineffability. By

15

supplying us with "new concepts and symbolisms" they make "…it possible to conceive of, think about, and ask questions about new types of possibilities."[35]

EXPERIMENTATION AND VALIDATION

A final area worthy of mention, if only briefly, is the ability of simulation models to test the adequacy of the explanations they model. For example, when texts detail transformative principles and make efficacy claims in terms of the causes behind and production of meditative states, such claims can be examined by regarding the model as an analogical or isomorphic model. Computation experiments can then be made with the model, which test either the accuracy of purported transformative principles or—given evidence for, or an assumption of the reasonableness of posited transformative principles—the goals posited for meditative techniques and ancillary conditions. In other words, hypothetical structures, cases, and conditions can be computed with a working model, and hence evidence the coherency, consistency, and accuracy of meditative literatures that describe specific results arising from specified causes and conditions.

In summary, the value and utility of simulation models and systemic explanations are many. Perhaps more relevant than any other use is their ability to help in explaining and determining real possibilities concerning human potentials.

SYSTEMS AND MODELS

In his primer on systems philosophy, *The Systems View of the World*, Laszlo writes of system-cybernetics analysis that, "It is a mode of organizing existing findings in reference to the concept of systems, and systemic properties and relationships."[36] He goes on to locate systems by drawing a distinction between the systemic arrangement of data and structuralist descriptions in which processes, rather than morphologies, respectively serve to organize sets of data. With respect to social systems, but generalized beyond that, Laszlo writes:

> To define the structure of the system…is to give an internal *state* description of it. The other mode of analyzing social systems centers on its *dynamic functions.* Here the internal set of constraints which give the system its specific morphological structure are related to sets of external factors, 'inputs' and 'outputs.'[37]

The "internal set of constraints" and "sets of external factors" act within any system as "control processes," which *channel* some input through a system and *determine* its various throughput modifications and final output state.[38] As a result, systemic analysis is concerned with the conceptual abstraction of "control processes" and the framing of systemic descriptions around specified control processes. Its focus of attention is accordingly on constancies and changes within and between systems rather than with the states of their components or elements. More specifically, systemic analysis locates species of order, elemental patterns and configurations, and, periodicities, constancies, and recursions with respect to these orderings and patterns. In the case of goal-directed and evolving systems, such as we have in the cognitive changes induced by insight meditation, systemic analysis is also concerned to discern patterns of hierarchy, stability, adaption, individuation, and unification.

SUBSYSTEMS AND ENVIRONMENTS

Consonant with the holistic tenor of Laszlo's thought, and as corollaries to the systemic assumption that all objects, real and ideational, are interrelated[39] are the additional assumptions that no systems are truly isolated and all may be interdependent and informationally and energetically interactive. System-cybernetics further assumes that non-transitive and non-symmetric dependencies can obtain between systems. From these assumptions system-cybernetics derives the concepts of hierarchical structuring, environments, and subsystems. These concepts make it possible to organize data in heuristically powerful ways. It means, for example, that any number of systems can be coordinated interactively such that they form subsystems within some holistic framework. If these subsystems are not related bi-directionally they can be ordered in terms of informational and/or energetic dependencies, and thus structured hierarchically.[40] Such integration of subsystems within systems and systems within environments[41] is a case of second-order analysis and description.[42]

INVARIANTS

The major contribution of Laszlo to the discipline of systemic organization is his specification of systems and their behavior by the device of "invariant properties." An "invariant property" or "organizational invariance" is defined as the "non-random regularity of the coactions" of systemic components.[43] Laszlo's rationale for defining systems in terms of invariances is that:

> There can be no science of a phenomenon in a constant
> state of flux: *some* parameters must remain constant, or
> invariant under transformation. These constancies and
> invariances furnish the systemic elements in reference to
> which theoretical structures can be built, mapping the
> fluctuating phenomena under investigation."[44]

He writes further that it is an assumption of science "…that *some* theoretical mappings are valid."[45]

The discipline of systematic analysis, then, is to locate and describe systematic invariances that can be discovered by selective screening of the observed data.[46] In his work Laszlo has mapped a handful of such systems properties and their appearance "under qualitatively divergent transformations".[47]

MODELS

Models are an important and powerful research tool in system-cybernetics. Well constructed and appropriately interpreted models can serve two principal functions. They can assist in the systemic interpretation and representation of data and can test the coherency and consistency of systemic constructs and explanations. In the first capacity they act as facilitator in the abstracting of invariances and their representation in an intelligible and comprehensible form. In the second, they test the adequacy of systems explanations vis-a-vis their underlying assumptions, structures, mechanisms, relationships between subsystems, etc. These heuristic and pedagogical functions of models make their use commonplace in theory construction and testing in the empirical sciences. Models may be of two types, conceptual and simulational. A conceptual model is a systemic fabric and infrastructure that has been abstracted from some data and embedded in a procedural literature that explains how the infrastructure is mapped from the data. Simulation models are working or functioning models that attempt to simulate, mime, or mimic the *behavior* of some natural system. They presume a conceptual model and are particularly useful for describing and testing meta- or second-order analyses, i.e., those in which some number of systems are placed in an interactive relationship. In all cases models are necessarily simpler than the data they map, though they should be isomorphic to the data, and reflect its essential structural and systemic properties.

COMPUTER MODELS

Simulated models of natural systems can be produced by appropriately programmed computers. Such simulation programming does not necessarily require quantified data in the form of numerical measurements, statistical distributions, etc. They can and do compute non-numerical concepts, symbols, and processes.

A system being simulated or modeled is described[48] in terms of decision algorithms—sometimes called rate equations—which are monitored and controlled by executive commands. That is, a command or executive program controls and directs the implementation of the computational algorithms. The algorithms can be supplied with state variables which determine their behavior and can be altered to produce different simulations or vicissitudes within the one system. Thus, like many naturally occurring processes, such simulations[49] contain a variety of subroutines, some of which may change with regularity while others may change as conditions warrant. In fact, the entire state history of a simulation can be drawn upon as a decision variable "...for scheduling, and/or canceling previously scheduled, event routines."[50] The behavior of each and every entity within a simulation, can, if necessary, be partially or wholly determined by the behavior (present and past) of *all* other entities within the system. Teleological processes can be modeled insofar as "...a programmed computer may include representations of itself, its actions, possible futures, reasons for choosing, and methods of inference...."[51] The phenomena and processes being modeled can be placed in realistic environments such that they maintain their own autonomy yet are appropriately influenced by, and influential on, environmental factors and changes. The stochastics or irregularities of the dynamics within systems are programmable, for example via recourse to random sequences. In fact, the balances between autonomy and interdependence and stochasticity and determination can only be computed electromagnetically. Even with comparatively simple natural systems their principles, recursions, and interactivities are too complex to be evaluated without recourse to computers. Computer directed simulations, besides producing facsimile models or isomorphic analogs of natural systems, can additionally serve as "...devices for constructing, manipulating, analyzing, interpreting, and transforming symbolic structures of all kinds, including their own programs."[52] As such simulation programs cannot only compute a complex and hence seemingly amorphous set of data but can interpret the raw data or rather structure or re-structure it to be then displayed or represented in a more intelligible, conceptually manageable and comprehensible form. In one sense, then, computers can also be viewed as *tools* for assisting in the re-conceptualization of data.

The utility of any simulation or model is limited by its ability to mimic or emulate the natural system. That is to say, the utility that can be extracted from any simulated modeling is dependent upon the degree of correspondence between the systemic or simuland (i.e., the natural system) properties and those of the similar (i.e., the computational model). High degrees of correspondence obviously ensure high utilities. The quality being sought, then, in all simulations is for a model which is concise, lucid, logical, and expressively unambiguous and a "...precise reproduction of the simuland's observable behavior."[53] The simular reproduction or miming of the simuland is guaranteed by the scientific procedures of scrutiny and confirmation.

Given that some degree of correspondence between the natural system and simular can be obtained, the resulting model

21

can be used for a variety of purposes, all of which will be elaborated later in this work. Presently it is sufficient to say that the
utility of computer produced models is primarily heuristic and
pedagogical, i.e., inferential and illustrative. In the latter role
they can produce diagrammatic, structural, systemic, typograph-
ic, taxonomic, etc., representations of natural systems, the existence and characteristics of which have already been evidenced.
In the former role they can be used as a research tool within
empirical scientific and philosophical methodologies. In that
capacity models can, amongst other things: make theoretical
analysis of possible explanations and hence test the effectiveness
of those posited explanations; hypothesize about possibilities
and the limits of possibilities; evidence possibilities via amplia-
tive inferences from actualities; and conduct computational
experiments.

SYSTEMS EPISTEMOLOGY

Though this study is making few if any claims to validity in the
systemic sense, it is worth our while elaborating the principles
and criteria of systems evaluation, for they form the epistemic
framework that has been borne in mind. They also show why no
substantive claims for verity or accuracy have been made.

The task of systems epistemology is to justify and validate
systems constructs. As principles for evaluating any systemic
construct, a systems epistemology is comprised of a set of invariant criteria that can be applied to any data that is systematically
organized. Through providing criteria for evaluation, systems
epistemology also implicitly gives guidelines as to *how* one should
systemically construct data, or more particularly, methods for
achieving a good and accurate organization of data, assuming
these as the goals of systemic construction.

The first point coming from this definition is that systems epistemology is evaluative only in regard to systems constructs.[54] As such, there is no question of verifying or falsifying the existence and characteristics of natural systems *per se*. In other words, it is a systemic assumption that natural systems exist as bodies of empirical data which are subsequently systemically organized. By definition, the presence of any organized data is indicative of a natural system, and the ontological question proper of whether or not the data exists is outside the scope of systemic analysis.[55] The question of what constitutes the natural system in this study we will answer shortly. This non-evaluative stance of systems epistemology toward non-systemic constructs means moreover that systems epistemology does not adjudicate between alternative organizations of some natural system even when one of the organizations is a systemic construction. As Laszlo writes:

> (Systemic) interpretations do not involve modifications of existing theories, merely their translation into the synoptic framework offered by our theory. There can be no question of adjudicating among scientific theories or of revising them.[56]

There are two reasons for this non-judgmental attitude *toward* non-systemic structures, and *between* these and systemic ones. One is that some of the criteria for assessing systems constructs are specific in the sense of being designed and having relevancy only for systemic constructions. Those are the criteria shortly to be discussed under the rubric "coherency." To apply them outside of their systemic domain would be to contravene our axiom that there may be different epistemic and methodological contexts and perspectives, each with its own criteria of validation.[57] The second and related reason is that contextualization adds a pragmatic element to justification such that what are valuable and heuristically warranted criteria in one framework of organization may not be in some other.

In the case of meditation texts, which we view as both systems in their own right and as giving a structured and conditioned account of some referent system, the above restrictions to systems epistemology dictate that the integrity of a text as one contextualization will not be queried, and further that no comparative judgment is entered into vis-a-vis which interpretation of some "natural system" is more preferable, the traditional or the systemic one. In summary, systemic reconstruction is descriptive and hence not evaluative with respect to traditional accounts of meditative development. Epistemological factors enter the picture in an effort to ensure that reconstructions are systemic ones rather than another sort, and that a reconstruction is accurate.

EPISTEMOLOGICAL CRITERIA[58]

Systemic reconstruction requires a two-pronged epistemology that emphasizes correspondence and coherency. These respectively ensure a matching or isomorphy between a natural system and systemic construct and the intra-systemic cogency of a systemic construct. They further correlate with empirical and rational sources. Before elaborating these two criteria their basic functions can be usefully illustrated by noting their relationships to Boguslaw's typology of design systems,[59] for each in isolation from the other can be seen as producing one of Boguslaw's systems. Hence in combination they result in an amalgamation of two of his systems, and in so doing give us an idea of the systems design envisaged here and as determined by these two epistemological criteria. The two systems designs of relevancy here are called "formal" and "heuristic" by Boguslaw.[60] The aim of a formal design is to produce models that are simplified representations of an existing situation (i.e., a natural system).[61] The task at hand is to draw connections between a real situation and systemic model, and so the criterion of correspondence or isomorphy is predominant. Where coherency, consistency, simplicity, etc., are the basic criteria one has the production of heuristic designs in which the state or condition of a natural system may be largely unknown and in which the one-to-one modeling of a natural system necessarily ceases to be the most important criterion. The task of heuristic designs is to take some broadly conceived subject matter and then to describe it within principles rather than "laws." The principles are transformational invariants and give a hypothetical description rather than claim empirical correspondences.[62] From this we see that coherency, etc., is concerned with intra-systemic formalities and that correspondence is concerned with accurately depicting a natural event.

COHERENCE

The criterion of coherence is more straightforward and less problematic than that of isomorphy, so we will discuss it first. Under the rubric "coherence" we refer to a criterion which stipulates that systemic constructs should be demonstrably coherent, cogent, consistent, complete, simple, and reasonable. By and large these criteria bear a non-technical meaning and hence require little explanation. Laszlo makes a fairly concise statement of the coherency and consistency requirement when he writes that "the task is to map...into a common internally consistent framework wherein...propositions become mutually reinforcing as descriptions and explanations of one reality with a rationally knowable, overarching, species of order."[63] "Complete" means to give a non-residual description. "Simplicity" means to furnish constructs that are economic and free of redundancies, irrelevancies, and repetitions.[64] "Cogency" refers especially to the heuristic power of systems models. These criteria are fulfilled by organizing constructs around invariant principles, for invariant principles—as we have defined and will use them—provide the necessary order and organizational infrastructure for ensuring their satisfaction. The faculty and ability of invariant principles to organize data in terms of these criteria is the very reason for their emergence as organizational facilitators and subsequent employment in the latter half of this thesis. The satisfaction of these criteria in the case of meta-systems or second-order constructs is obtained by the testing of working models. If a simulation model works, i.e., displays the desired invariants and produces the relevant results, it shows that a functioning systems description can be given and evidences an internal validity for the described system's dynamics.

ISOMORPHY

The criterion of correspondence is a little more complex than the preceding one. A criterion of correspondence or isomorphy is introduced in order to ensure that, when a system-cybernetics description claims to be describing some natural system, it is in fact describing that natural system. This requires that there be demonstrable analogies between a natural system and its systemic description. As Streng writes with respect to religious systems, "The 'structure'…is a mental 'construct' that has its empirical base in the data, and that describes in an isomorphic way an infrastructure of religious transformation."[65] The degree or resolution with which the natural system's infrastructure is displayed in the systemic construct cannot be strictly specified for it depends on many factors, such as the clarity and data with which a natural system is known and the purposes for which a systemic organization is made. A minimum requirement is that the crucial and essential features of the natural event must find systemic counter-parts. Streng writes that: "The categories of description...are like the directions of a map that should give approximate indications of the terrain."[66] The requirement of isomorphy, then, is fore-mostly an empirically based criteria in that reference is made to empirical data, i.e., a natural system.[67]

In many circumstances there is little ambiguity and few grounds for equivocation over what constitutes a natural sys-tem.[68] This is because the parameters whereby one system or event is demarcated from others are easily located and the details of its internal characteristics are able to be well defined. This is not so with meditational phenomena for there are a number of ways in which the "natural system" can be defined. For our pur-poses we take the view that the natural system is a cognitve reali-ty, some features of which can be distinguished in language and other descriptive media, such as graphic models. In this study the system-cybernetics model will seek to map key features of Middle Path analysis as this has been described in traditional Middle Path literature. The model is also supplemented by speculations about the cognitive transformations induced by Middle Path analysis.[69]

VARIANCES AND EMPHASES

The two prongs of a systems epistemology, namely, systemic coherency and correspondency, can result in disparities and dis-crepancies between traditional literature descriptions and sys-temic models. Such variances between a traditional description and a systemic one are to be expected and to a degree tolerated, for differing criteria of validation and methods of description will naturally produce different presentations of the same body of data. An acceptance of a degree of disparity and also some means for reconciling differing interpretations is provided by a neutrality inhering in systems epistemology in regard to the emphasis that each criterion commands. This is to say that though the epistemological criteria are invariants for guiding and assessing any systemic construction, the emphasis or weighting with respect to each may vary. The systems epistemology of Laszlo, for example, expresses this epistemological relativity by accepting as valuable and legitimate a wide range of epistemological positions. He specifically excludes only radically bifurcating theories of knowledge such as one finds in radical empiricism (where the cognizer adds nothing to cognition) and ultra-rationalist or phenomenological theories (where sense cognosundum have no bearing on the acquisition of knowledge).[70] Within the *Introduction to Systems Philosophy*, for example, Laszlo advocates a firm empirical base when and wherever hard-data is available.[71] On the other hand, in the case of metaphysical systems, which have a paucity of empirical data, Laszlo advocates as primary the criteria of "intrinsic coherence, simplicity, and adequacy—in one word—elegance."[72] His systems philosophy accommodates different epistemic emphases but no one to the exclusion of the others.[73]

The tolerance and modification of variances derives, then, from a knowledge and appreciation of the fact that emphases vary not only by choice but in dependence on the subject matter being systemically analyzed. This is to say that natural and necessary correlations obtain between the relevancy of criteria and different subject matters.

2

ANALYTICAL MEDITATION

INTRODUCTION

IN THIS CHAPTER WE WILL DESCRIBE how Buddhist Middle Path practitioners (*Mādhyamikas*) use a particular form of logical analysis as an integral and essential technique within their practice of insight, or discernment (*vipaśyanā*) meditation. The form of logical analysis that Middle Pathers use is called paradoxical analysis (*prasaṅga-vicāra*)[74] and according to practitioners a state of liberation (*mokṣa*) or unconditional freedom (*nirvāṇa*) can only be gained through the skillful and diligent use of paradoxical analysis.

The chapter will be divided into three main sections. The first sections will lay out the logical structure of the paradoxical analyses used in Middle Path insight meditation. The structure outlined is common to all paradoxical analyses and elementary in that all analyses follow a single set of basic logical principles.

The middle sections of the chapter outline some traditional Indian formats of Middle Path analysis and then develop a set of generalized analytical principles. We will find that all Middle Path analyses can be resolved into the more general structure. The final sections make some observations about the relationship between paradoxical analysis and the experience of insight that occurs within the Middle Path methods of meditation.

According to Middle Pathers insight into openness is developed through analysis (*vicāra*). For example, the great seventh century Indian Middle Path philosopher Candrakīrti [MA: 6.116–117] wrote that:

> When things [are conceived to intrinsically] exist, then conceptuality (*kalpanā*) is produced. But a thorough analysis shows how things are not [intrinsically] existent. [When it is realized that] there are no [intrinsically] existent things, conceptualization does not occur, just as for example, there is no fire without fuel.
>
> Ordinary people are restricted by their conceptualizations, but practitioners [by achieving a] non-conceptual [realization of the nature of things (*dharmatā*)] become liberated. The learned have said that the result of analysis (*vicāra*) is the reversal of conceptualization.

These verses are quite unequivocal and clear: conceptuality arises when we perceive things to be intrinsically real, and conversely, conceptuality also ceases when this false perception is removed. The rationale behind the cognition of the openness of entities and the cessation of conceptualization is that when the things referred to by thought (i.e., its referents) are not presented to consciousness, thought (or conceptualization itself) has no basis. It has nothing to rest on and work with (i.e., it is unfuelled), and so it also stops.[75]

The reason here is explained by Śāntideva in the *Introduction to the Evolved Lifestyle* [BCA: 9.34–35] who writes:

> When one asserts that nothing exists [and there is] no perception of the things that are the object of investigation, then how can existence, being separate from a basis, stay before the intellect? When neither things nor non-things are placed before the intellect, then there is no other route, it lacks any support [and achieves] the supernatural peace.

Candrakīrti's *Commentary to the Introduction to the Middle Path* [MABh] makes the point that the disappearance of conceptuality comes as a direct result of analysis, and such dissipation of conceptuality is concomitant with the onset of the insight into reality (*tattva*). This last point also accords with the Expansive Career path-structure where for example, advanced practitioners (*bodhisattva*) at the level called Immovable (*acalābhūmi*)—the point at which henceforward they cognize openness uninterruptedly—are free from conceptuality (*vikalpanā, rnam rtog*). The absence of conceptuality that is talked about here is not the removal of all thought and ideation. Rather it is the eradication of a cognitive substratum that is responsible for *ontologizing* types of conceptions.[76]

Śāntideva in his *Introduction to the Evolved Lifestyle* [BCA] confirms Candrakīrti's claim that Middle Path analysis leads to liberation. In reply to a query that analysis may get bogged down in an infinite regress with no natural conclusion he writes (9.111) that,

> Once an object of investigation has been investigated, there is no basis for investigation. Since there is no basis [further analysis] does not arise, and that is called unconditional freedom (*nirvāṇa*).

MIDDLE PATH ANALYSIS

In the Middle Path, analysis (*vicāra*) refers to a particularly rigorous form of rational investigation. By "rational" we mean that it is based on conceptual analysis (*rtog par dpyod*) in contrast to say the *perceptual* examination of some entity that may result in an increased understanding of its composition and behavior. This is to say that Middle Path analysis is concerned with the *status* of the various things that we say exist as opposed to their empirical details.

"Analysis" refers to a method of inquiry that is designed to counter the natural tendency for thinking to automatically proliferate and perpetuate itself. Thus, the type of conceptual analysis used in Middle Path insight inquiry (*vipaśyanā*) is designed to progressively break down and finally bring a complete halt to ontologizing ways of thinking. The gradual breaking down of ontological forms of conceptuality is the same as a progressive induction of the insight into openness (*śūnyatā*). As Robert Thurman writes, "...enlightenment as wisdom is perfected as the culmination of the most refined rational inquiry, not at the cost of reason."[77] In summary, Middle Path analysis is a form of rational investigation that aims at inducing insight into the open texture of reality by exposing, at an existential level, the insubstantiality or non-intrinsic existence of entities.

Thus, analysis induces the very insight that is understood to free people from the bonds of suffering, pain, and confusion (*samsara*). Analysis involves searching for intrinsically existent entities and failing to find them. This is accomplished by the use of paradoxical consequences (*prasaṅga, thal 'gyur*). Paradoxical consequences expose logical contradictions (*rigs pai 'gal pa*) that naturally and necessarily inhere in *all* ontological positions. By an ontological position we mean a viewpoint that "This IS such-and-such," or "This ISN'T a such-and-such," or "This IS how it is," or "This ISN'T the case."

In other words, an ontological position makes a univocal, existential claim. It is any position that is asserted as though it is definite, absolute, and certain. While the notion of an "ontological position" does include the dogmatically asserted opinions and claims that we and others may make in our conversations about religion, ethics, metaphysics, politics, business, etc., it also includes a set of automatic and background assessments about which we are *so* certain that we do not even need to talk or think about them. These are assessments such as, "The world is external, physical, and real," or the proposition that is the focus of all Buddhist practice, "I exist." We are so sure we EXIST that it is as though the proposition "I exist" is present to us even without our having to think about it.

These are the types of assessments that Middle Path analysis examines. In the terminology of Middle Pathers, these are positions that assume that things exist in-and-of-themselves, i.e., that they have an intrinsic existence (*svabhāva*).

The rationale for using logical contradictions to disclose the non-intrinsic existence (*niḥsvabhāva*) of things is that if something exists intrinsically, then it cannot contradict its own mode of existence. And conversely, if something's mode of existence is self-contradictory, it cannot exist intrinsically.[78]

In exposing contradictions Middle Pathers act not as protagonists with their own position but as a catalyst and prompt for the analytical exercise. They invoke an analyzing mentality in themselves and offer their critical resources for others who may wish to question their ontological assumptions.

In summary, Middle Path analysis is a logically rigorous method for disclosing the open texture of reality through an insight that acts against the habitual tendency to make things real, definite, and substantial.

CHARACTERIZATION, DISCRIMINATION, AND THOUGHT FORMATION

Middle Path analysis is best understood in terms of the classical or Aristotelian model of predication.[79] On this classical model thoughts arise in a mind-stream in dependence on conceptually identifying things. In turn, entity identification depends on the ascription of characteristics or predicates to an entity. The ascription of characteristics serves to define things. Characteristics give something the boundaries that mark it off from other things. In the absence of characterization there are no entities and hence there is no basis for conceptual elaboration.

This view accords with the Buddhist theory that recognition or discrimination (*saṁjñā, du shes*) is predicative in form. According to the *Collection on Phenomenology* [AK: 1.14b], discrimination is apprehending the features (*nimitta, mtshan ma*). This position is echoed by Candrakīrti in the *Introduction to the Middle Path* [MA: 6.202]. Under this definition entity recognition depends on a conceptual (pre-verbal and often unconscious) location and ascription of features to an entity (*vastu*) that make that entity a member of a class. Thus entities are abstracted from the field of experience in dependence on their perceived possession of characteristics appropriate to entities comprising different classes of entities. This structure of recognition is thus propositional and predicative for it depends on the linking of characteristics (predicates) to entities (subjects).

Thus, conceptual discrimination depends on predication, i.e., on things being defined through their possession of qualities or characteristics (*nimitta, (sva-)lakṣaṇa, dharma, ākāra, viśeṣya*, etc.).

When entities are undefined, i.e., uncharacterized, they are inconceivable. They cannot be thought about, and so they are unable to provide a basis for conceptual discernment and thought construction. Hence, discrimination creates entities through a categorial abstraction. Once there is a conceptual discernment of entities, conceptuality (*kalpanā*) is established and from this the full gamut of elaboration (*prapañca*) takes off, weaving a dense and complex web of beliefs, judgments, inferences, opinions, theories, etc., some of which we verbalize.[80] We could say that consciousness ceases to be strictly phenomenological in its activity but engages in ontologizing and evaluative activities that lead to proliferation. Once entities have been distinguished by the process of characterization, conceptuality complexifies and becomes progressively more removed from its perceptual basis.

Still, at root, conceptual proliferation and elaboration depends on and is subsequent to discriminations (*saṁjñā*) which can be analyzed in terms of subject-predicate propositions.[81] The significance of this is that nirvāṇa is the reversal of elaboration and this is accomplished by a ceasing of discriminations.[82]

THINGS ARE DEFINED BY WHAT THEY ARE NOT

Given that concepts and hence thought formation depend on characterization, the next question in tracing the evolution and involution of conceptuality is, on what does characterization depend? The insight of the Middle Path philosophers (and others such as the Taoists, Saussure, Levi-Strauss, P. Winch, G.A. Kelly) is that characterization arises in an oppositional structure.[83] According to these philosophers predicates or characteristics arise in and through a formal oppositional relation. As Paul Williams writes, "the referent of a *vikalpa* exists only as the negative of what it is not and vice versa."[84] This means that all terms are *necessarily* defined (and hence gain their meaning) with reference to what they are logically not (i.e., their logical opposite). Likewise a logical opposite is defined only on the basis of the affirmed term.[85] Each is defined, and so comes into being, in mutual dependence (*parasparāpekṣa*) on the other. Entity-characteristics are thus "other-defined" and not "self-defined." This is a principle of definition via logical opposites: that concepts are formed in the context of pairs of logical opposites. The concept of A is formed if and only if the concept of –A is formed and vice versa. In its predicative form an entity A is defined and hence identified by some characteristic **P**, where **P** is defined in relation to −**P**. This then is how the Middle Pathers interpret the Buddhist concept of relational origination (*pratītyasamutpāda*). It is the insight that all entities *depend* ontologically on their logical opposites, i.e., *all* that comprises the class of what they are not.

DICHOTOMIZATION

The creation of terms or concepts—and hence entity identification—comes about, as we have said, by a bifurcating type of conceptuality (*vikalpa*). As Paul Williams writes, the prefix "*vi-*" in *vikalpa* emphasizes "the creation of a referent through the ability of language to partition and create opposition, to divide a domain into mutually exclusive and contradictory categories."[86] That is to say, entities gain their identity only within an act of dichotomization in which the defining characteristics of an entity are located in terms of *not* being their logical opposite, i.e., not being logically *other* than what they are. Though predicates arise in the context of and in dependence on their logical opposites the two mutually defining predicates that constitute the pair, **P** and −**P**, become bifurcated in the act of ascribing *one* predicate to an entity. The two contrary predicates which naturally arise together, in a relationship of reciprocity, are pared apart in order to gain a degree of predicative consistency such as is necessary if there is to be discourse and thought about experience. There is a progressive distancing of the two contrary predicates that is artificially maintained at the expense of psychological effort (and pain). The reciprocal dependency or relational origination (*pratītyasamutpāda*) of predicates is lost sight of, **P** and −**P** come to function independently of each other, as though they were self defined, and their referents take on an independent existence of their own, i.e., appear to have an intrinsic reality.

36

In summary, where predicates first arise in the context of two mutually defining contraries, thus:

$$P - P$$

The dichotomizing faculty (*vikalpa*) bifurcates the two predicates and latches onto one of them in an effort to gain an entity that is serviceable as a conceptual referent.

$$P \longleftrightarrow -P$$

Entity identification is henceforward dogmatically rather than logically based. Such bifurcation and creation of seemingly independently defined referents is *drawn out* and reinforced by elaboration (*prapañca*) in the sense that the dynamic of elaborative thought feeds on an input of concepts which become embedded in a conceptual framework by the functional role they continue to play. Hence bifurcation (*vikalpa*) provides the concepts that can be conceptually synthesized and woven by *parikalpa* into a self-perpetuating stream of elaboration by the addition, attrition, modification, deepening, etc., of the relationships between concepts. Here then is the real *locus* for the creation of samsara: dichotomization providing the referents for elaboration and in turn elaboration feeding back to provide the concepts that are necessary for the creation of "absolute categories" in the first place. This spiral of mutual reinforcement between dichotomization and elaboration is broken, for Middle Pathers, by the tool of logical analysis.

This concludes the explanation of the genesis of conceptuality to the level of elaboration (*prapañca*). To summarize: (1) Conceptuality depends on entity recognition, which in turn (2) is dependent on the ascription of characteristics, or predicates, to entities, such characteristics that define them. Characteristics are (3) created in dependence on their logical opposites, and (4) predicative consistency (such as is necessary for recognition) is gained by hypostatizing two contrary predicates or characteristics so that they can be definitionally separated and made autonomous from each other. The isolation of conceptual opposites then enables us to use each characteristic as a predicate for defining different things.

The fact that concepts arise through logical contrariety goes unnoticed for a pre-analytical consciousness and the act of dichotomization, wherein the characteristics which make up a pair of concepts are latched onto and reified, occurs at a subliminal level. Only the fruition state in this process is discerned, where concepts have already gained an autonomous identity, i.e., at a point where concepts have been reified and able to enter into the flux of elaboration at the level of naming and verbalization. The subliminal or unconscious nature of concept formation contributes to the innate (*sahaja*) quality of delusion as does the *habitual* way in which concepts are reified. A whole network of concepts is maintained in a reified state. These represent a continuous undercurrent of fixation that is relatively uniform in nature given the quantity of concepts that are entertained by people and the complexity of the relationships between concepts. Any changes and vicissitudes in thought are relatively minor and superficial when compared to a dense background of conceptuality. This is the basis for the Buddhist claim that ignorance and confusion are trenchant and deep-seated.

The above account provides the basis for the Middle Pathers' claim that logical analysis is an appropriate tool with which to separate ontologizing forms of thinking, thereby disclosing the open texture of reality (*śūnyatā*).

THE PARADOX IN CHARACTERIZING THINGS

The assumption on which paradoxical (*prasaṅga*) analysis hinges is that characterization is logically paradoxical in virtue of being embedded within a structure of logical opposites. The notion of identifiability via characterization is inconsistent and without any sanction in logical thought because the reciprocal dependence of terms on their logical opposites means that the two terms that make up any oppositional structure must *both* be present in order for either one to be present. This is a *strong* interpretation of the principle of logical opposites in which reciprocal dependence means that one cannot have single terms, in isolation with respect to their opposites: either both or neither are present. The paradox of characterization, then, is that in the instance where something is characterized there must be a simultaneous ascription of logically contradictory characteristics to the *one* entity. Hence, in the very act of gaining their identity entities lose it as the presence of any attribute entails its absence. And in the very act of losing it they gain it since a negation of a characteristic affirms it. The affirmation of any characteristic logically entails the affirmation of its negation and vice versa. Wittgenstein seems to be making this same point from one angle when he speaks of a feeling "as if the negation of a proposition had to make it true in a certain sense in order to negate it."[87] And conversely, an affirmation is simultaneously a negation, meaning that an entity must be cognized as *not* what it is in order for it to be known as what it is. Thus contrary to its aims, entity identification is lost at the expense of characterization, rather than gained. (On this interpretation the insight of relational origination [*pratītyasamutpāda*], as the dependency of terms on their logical opposites, serves to negate the intrinsic identifiability of entities and this explains the Middle Path equivalence that is drawn between openness and *pratītyasamutpāda*.)

Some may query that while terms are defined in an oppositional structure, it is not necessary that contradictory characteristics are coaligned, i.e., *both* placed or located on the same entity. They may argue that it is sufficient for the two terms comprising any pair of logical opposites to be at different *cognitive* loci. This is the weak interpretation of the principle. (We should remember that we are talking here about concepts and not the premediated features of objects, if such can be talked about, and hence that it is not a question here of assigning mutually contradictory features to entities *themselves*.) The reason for the stipulation by Middle Pathers of the co-presence of two mutually negating characteristics, is an adherence to the letter of the principle of definition via logical opposites: that the concept −P has to be *present whenever and wherever* the concept of P is present, for otherwise P could not be sustained and vice versa. If they did not occupy a common spatio-temporal locus the two opposing terms would be separate from each other and so unable to define each other. In other words, P can only be defined *where* −P is defined (and vice versa). For Middle Path philosophers the co-presence of opposites is logically entailed by the reciprocity of concepts involved in creating a definition.

The aim of analysis is to clarify and expose the formally paradoxical structure of predication. In the pre-analysis situation conceptual bifurcation (*vikalpa*) is operative; Middle Pathers would say it is rampant. It is a state where entities are identified through a process of attribute fixation. That is to say, the features of entities are fixed and assume a seemingly autonomous existence, and there is no knowledge or recognition of the principle that predicates imply their opposites. If there is an awareness of predicates *and* their negations, they appear at different cognitive loci, i.e., at different levels of awareness and accessibility. This way, predicates are isolated from their opposites and consistency of predication is maintained. Or alternatively it may be that the paradoxical structure of predication surfaces as an unconscious (or even conscious) toleration of a certain degree of predicative ambiguity that manifests as an equivocation at different points in time and/or with respect to different aspects of an entity as to its defining features.

Analysis demonstrates a paradox of predication that is opaque for a non-analytical intellect. Since the structure of the subject-predicate relation is basic to analyses, any position, opinion, viewpoint, or cognitive perspective (*dṛṣṭi*) can become an object of analysis once such a viewpoint reaches a sufficient degree of articulation and formed precision, i.e., once it becomes a formal position (*pratijñā*). Some commitment to a position is required of whoever holds it. Philosophical positions are fairly formal from the outset. Natural or uncultivated positions, by which we mean innate cognitive and effective responses, require a fair degree of investigation before they can be formalized with sufficient precision to make analysis appropriate. Various sorts of positions can be accommodated within the subject-predicate arrangement. The basic structure would accommodate *simple* position—where single or multiple conjunctively joined predicates are attributed to a subject. It also accommodates *substantive* positions, i.e., those which involve nominative or substantial identifications or differentiations between entities. It also accommodates *complex* positions which may include detailed descriptions of the behavioral characteristics of entities.

In any instance the paradoxical structure of a position is said to be clarified and made transparent by deriving an opposite position from the position that is initially being advanced.[88] The paradox is that a position can *only* be taken at the expense of affirming a logically contrary position. In terms of the subject-predicate structure paradoxical analysis claims, then, to generate antilogisms, i.e., the simultaneous affirmation of **Pa** and **−Pa**.

The basis for deriving an opposite position from any position that is formulated, and so generate a logical contradiction, rests on the fact that the copula itself, such as figures in *any* position which takes the form of **A** *is* **P** or **A** *is* not **P**, is embedded in an oppositional structure of is/is not. The two existential or ontological qualifiers mutually define each other and hence for Middle Pathers also mutually negate each other. Any affirmation such as is captured by the copula "is" (in either nominative or adjectival constructions) in linking predicates to a subject, derives its *affirmative import* in opposition to the denial "is not." And likewise a denial of the form "**A** *is not* **P**" derives its import from the thesis "**A** *is* **P**." Hence the existential category: "is *and* is not," is comprised of terms that must be mutually present for either one to be present. And on this basis Middle Pathers draw out a logically contrary position that they claim is *logically entailed* for any position that one wishes to assert.

In Middle Path analysis the logical contradictions typically turn on a paradox that inheres in the *function* that the copula plays in *relating* the subject and predicate(s). The copula serves to *identify* some predicate substantively or attributively with a subject. (Given these substantive and attributive uses of "is" we may prefer to think of the relationship generically as one of *joining* rather than identifying which has a substantive ring to it.) The negation of the copula, on the other hand, serves to differentiate (or we may prefer, divide) either substantively or attributively

42

some predicate(s) with respect to a subject. Hence, the copula and its negation function *relationally* to identify and differentiate respectively. Identity and differential relationships mutually imply each other, and hence, as logical opposites, mutually contradict (*pun tshun 'gal ba*) each other. As such the whole notion of a relationship is nonsensical. A relationship of difference logically implies a relationship of identity or sameness (at least under the definition of intrinsic existence [*svabhāva*] in which intrinsically or genuinely different things are necessarily *unrelated*) in that different things have no characteristics that are in common, and hence have no provision of a basis for any interrelationships at all, including that of difference. It is only where there is a similarity in the strongest sense of an identity that there can be a difference. Otherwise there is no point of commonality, and hence no *basis for a comparison* whereby things can be judged to be different. Hence Middle Pathers have argued that whenever and wherever a relationship of difference is affirmed, so a relationship of identity must be affirmed, as the notion of a difference implies a point of commonality where terms in a relationship must be the same. Conversely, Middle Pathers have also argued that a relationship of identity implies a differential relation, as relationships exist, by definition, in dependence on terms of the relationship that are differentiable, i.e., that are different. Hence, wherever there is a relationship, there must be a difference. In the case where the terms of the relationship are the same, they cease to function as two terms in a relationship, and so there is no relationship.

In summary, then, for Middle Pathers relata are the same *where and to the extent* that they are different and vice versa. Any relationship is paradoxical as it simultaneously affirms an identity *and* difference between the terms being related in a relationship. Hence, in the context of their analyses, the relationship within a subject-predicate structure that is governed by the copula "is" implies its converse relationship, and on this basis it is considered that a logically contrary position can *always* be derived from any formalized position.

THE DESTRUCTURING OF CONCEPTUALITY

The simultaneous affirmation of a thesis and its negation is the logical fruit of the Middle Path analysis and it is here that the destructuring of conceptuality occurs.

The process of paradoxical analysis, where a position and its opposite mutually entail each other, can be thought of figuratively as a series of logical steps that serve to cause or induce logical opposites, positions, and their opposites (i.e., a predicate(s) and its negation with respect to the same entity) to *coalesce* at a common spatio-temporal locus. As Shohei Ichimura writes, "the predicament created by this dialectic is due to the unexpected contradiction which our convention implies, and this feature is suddenly disclosed by the particular context in which two contrary entities are *juxtaposed over the same sphere and moment of illumination.*"[89]

A position and its opposite, which have previously become reified in relationship to each other and achieved an *artificial* autonomy, collapse into each other (as the affirmation of either is seen to imply the other) and mutually negate each other (as they are logical opposites).

$$P \longrightarrow \longleftarrow -P$$

On this interpretation the bifurcating activity (*vikalpa*) of the intellect would be opposed or countered by analysis, in the sense that analysis would act to show that the separation of logical opposites is constructed and artificial and that intrinsic- as opposed to inter-identifiability is a reification that is mentally imposed on experience.

Intrinsic identification would be negated because the only point at which there could be a real or analytically credible entity identification would be at an *interface* between P and −P but at an interface they would also mutually negate each other, (on the Middle Path assumption that P and −P, in order to define each other, are logical opposites). The real cutting edge of analysis, then, occurs at the cognitive interface between P and −P, at a *coincidentia oppositorum* where P and −P negate each other.

Though effort and application is required on behalf of an analyst to counteract the bifurcating tendency, in fact, bifurcation, being an artificial condition, is maintained only at the continual investment of effort. When such effort is relaxed, conceptuality would tend to naturally fold in on itself and dissipate. This makes sense of the idea that openness is a natural, effortless, and primordial condition of consciousness and that samsara is characterized by the continual expenditure of effort.

This explanation for the destructuring of conceptuality by the Middle Path analysis assumes as we have said that terms arise in dependence on their logical opposites: the principle of terminological reciprocity. The explanation also assumes that the structure, formation, and development of conceptuality in the analytical context conforms to the three Aristotelian principles of thought, viz., contradiction, identity, and the excluded middle.

These principles are implicated by the Middle Pathers not simply as logical axioms but also as principles of thought that are *descriptive* of the thought activity encountered in analysis. That is, they describe certain structures that govern the train and development of an analyst's thought at the time of debate and meditation, and so are *psychological* principles as well as formal axioms. And insofar as analysis produces insight, they are also *prescriptive* principles, in that they represent an advocated structural basis for guiding the course of conceptuality. Middle Pathers hold that the structure of thought can be made to approximate to these principles in varying degrees and that in a pure form of paradoxical analysis, thought is guided by them.

It is useful to examine how these three principles function in the analytical context as logical axioms that are modeled or replicated within the conceptual development of an analyst, and how they constitute *conditions* for the *formation* of thought and, when *infused* with the principle of terminological reciprocity, a condition for its dissolution.

THE PRINCIPLE OF NON-CONTRADICTION

The principle of non-contradiction states that for any subject **A**, any given predicate **P** cannot be both affirmed and denied at the same time and in the same respect. The principle is stated formally[90] and used materially[91] by Middle Pathers such as Nāgārjuna and Candrakīrti.

In the context of paradoxical analysis the principle of non-contradiction is used as a structure for dichotomizing the possible positions that can be assumed with respect to any matter into two contradictory and mutually excluding positions, i.e., **A** is **P** and **A** is not **P**, and in doing this the principle is structurally identical with the principle of definition by logical opposites except for the crucial fact that the principle of non-contradiction holds that **A** cannot be **P** and −**P**, where the principle of definition by logical opposites holds that **A** must be **P** and −**P**.

The principle of non-contradiction is used in the analytical context in order to commit someone to a position at the expense and in terms of rejecting its logical opposite. In other words, a commitment to the truth of some position is gained in parallel fashion to the identification of entities, by assigning a false truth-value to an opposite position. And vice versa, the assignment of a false truth-value to a contrary position is possible only on affirming the truth of an initial position. The principle of non-contradiction is thus a *precondition* for the formation of any position and in a *pre-analytical* situation this serves to (seemingly) provide a basis validating a position.

In the analytical context, on the other hand, the principle of non-contradiction comes to fruition in *conjunction* with the principle of definition via logical opposites in its *strong* interpretation by the Middle Pathers. This latter principle functions as a *condition* for analysis rather than as a precondition, though the principle of non-contradiction rightly acts as a condition *for* analysis also. The difference is that the principle of non-contradiction is at work in the non-analytical state-of-affairs in the sense that it is a tacit (and in logic a formal) assumption where the principle of definition by logical opposites is not. Together these two principles account for the destructuring of conceptuality.

These two principles force a dilemma upon the mind of an analyst. On the one hand, the principle of definition by logical opposites structures conceptuality *in the direction* of simultaneously affirming a position and its negation (i.e., simultaneously affirming the presence *and* absence of predicate(s) with respect to the one entity: that **A** is and is not **P**). And, on the other hand, the principle of non-contradiction structures conceptuality in a way that formally and prescriptively (and perhaps also psychologically) precludes consciousness from simultaneously affirming a position and its negation (i.e., it disallows that predicate(s) can simultaneously be affirmed and denied of the same entity in the same respect: that **A** is not both **P** and not **P**).

When conceptuality is formed by both these principles its structure is forced in the direction of assuming two mutually contradicting and excluding states to which there would seem to be two possible avenues of resolution. One, a non-analytical (and for Middle Pathers regressive) resolution which is to retain the structure formed by one principle at the expense of revoking the other principle, *or* alternatively, an analytical (and psychologically progressive) solution that adopts neither structure (given an analyst's commitment to the validity of both principles). The resultant effect of this last solution would be to introduce a cessation within a stream of conceptuality. In other words, the tension between the two principles can be relieved either by an analyst backtracking, as it were, to a non-critical standpoint where one or other of the principles lapses from its role as a structural form of conceptual development (one guesses that the principle of definition via logical opposites would be discarded), or by a dissolution of conceptuality. This last solution would take place, as we have said, at an interface between two mutually contradictory conceptual structures where conceptuality would cease as the only logically forthright response to the dilemma of having to simultaneously identify and differentiate **P** and **−P**.

The principle of non-contradiction is revoked in this interpretation, on the insight that two logical opposites are not contradictories of which one is true at the expense of the falsity of the other, but rather are logical contraries in which both are false. In other words, the pre-analytical assumption that **P** and **−P** are contradictories is analytically rejected on the discernment—propelled by a strong interpretation of the principle of definition by logical opposites—that the two opposites mutually negate each other.

Though Middle Pathers reject an identity between the mind and brain it is interesting to note that the mathematician Ludvik Bass has hypothesized that the *reductio ad absurdum* method of proof may have "a radically distinct structure at the neural level"[92] when compared with constructive methods of proof. Where with the latter, neural modes may be characterized as achieving a point of stabilization or a lack of conflict, in the case of *reductio* arguments, he suggests that the conflict between premises may have a neural analog as a "persisting conflict between modes."[93] If the conflict between premises is mirrored at the neural level we could further speculate that this would involve a tendency for one neural structure to be formed or activated into two mutually excluding states, a tendency which could be responded to by assuming one state and relinquishing the other (this would be the Middle Pathers' regressive option, and would be exhibited as a failure to conclude a proof) or by a destructuring of the neural state due to its being formed into an impossible condition (this would manifest as a conclusion to a proof).

The significance of conceptuality becoming unstructured is that it cannot be identified with a concept in either its positive or negative formulation and so becomes vacuous with respect to that concept. The dissolution of conceptuality that such a vacuity of reference amounts to, is what we are interpreting as an insight into the openness of the concepts being analyzed. In other words the confluence of logical opposites and the resultant breaking up of conceptuality is insight into openness. The notion of identifiability is inconsistent, and when it is seen that entities lack an intrinsic identity conceptuality dissipates. The doctrinal distinction made by Tibetan Middle Pathers between certified and inferential cognitions of openness will be raised later.

An assumption in this explanation is that the logical falsity in simultaneously taking a position and its negation also reflects a psychological impossibility, such that two logically contradictory concepts cannot be *held* within a unity of consciousness. David Armstrong[94] (among others) has questioned the impossibility of the co-temporal entertaining of contradictory beliefs and it is worthwhile briefly considering what he says as it helps to highlight the position of the Middle Path.

Armstrong's first observation en route to his final position is that a person can hold contradictory beliefs but fail to discern the contradiction. He writes: "It [the mind] is a large and untidy place, and we may believe 'P' and '−P' simultaneously but fail to bring the two beliefs together, perhaps for emotional reasons."[95] The Middle Pathers would agree with this as a description of a non-analytical intellect, where in order to maintain predicative consistency, perhaps so as support cathexis toward some object, any indication of a possible predicative inconsistency would be unconsciously or consciously repressed. An individual, on realizing an inconsistency, may decide that the emotional attachment (or aversion) to be lost, or gained, or at least attenuated, is not worth forsaking and so prefer to remain oblivious of any inconsistency, save such an awareness destabilizing and undermining an affective response. A difference, on this point, between Armstrong and the Middle Pathers is that Middle Pathers would say that *all* rather than just some beliefs may be contradicted within an individual's fabric of beliefs.

Armstrong goes on to suggest that "it seems possible to become aware that we hold incompatible beliefs."[96] The (apparently) contentious part of Armstrong's claim (it seems) is that such an awareness need *not* result in any structural or categorial change to the belief situation. (He agrees that in some cases it would result in some modification in the situation, such as the revoking of one belief.) The point for Armstrong, though, is that the logically incompatible beliefs represent *two different states*, and hence the co-presence of beliefs in the one mind is not their *co-alignment*. Hence, there is no real conflict in his account with what Middle Pathers would say. He is not proffering the "confusing situation" where two states are *actually* coaligned, but rather has described two or three situations of contradictory beliefs that Middle Pathers see as stages either prior to analysis or at some point within an analyzing context but prior to the co-alignment (and concomitant destructuring) of contradictory structures. There is still to explain the roles that the principles of identity and the excluded middle play in paradoxical analysis.

THE IDENTITY PRINCIPLE

A principle of identity is presupposed in the other two Aristotelian principles and in the principle of definition by logical opposites. The principle figures as a *precondition* for analysis, and serves to guarantee predicative consistency with regard to an entity being analyzed. Though it is not formally stated in Middle Path texts as a precondition, the notion of intrinsic existence (*svabhāva*) as the "object to be negated" in an analysis states a tacit if not formal assention to the principle of identity, since whatever has an intrinsic existence cannot change its identity, i.e., cannot become something else without losing its intrinsic existence. In other words, intrinsic existence presupposes intrinsic identity. In the meditative manuals of the Tibetans that outline stylized procedures for the private contemplation of openness (as opposed to analysis through the medium of debate), an initial procedure is "ascertaining the mode of appearance of what is negated,"[97] which in part amounts to an analyst *committing* him- or herself to the identity criteria for an entity being investigated—for example, that a certain configuration of forms, percepts, affections, etc., is a self and *regarding* that configuration to be just that self. It is reasonable also to suppose that dialecticians in the course of their debates would likewise try to irrevocably commit an opponent at the very outset to specific identity criteria for the entity(s) figuring in an investigation. The rationale behind this extraction of identity criteria is clearly an *attempt* on behalf of an analyst to *guarantee* a fruitful result to an analysis by ensuring that there is no equivocation on what is being analyzed at some point during an analysis, and to forestall the invoking of changed identity criteria, either of which would act to *dilute* an analysis to the qualitative extent of any changes in identity criteria (given the stability of other conditions for analysis). In other words, were the identity of an entity that is being analyzed to be revoked in any degree *subsequent* to being established as an object to be refuted but *prior* to its being refuted, a conclusion would fail to bear on the changed entity with its revised identity criteria to whatever *extent* it was a *new* entity. Thus, in dialogical texts we see Middle Pathers being uncompromising with their opponents who proffer potentially ambiguous identity criteria or introduce mobile concepts, the definitions of which vacillate, and so undermine the full force of a Middle Path analysis.

THE PRINCIPLE OF THE EXCLUDED MIDDLE

The principle of the excluded middle is upheld by Middle Pathers, in order to account for the *complete* dissolution of conceptuality and so substantiate the possibility of a thoroughly pure and totally pervasive insight into reality. The principle says that any entity **A** is either predicated by **P** or not predicated by **P**, and that there is no other, third alternative. The principle is very clearly stated by Nāgārjuna (for example, MK: 2.8b[98] and 2.21). Candrakīrti also says in his *Commentary to the Introduction to the Middle Path* [MABh: 100.16–17] that "through the pervasion [by existence and non-existence] there will not be even the slightest particularization [remaining] (*bkag pas cung zad kyang khyad par du mi 'gyur ro*)."[99] Śāntideva writes in the *Introduction to the Evolved Lifestyle* [BCA: 9.35] that, "When neither things nor non-things are placed before the intellect then there is no other route [for the mind to take], it lacks any support [and so achieves] the supernal peace." In the Tibetan meditative manuals[100] the principle is included as a second essential step (after the commitment to the predicative configuration and consistency of any entity that is to be analyzed). It is called "ascertaining the pervasion" and is a commitment to the principle that outside of two mutually contradictory modes of existence there is no third mode; or in what is the same thing, two logical opposites pervade all modes of predication.

The principle, as Śāntideva clearly shows above, is utilized to rule out the possibility that a residuum of conceptuality remains after the dissolution of two logically opposed concepts. For example, were there to be a third conceptual position outside of a concept's positive and negative formulations, then that third position would still be retained after the positive and negative forms were analytically dissolved. It would mean that some remnants of conceptuality would fall outside the compass of paradoxical analysis in the sense that they could not be analytically removed. Hence, the ascription of contradictory attributes to the one entity jointly exhausts all possible modes of predication with respect to that attribute. Thus, when the paradox of characterization is exposed, an entity is uncharacterized (positively or negatively) with respect to that characteristic.

It may be useful briefly to summarize what has been a fairly elaborate explanation up to this point. I have (1) isolated certain assumptions that are intrinsic to Middle Path analysis, and (2) described an infrastructure to consequential analysis which explains how this form of analysis dissolves ontologizing conceptualizations.

The assumptions that undergird the Middle Path analysis are these: (1) Conceptuality depends on the *consistent* ascription of characteristics to an entity. (2) Characteristics arise in the context of their logical opposites, which in its strong interpretation, as is required by the Middle Pathers, means that the presence of a characteristic implies its absence (and vice versa). This principle assumes a status equal to the Aristotelian principles and it is significant in that analysis is effective to the *extent* that this principle is structurally formative (*in its strong interpretation*) for conceptuality. (3) The logical validity and formative influence and role of the three Aristotelian principles of thought in structuring the development of conceptuality.

Given these assumptions, it can be seen that paradoxical analysis is a technique for taking a stream of conceptuality that is (artificially) structured by a principle of non-contradiction (and loosely also by the principles of identity and the excluded middle) and then introducing within that conceptual stream an awareness of a paradox inhering in conceptuality. A stream of conceptuality, in other words, is redirected by paradoxical analysis into becoming aware of an inherent paradox in predication that, by its tendency to compel consciousness to assume the psychologically impossible and structurally unstable condition of forming two mutually contradictory structures, results in a failure in the ability to predicate, and in consequence a destructuring and dissolution of conceptuality that can be interpreted as the insight into openness.

PATTERNS OF PARADOXICAL ANALYSIS

The above explanation shows the *structural foundations* upon which the methods of analysis used in Middle Path insight meditation (*vipaśyanā*) are based. Our next step is to describe the actual procedures of analysis used by Middle Path meditators. We will then be in a position to develop the speculative model in the next chapter that will link the role of analysis to the notion of a progressive liberation that accords roughly with the Middle Path path-structure. This will result in a fully fledged model that integrates Middle Path analysis within a path-structure.

We will begin by outlining the analytical procedures that are used by Middle Pathers in traditional Indian and Tibetan settings. From there we will develop a more generalized account of the procedures that direct any analytical inquiry that is based on paradoxical consequences. We will thus effectively be describing how Middle Path analysis can be applied in any culture and for any position and worldview.

TRADITIONAL ANALYTICAL PROCEDURES

The traditional forms of Middle Path analysis are based on the Buddhist worldview that was formalized in the meta-psychological texts (*abhidharma*). One of the first divisions this worldview makes is between persons (*pudgala*) and things (*dharma*). And this distinction serves as a basis for the two main analytical templates used by traditional Middle Pathers. Fortunately, the distinction between self and other is a transcultural distinction. It is also ahistorical and holds for all mature humans. As such the traditional analyses are just as relevant to our own lives and times as they were in classical India and Tibet.

The two analyses that we will outline here will serve to show

how logical contradictions are generated using exactly those principles that we have described in the preceding sections.

The pattern we will observe, in which the positive and negative formulations of a position mutually entail each other, is to be found in all Middle Path analyses that are based on paradoxical consequences.

TWO PRELIMINARY STEPS

Logical analysis of the type we are outlining here is, as we have already said, a tool that is used privately by Middle Path philosophers in their meditations on openness. In fact, according to Middle Path meditators, insight into openness can be only be induced through analytical meditations. When Middle Pathers are meditating on openness they first begin by developing their concentration so that they can focus their thoughts in a firm, precise, and sustained way. This is the practice of serenity (śamatha) and mental integration (samādhi).

When Middle Pathers begin an analysis designed to generate a paradoxical consequence they start by clearly establishing the logical principles upon which the analysis will be based. That is to say, they commit themselves, as we have just explained, to basing their analysis on the principles of identity, non-contradiction, and the excluded middle. In the traditional meditational manuals this commitment is established in two steps, called (1) determining what is to be refuted, and (2) ascertaining the pervasion.

In the first step the Middle Pather distinguishes an object to be analyzed and then determines that it is *this* object and not something else that is to be analyzed. This involves making a firm commitment about the defining characteristics (svalakṣaṇa) of the object in question and deciding not to reconsider this definition during the analysis, nor to query the identifying characteristics or introduce any ambiguity about what it is that he or she is analyzing once an analysis is under way. In other words, the analyst decides that his or her analysis will be structured by the principle of identity: that if **A** is **A** then it is not something else.

In doing so the analyst also upholds the principle of non-contradiction: that the object to be analyzed cannot be both **A** and not **A**.

Thus, if the meditator is examining him or herself, he or she will, as it were, take a fix on what, for the purposes of any particular analysis, will be regarded as the self. He or she may decide to focus on a set of feelings, or memories, or ambitions, or physical appearance, or all of these and any other aspects of what he or she considers him or herself to be.

Similarly, if the meditator is going to develop insight into the non-intrinsic existence of an object such as a house, he or she will first decide if it is a particular house or the class of houses, and then search for and commit him or herself to the defining characteristic(s) of the house.

In the second step, called "ascertaining the pervasion," the Middle Pather selects a logically contrasting relation within which to analyze the object that is chosen in the first step. "Ascertaining the pervasion" involves the analyst in committing her or himself to the validity of the principle of the excluded middle or what is alternatively called the principle of joint exhaustion. This principle says that **A** and not **A** exhaust *all* the possible ways in which something can exist. As we explained, this principle is invoked in order to ensure that no residue of a concept remains at the completion of an analysis.

In a traditional setting the meditator will usually choose a contrasting relation that has come to be associated with the object being analyzed. Thus, if the object is a "thing" the analyst may look at "modes of production" as the relation with which to analyze the "thing" in question. In this case the two contrasting relations are: (1) that the thing is produced, or brought into being, by itself, and (2) that the thing is brought into being by something other than itself, i.e., by something which is not itself.

If, on the other hand, the analyst is seeking to develop insight into the open nature of his or her own person, then he or she will look at their sense of selfhood in relationship to their psychophysical organism—what we will call the "body-mind." The two contrasting relations with which to structure the analysis will be: (1) that they *are* their body-mind, and (2) that they *are not* their body-mind.

At this point we will outline the two particular forms of analysis we have just mentioned and show how logical contradictions are generated. As we have said, these two particular formats of analysis are employed frequently by Middle Path analysts in their contemplations on openness.

THINGS AND THE PRODUCTION ANALYSIS

The analysis of things (*bhāva, dharma*), in terms of how they are produced or brought into being, was first detailed by Nāgārjuna in the second chapter of his *Principal Stanzas on the Middle Path* [MK].

Things are analyzed through their possible modes of production. The two contrasting and jointly exhaustive modes are that things are produced from themselves or from something else.[101]

PRODUCTION FROM ITSELF

In the case of something being produced from itself, the analysis raises two jointly exhaustive alternatives as to how something could produce itself. These are: (1) that the thing which is produced (i.e., the product) retains the nature of the thing that produced it (i.e., the producer), or (2) it adopts a new nature.

If the product doesn't assume a nature different from that of the producer (which is viewable as either the product being the same as the producer, or vice versa) then as there are no perceivable differences between the producer and product, one doesn't have an instance of production, for by definition this requires a product that can be discerned from a producer. Thus, here there is no production qua production and so no production from self. In the absence of being able to discriminate between a "producer" and a "product," there can be no function of production, and hence the "product" cannot be said to have been produced. The implication here is that production requires that there be *two distinct* things, one acting as the producer and the other as the product. Candrakīrti writes [MA: 6.13a–c]:

> If self-production is asserted, then product, producer, the object (produced), and the agent alike are identical. Since they are not identical, production from self cannot be maintained.

The other option is that the product does lose its former nature. This option fulfills the requirement that products are different from their producers. Here, however, the product ceases to be identical with the producer and hence is an "other" with respect to the producer. As such, production from self (insofar as we are talking about production) requires that products and producers differ and so all production is production from another, including production from self if we wish to confirm the presence of a *productive* process.

Thus, in the first option "production from self" is said to logically imply that there is *no* "production from self" since the process of production requires that the producer and product are

59

different. The second option draws the logical absurdity that "production from self" implies "production from another." Thus this position implies its negation.

PRODUCTION FROM SOMETHING ELSE

The second way in which things can be produced is through a "producer" that is different from the "product." This theory appears on the surface to be plausible, but it too entails a logical contradiction.

The analysis of this theory again proceeds by way of raising two mutually exclusive and jointly exhaustive possibilities. These are: (1) that a producer (or cause) is connected to the product or (effect), and (2) that these two are unconnected. The concept of "connection" in this analysis is taken in two ways: in a temporal sense and in terms of a linkage that connects a producer and product within the same continuum or stream of production. In the temporal sense the two options are between whether a producer decays and a product arise simultaneously or non-simultaneously. In the non-temporal case it is a question of whether or not a producer and product (or cause and effect) interface or remain separate.

The first set of arguments claims to reject the option that causes and effects or producers and products can be unconnected on the grounds that this option forfeits the concept of production or causation. The claim is that if the two are separate, then the "producer" or "cause" cannot be distinguished from "non-causes," in which case they cease to be "causes" or "producers." The idea is that the notion of "difference" doesn't partake of degrees or graduations: things are either the same or different. If, for example, two things are really or intrinsically different from a third thing, then they are *equally different* from that third thing.

This makes nonsense out of the notion of production, as *any* "other" could be posited with equal reason as the cause of anything else.[102] There would be no restriction on what can cause what, outside of the requirement that causes and their effects be different. If there *is* birth from another, then everything would cause everything. Thus from this angle, the notion of production or causation would be unspecified in the extreme and for this reason effectively forfeited. This conclusion can be obtained from another angle. Production, if it is to be at all meaningful, has to be a specified relationship in the sense that some "others" have to be precluded from being causes or effects in instances of causation or production. Citing a traditional example, Candrakīrti writes (MA: 6.14a–c) that, "If something were to arise in dependence on something else, then thick darkness could arise even from a flame. Furthermore, everything could be produced from everything else." The implication here is that since neither light nor darkness are identical with a flame, both are equally different from the flame, and hence a flame could just as well cause darkness to occur as it does illumination.

We see here that Middle Pathers work with an assumption that things are either the same or different from each other, and that there is no conceptual basis for our suspicion that things may be more or less different from each other. It is bogus to claim that things have a defining characteristic yet claim that they may be more and less different from each other. Thus, the productive relationship cannot be delimited and hence the concept of production of causation is meaningless. In this argument, no consequence (*prasaṅga*) has been offered; instead, one option has been excluded on the grounds that it forfeits the concept of production.

The second option is that production from another can only

occur when there is some form of interface or connection between the producer (or cause) and product (or effect). This again is considered in a temporal and non-temporal sense. The suggestion that the producer and product can exist simultaneously is refuted on the grounds that such a producer could not give rise to a product, for if they are simultaneous, i.e., co-existent, the producer would have existed for as long as the product had. Further, if the product exists prior to the producer, there is no need for it to be produced, hence it would not be a product. If the product arises after some time lag, then the producer cannot in fact have produced it.

The argument is clearer when we consider production in terms of an interface between causes and their effects. If there is to be a genuine meeting between causes and their effects, then at the point where they meet one must merge with the other. Were they not to be so connected, one could not become the other. In other words, at the point where the producer is becoming the product two things become one thing. As Candrakīrti writes (MA 6.169ab): "If a cause produces an effect when they meet, then at the time they are a single potential, and therefore the producer would not be different from the effect." And because the producer and product are identical in this case one has an instance of "production from self." Hence, the position of "production from another" implies its negation.

In both of these cases, of refuting production both from self and from something else, one alternative is rejected on the grounds that it forfeits the notion of production, and hence could not be what is meant by *birth* or *production* from self or other. A paradox is then drawn out on the assumption that the only viable alternative (i.e., the one that retains a meaningful notion of production) is correct. If this alternative is affirmed, it is claimed that it negates itself and so establishes its opposite.

In the first option there is no production, since the effect cannot be distinguished from the cause. In the second option any cause could equally serve to produce the effect.

The conclusion to this analysis is that there cannot be any "produced things," since "being produced" is an essential characteristic of "produced things," yet the ways in which something could have been produced are impossible. Thus, there are no "intrinsically existent" products.

While the analysis we have outlined may seem quite complicated, our concern has been to show the full elaboration of alternatives and to present the assumptions behind the logical contradictions. When the analysis is used by Middle Pathers who are familiar with this and other analyses, it appears much more simple and straightforward since the analyst knows how to reach a conclusion swiftly.

PERSONS AND THE SAME-OR-DIFFERENT ANALYSIS

The contrasting relationship in the personality analysis is between a position which asserts that there is a substantive identity between the self and the body-mind and a position which asserts that a person and their body-mind are genuinely different things. These two positions are the logical negation of each other since to say that a person is *other than* the body-mind is logically equivalent to saying that a person *is not identical* with the body-mind.

This analysis was fully developed by Candrakīrti in *The Introduction to the Middle Path* [MA]. This particular analysis constitutes the most important set of arguments in all of Buddhist philosophical literature. The arguments are in fact an extension and elaboration of proofs that Nāgārjuna outlined in the second century.[103]

63

THE SELF AS DIFFERENT FROM THE BODY-MIND

The first section of the analysis refutes the view that the self is different from the body-mind. That is to say, it rules out the possibility that a person could be something that is different from their body and mind. These are referred to as "transcendental" conceptions of the person.

The analysis here follows the same structure as the analysis of things in that two subsidiary possibilities are adduced, namely, that a self which is different from the body-mind can be either known or not known. If it is not known, it cannot be known as an "other" with respect to the body-mind, so this option drops out straightaway.

The other option, and one from which a paradoxical consequence is derived, is that a self that is different from the body-mind can be known. Middle Pathers argue, though, that if that self is known, which it must be in order for it to be known as "different from the body-mind," it must be the body-mind for the body-mind defines the limits of knowledge in the sense that whatever can be experienced is experienced in terms of the body-mind, specifically feelings, discriminations, and consciousness. An assumption is that if the self is not included in the body-mind then it can be known, located, and described, etc., independently of and without reference to the body-mind, and that if this is not possible then the self is included within, and so is not different from the body-mind. If the self is different it is unrelated to the body-mind and hence cannot be known through the psychophysical apparatus. The argument here is that the body-mind mediates *all* cognition through the sense and mental consciousnesses (*citta-skandha*) and the body (*rūpa-skandha*). Thus, a self that is totally unrelated to the body-mind cannot be known.

Hence, given that we are talking about a self that can be known such a self cannot be intrinsically different from the body-mind. Thus, the position that the self and body-mind are different is seen to imply its negation.

THE SELF AS THE SAME AS THE BODY-MIND

The second alternative, that exhausts the modes in which the self could exist, is that the self is the same as the body-mind. This is a negation of the preceding position. The refutation of this position hinges on whether the self and the body-mind are individually discernible in the instance of their being the same thing. They either are both discernible, or they *both* are not.

If they are not discernible, one from each other, as the thesis seems to imply, then one could not say that the self is the same as the body-mind for this supposes that there are *two* things which are one. There could be a self, *or* a body-mind, but if both of them are in fact just one thing, then there can't be the two of them. This thesis collapses because for Middle Pathers there is no such thing as a genuine identity relationship, since a relationship requires at least two discernible objects to be related. Thus, this interpretation of the thesis is not consistently formulated, and in fact describes a logical impossibility.

Hence, this position must mean that though the referent of the term "self" and referent of the term "body-mind" are the same, the referents can be distinguished from each other. On this interpretation, though, the identity relationship is forsaken for if things can be genuinely distinguished from each other by having different properties (such as being divisible in the case of the body-mind and indivisible into parts in the case of the self) then they are different. Thus, when a relationship is *retained* rather than forsaken as in the first interpretation, the position that the self and the body-mind are the same, implies that they are different.

Thus, in the analyses of the person and things we find pairs of consequential arguments that purport to logically derive a negation of a position from its affirmation. This works for both the initial position and its negation and so the two positions from each of the two sets mutually negate each other.

TEMPORAL AND ONE-OR-MANY ANALYSES

Traditional Middle Pathers also commonly make use of an analysis based on investigating when something arises. Such an analysis uses a "temporal" template. The contrasting positions are that something exists before its defining characteristics, or the defining characteristics exist prior to that which they define. The first position leads to the contradiction that a thing (which is undefined) is not a thing. The second position entails the conclusion that something has to exist before it exists, since something cannot be characterized when there is nothing to characterize.

Middle Pathers also equip themselves with an analytical template called "one-or-many." This template is based on the contrasting positions that **A** is one thing, or **A** is many (i.e. not just one). The analysis generates the paradox that to be one something must be many, and to be many it must be one.

While the self is typically analyzed using the "same-or-different" template any other template can also be used. Thus, the self can likewise be examined using a one-or-many analysis, or by looking at whether it was produced from itself or another. Likewise, things can be analyzed under any template.

ROUTES OF ANALYSIS

These traditional patterns of analysis can be presented as a flow

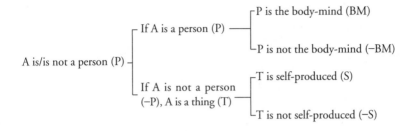

Figure 2.1 Traditional patterns of analysis as flow chart.

chart (*Figure 2.1*) that traces the routes that were suggested for traditional Middle Pathers in the course of their private contemplations on openness, and also in the dialectical context where Middle Pathers debated with colleagues and others. In this debating context a Middle Pather acts as an analyst for an analysand, who may be either another Middle Pather, or someone from another philosophical tradition.

The chart reads from left to right. As an analyst works through, or *directs* his analysand to work through the procedure, she or he is confronted with a series of alternative categories that are logical opposites and which exhaust a universe of conceptuality, or some well defined category structure within that (if the principle of the excluded middle is a structural former of conceptuality). He or she is confronted, as it were, with a series of Y intersections, at which she or he decides which route to take in dependence upon the definition of the concept being analyzed. One route or another is traced out depending on the concept that is chosen for analysis and each route leads into the Middle Path method of analysis that is appropriate to the concept being analyzed. The paradox, which consists of refuting a position and its negation that purport to define the concept in question, is applied to the concept. The refutation of both the position and its negation render the concept to be void of any intrinsic or self-referential identity. In other words, each route leads finally to a consequential proof for the openness of the concepts in question. All branches for all concepts that comprise the universe of discourse are in theory closed by the Middle Path analysis. The different routes serve to locate the position within which the intrinsic existence of a concept will be refuted.

If a Middle Pather is analyzing his or her own conceptual makeup, the procedure is straight forward. She or he knows the definitions of the conceptual categories that are used in Middle Path texts and thinks in those same categories. Thus, any concept is allocated to its appropriate category and analyzed in terms of the analytical structure that is suggested for that category. If traditional Middle Path schema are used to guide the analysis then the analyst will first decide whether he or she is dealing with the concept of a person or a thing. The appropriate "contrasting relation" would then be selected. Thus, rather than working through a route on the flowchart from its very beginning at the person-thing distinction until locating the appropriate category and its method of refutation, the knowledgeable Middle Pather would be able to go directly to the appropriate category and refutation.

In the case where the Middle Pather is unclear about the alignment of some concept within the Middle Path categories of analysis, she or he would start at the beginning of the schema with the person-thing distinction or at some subsequent distinction where he or she was sure, or able to easily ascertain, in which category his or her concept was included.

ANALYSIS BETWEEN MIDDLE PATHERS AND OTHERS

The above procedure differs when a Middle Path analyst engages a non-Middle Pather in an analysis, since such a person operates with a different worldview. The most significant difference is that the analyses could not presuppose the Middle Pathers' categories. At the start of an analysis, at least, they must assume the details of the analysand's categories. That is to say, the Middle Pather would have to agree (if there were to be any point to an analysis at all) that the concepts being committed to an investigation in an analysis were the entities defined by the positions taken by their analysands.

The procedure of the Middle Path generally is that *any position* about any thing, be it referring to an entity or a process, can be allocated to one or other of a pair of categories that exhaust the universe or a well defined domain of concepts. The pervasion of all possibilities by a pair of concepts, such as person and things, self-produced and other-produced, etc., ensures that no concept of an analysand can fall outside the categories used by Middle Pathers. This guarantees that all positions are accommodated within Middle Path schema.

With regard to who is responsible for assigning the analysand's position to one or other of the Middle Pathers' generic categories, we can assume that this is negotiated at the beginning of an analytical session. In theory at least, there is no need for the Middle Path analyst to assign an analysand's position to one of her or his own generic formulations. It is valid for an analysand to make his or her assignment (and one would think most skillful for the Middle Pather to do it this way, for then there is presumably no question of coercion by the Middle Pather). Even so, we can expect that a Middle Path analyst often takes the categories of the analysand to be instantiations of his or her own primary categories, even though this may involve some deformation of the analysand's categories.

An important point to appreciate, though, is that Middle Path analyses require (and demand) a rigid designation of whatever concepts are analyzed. Middle Pathers speak in blacks and whites, of things existing or not existing, being one or many, the same or different, etc., for the reasons mentioned earlier when detailing the role of the principle of identity. Their analyses also demand a rigor of logical development.

We should appreciate also that an analysand may not wish to be directed through the various decisions that need to be made en route to a final consequential refutation of her or his position. At the least the analysand may *hesitate* at the various intersections on the flowchart, or even refuse to proceed. He or she may *resist* in various ways the attempts by the Middle Pather to analytically process her or his positions. This may manifest as an analysand's failure to commit her or himself to a sufficiently rigorous and syntactically precise elaboration of a position, i.e., by obscuring his or her philosophical and unconscious commitments, as it were, and by *refusing* to clarify opaque concepts when asked to by the Middle Pather. Finally, an analysand may change the definitions or identity criteria of the concepts being analyzed part of the way through an analysis, possibly when she or he feels on tenuous ground with respect to the integrity of her or his concept(s). Any of these moves serves to avoid the Middle Path logic.

In summary, then, the schema as presented in the chart applies to analysis conducted within the Middle Pathers' own school and also *guides* their dialogical exchanges with analysands. For Middle Pathers, who are committed to the worth and validity of paradoxical analysis, the procedures are presumably followed in a stepwise and fairly methodical fashion. For non-Middle Pathers the assumptions and logic underlying paradoxical analysis are at variance with their own epistemologies, with the tension between the two meaning that analysis would tend to be labored, and from a Middle Path perspective perhaps oftentimes incomplete.

ANALYTICAL VARIATIONS

Some of the particular analytical procedures we have outlined above (such as in the analysis of people and things) display structural differences from each other. Some of the differences are less important than others. Thus the reader may wish to gloss over the next three sub-sections. However, a full appreciation of section 6.0 depends on at least a surface reading of these sections.

RESTRICTED AND UNRESTRICTED ANALYSES

One point worth noting from the above explanation is that analyses can proceed through what we call "restricted" and "unrestricted" categories of analysis.

A category restricted analysis is one in which the characteristic or predicate in terms of which a concept is analyzed is the concept's defining characteristic (*svalakṣaṇa*). Thus, for example, in analyzing things (*bhāva, dharma*), Nāgārjuna and Candrakīrti analyze their defining characteristic of "being produced" and adduce two primary possibilities that are opposites and which exhaust *only* the ways in which things can be produced, viz., from themselves or others.

On the other hand, in the case of non-category restricted analyses, the actual characteristic(s) within which an entity is analyzed are immaterial. The only requirement is that the characteristic(s) exhaust the entire field of discourse. Thus, the analysis of the person could, hypothetically, be carried out not only in terms of its identity or difference with respect to the body-mind, but for any characteristic at all. The body-mind (*skandha*) was traditionally chosen as it is a stock rubric for Buddhism. Theoretically,

71

any characteristic would suffice to prove the non-intrinsic charac-terizability of the person, so long as it is affirmed and denied of the person, and that the denial or negation of the characteristic extensionally includes everything else in the universe. In other words, any **P** is suitable, since **P** and **−P** comprise the universal set.

ABSTRACT AND INSTANTIATED ANALYSES

The procedure for analysis is again different depending on whether an analysis investigates a member of one of the basic cat-egories or the class circumscribed by the category itself. This is the difference between an instantiated analysis that, for example, investigates the status of a particular tree, house, person, etc., and an abstract analysis that investigates a class of concepts such as things (*bhāva*), the concept of personhood, etc. The former analyses purport to demonstrate the openness of the concept, or instance in question, and the latter claim to prove the openness of an entire *class*, i.e., show that the class is void of any members.

The analysis proceeds a little differently in both cases due to the structural differences that we noted between category-restrict-ed and category unrestricted analyses. When one is analyzing a class of concepts it is sufficient that an analysis is confined to the two positions that make up a pair of logically opposed positions, even when they exhaust the modal characteristics of just one cate-gory, such as in the analysis of things (*bhāva*). Using this exam-ple, if the object of refutation is the class of "things" then a refu-tation of the defining characteristic of "being produced" serves to prove that the class of "things" is empty of any members because there are no produced things. And the analysis is complete with no other category option needing to be considered for the object of analysis was the class of "things."

On the other hand, if an instance of a produced thing, such as a sprout, chair, etc., is being analyzed it is analytically incomplete to merely refute its failure to have been produced from itself or other, for though "being produced" is the defining characteristic of the class of "things" it is not the defining characteristic of any instance of a "thing." For any individual "thing being produced" is one among many characteristics. Its defining characteristic is whatever makes the individual "thing" that particular "thing" and clearly, "being produced" doesn't demarcate it from other produced things. Thus, if an analysis takes as its object of negation an individual that is proffered as a "thing," an analysis that refutes the characteristic of "being produced" serves only to show that the object is not a "thing." It doesn't negate the individual as such for "being produced" is not its defining characteristic. At most, such a restricted analysis shows that it is empty of being a product. To show that the individual in question lacks any intrinsic existence the logical opposite to its being a "thing" would have to be considered.[104] Once it was shown to be neither a product nor non-product, its openness would be ascertained.

Hence, in instantiated analyses it is necessary that the theses within which a concept is analyzed exhaust all the categories, i.e., that they are extensional opposites. Whereas with an abstract analysis that takes a defining characteristic as the characteristic or predicate in a formal position, an analysis can be completed, i.e., show a class to be empty, just by analyzing within category restricted opposites.

MODAL ANALYSIS AND SUBSTANTIVE BI-NEGATIVE CONCLUSIONS

The two key analyses we have outlined (i.e., the "same-or-different" and "production" analyses, and the "temporal" and "one-or-many" analyses we very briefly described) are modal in structure for they analyze an entity in terms of its modalities or characteristics.

That is to say, the consequences refute positions that establish entities as having certain modal properties, such as being born from themselves, different from some other entity, etc. In doing so, they reflect the predicative structure of conceptuality. Though the analyses are modal in structure, their conclusions have a substantive import. That is to say, though the analyses *directly* take up the question of the presence or absence of the characteristics of entities, the conclusions made with respect to their characteristics bear on the ontological status of the entities themselves. This is because for Middle Pathers there is an ontologically reciprocal dependence (*parasparāpekṣa*) between the status of that which is characterized (i.e., a subject) (*lakṣya*) and the characteristics (*lakṣaṇa*) themselves. The dependency at work in the case of claiming a substantive import to these analyses is that the existence of entities depends on the ascription of defining characteristics to them.[105] Thus, the event of a modality being simultaneously neither affirmed nor denied of an entity takes it outside the realm of characterization (with respect to the modalities in question) and so beyond findability or knowability. Such an entity cannot be known, though this does not imply it is unknown.

It is important to see that non-characterizability is different from a negative characterization. Whereas the absence of a characteristic tells us *something* about an entity (it gives information that can help in the identification of an entity), non-characterizability, as expressed in the logical syntax of the bi-negative disjunction, does not help in the identification of an entity. In other words, it does not give us *any* information that could help in ascertaining whether or not an entity exists. Thus the bi-negation leaves the ontological status of a concept completely undetermined.

The substantive conclusion is derived differently depending on whether an analysis is category restricted or unrestricted. In the case of category restricted analyses the characteristic or modality chosen to be analyzed is the defining characteristic (*svalakṣaṇa*) of some entity. The conclusion to a category restricted analysis is that the defining property of some entity is neither present with, nor absent from, the entity in question. The substantive import of this conclusion derives from the fact that if the defining property is not present the entity *cannot* be affirmed to exist. If the defining characteristic is present the entity *must* be affirmed to exist. Thus, if the defining characteristic is neither present nor not present the entity which is identified by the property neither exists nor doesn't exist. This amounts to saying that the entity lacks an intrinsic identity.

In non-category restricted analyses an entity is shown to be non-intrinsically identified rather than non-existent through the exclusion of *all* possible characteristics as being inapplicable to an entity. The entity A is neither a P nor not a P where P and not P exhaust the universal set of modalities. The nihilistic conclusion that A doesn't exist would be mistakenly drawn from the modal conclusion for the non-existence of something presupposes the applicability of characteristics to an entity which are actually absent. In other words, in order to determine that A is non-existent we would have to know what A is, such that we could know that it didn't exist. If A goes uncharacterized because all characteristics are inapplicable to it, its existence or non-existence is unascertainable as the entity itself would be unidentifiable. In other words, A couldn't be a non-existent entity for it wouldn't be an entity at all.

The bi-negative conclusion is also arrived at more directly, it seems, by reflecting on the dependency of concepts on their logical opposites. Thus, when it is ascertained that there is no existence, no non-existence is also ascertained for in the absence of existence there is nothing to be negated. Thus, the negation of existence in Middle Path analysis implies the negation of non-existence. In the next chapter this will be explained in terms of analysis beginning at a refined level.

Reflecting directly in this way, from a negation of existence (or an existent) to the bi-negative conclusion that there is neither existence nor non-existence, (or neither an existent nor a non-existent) is what I would call a substantive analysis for it goes directly to the bi-negative conclusion without analyzing the modality involved in *analytically* ascertaining the *lack* of non-existence. (It relies on the fact that the concept of non-existence logically implies "existence" insofar as a negative implies the concept that is negated.) A substantive conclusion is tacked onto one prong of a paradoxical (or partitive) analysis[106] that establishes non-existence qua existence, or the non-existence of the proffered existent.

Nāgārjuna, for example, analyses directly to the bi-negative conclusion from one half of a paradoxical analysis on several occasions in the *Principal Stanzas on the Middle Path* [MK].[107] Perhaps this method of analysis represents an insider's technique for it *presupposes* a commitment to an awareness of the principles of the reciprocal dependence of concepts and their logical opposites and the transference of characteristics between logical opposites. Thus, when existence is negated so is non-existence. On the other hand, a modal analysis (which is genuinely paradoxical in structure) doesn't presuppose an appreciation of these two principles even though they are integral to the paradoxical method of proof.

A GENERALIZED ANALYTICAL PROCEDURE

By way of summarizing the overall procedure of paradoxical analysis we will now briefly describe a generic template that undergirds Middle Path analysis. Again, we can best achieve this by beginning with a chart (*Figure 2.2*). The facing pages are to be read together and from top to bottom.

Step 1. Identifying a universe of discourse (U of D)

The first step consists of identifying everything that is and isn't. This involves privately and briefly surveying the full range of conceptual distinctions that make up a view of the universe. This first step provides a backdrop or context in paradoxical analysis occurs.

Step 2. Dividing the U of D into mutually excluding classes

The second step consists of specifying a class or specific distinction (= object) to be analyzed by dividing the universe of discourse into that class or object (A) and everything that is not that class or object (−A).

Step 1'. Identifying the class by a characteristic

The third step involves identifying the class or object by some characteristic (in the case of category restricted analysis) or applying the presence and absence of any characteristic to the class or object (in the case of category unrestricted analysis).

Step 2'. Selecting two logically opposite positions

The fourth step involves selecting two logically opposed positions which describe how the characteristic can exist. (In the case of a category unrestricted analysis a pair of opposed positions is generated for both the possessing and lack of possession of the characteristic by the class or object.

Steps 3a and 3b. Demonstrating the paradoxes

The next two steps involve generating paradoxes for each of the

A GENERALIZED TEMPLATE

Step 1. Identifying a Universe of Discourse (U of D)

Step 2. Divide the U of D into Two Mutually Excluding Classes

Step 1'. Identify the Class to be Analyzed

Step 2'. Divide the Class by Way of Two Mutually Excluding Characteristics

Step 3a. Generate a Contradiction for the First Position

Step 3b. Generate a Contradiction for the Second Position

Step 4. Modal Conclusion drawn from the Conclusions to Steps 3a and 3b

Step 5. Substantive Conclusion

Figure 2.2 A generalized template [I]

two logically opposed positions. That is to say, a demonstration is offered for how each position entails the other. **A** is **P** is seen to entail that **A** is **−P**. and **A** is **−P** is seen to entail that **A** is **P**.

Step 4. Drawing a modal conclusion
The next step draws the conclusions generated by steps 3a and 3b into the bi-negation that **A** is neither **P** nor **−P**.

Step 5. Drawing a substantive conclusion
In the final step a substantive conclusion is drawn. If **A** is neither **P** nor **−P** then A neither exists nor doesn't exist. This is the openness of **A**.

We will demonstrate how to use this template by installing a set of substitutions. With these substitutions the template constitutes

78

A GENERALIZED TEMPLATE

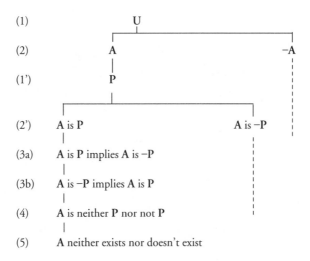

Figure 2.2 A generalized template [II]

an actual paradoxical analysis. For this demonstration we will follow the procedures for a "category-restricted analysis."

We begin by deciding to analyze a class of things that we find problematic or troublesome. For this example we will choose the class of "enemies." Since this is a category-restricted analysis, we need to choose a defining characteristic for the class of "enemies." Thus, membership of this class will be made up of all things that possess this characteristic. We will begin with a general understanding of what an enemy is and then narrow this down to a simple characteristic that is suitable for the purposes of performing a rigorous analysis. In general terms, an enemy is a person who I assess is out to do me harm. They wish to damage possibilities that I value. These could be material, physical, emotional, or intellectual possibilities. Thus, the concept of an enemy defined in this way is fairly general. It can include a competitor in business, a colleague at work, a partner in an intimate relationship, or a thug who is about to mug me.

Step 1'. In order to formalize this characteristic in a form that is suitable for analysis, we need a shorthand definition. The key feature of the above description is that of "intending harm." An enemy (**A**), then, is someone who intends us harm (**P**). Anyone who possesses the characteristic of "intending us harm" is an enemy.

Step 2'. Having formalized the opinion or position that the class of enemies are those people who intend us harm, we now select two mutually excluding and logically opposed ways in which someone could intend us harm. Two ways in which someone could intend us harm are "right now" in the present, or at some other time, i.e., "not right now." These two modes fulfill the requirement that each is a logical negation of the other. The task now is to produce a logical contradiction for both of these alternatives.

Step 3a. The first alternative is that an enemy is someone who intends to harm us at this very moment, i.e., "right now."[108] However, no one can harm us in the present because "right now" is past before they have time to harm us. Therefore, the person who intends to harm me "right now" must intend to harm me in the past or future (i.e., "not right now"). Intending to harm me at the present entails intending to harm me at some time other than the present.

Step 3b. The second alternative is that an enemy is someone who intends to harm me "not right now" but at some other time (i.e., in the past or future). However, no one can intend to harm me other than in the present because (1) they cannot harm me in the time that has already elapsed, and (2) they cannot harm me in the time that is yet to come. Therefore, the person who intends to harm me but not "right now" (i.e., who intends to harm me in the past or future) must intend to harm me right now.

Step 4. Drawing the two conclusions from steps 3a and 3b together we conclude therefore that the person we are calling an enemy can harm me neither in the present nor at any other time.

Step 5. From the modal conclusion at step 4, we draw the substantive conclusion that a person who can harm me neither now nor at any other time neither exists nor doesn't exist. In other words, we cannot make a claim about the existence or non-existence of an enemy who harms me right now or at another time.

Finally, we can note that because this is a category-restricted analysis it is sufficient to analyze the class "enemy" simply in terms of the defining characteristic of "intending harm." Since it is the defining characteristic it is not necessary to analyze the class "enemy" around the characteristic of "not intending harm."

Had we chosen a non-defining characteristic such as the identity or non-identity of an enemy with a body-mind then we would need to analyze the two positions: (1) that the enemy is their body-mind, and (2) that the enemy isn't their body-mind.

IMPLICATIVE AND NON-AFFIRMING NEGATIONS

A rounded understanding of Middle Path analysis depends on an understanding of two different types of analytical negation that are recognized by Middle Pathers. This is especially the case when examining the practical aspects of Middle Path. Hence, in this section we will make some basic observations regarding the distinction between implicative (*parudāsa*) and non-affirming negations (*prasajya-pratisedha*) and their use in the context of Middle Path praxis.

The distinction between these two types of negations in Middle Path logic is well defined.[109] An implicative negation implies the affirmation of a logically opposite position by the negation of the original position that is being put forward. A non-affirming negation negates the initial position without implying the affirmation of the opposite position. In other words, it is a pure and simple negation that doesn't establish anything positive. It may be difficult at first to see how the negation of a position can fail but to affirm the negative of this position. The idea of a non-affirming negation, though, is that it *removes* the original position but does not affirm its opposite. In other words, in the non-affirming negation the original position simply lapses. It is simply no longer affirmed. However, this lack of affirmation does not imply the adoption of the negation of the position. The capacity to non-affirmingly negate a position depends on an appreciation of the principle of non-contradiction and a thorough understanding of the principle that every position mutually entails its negation and that the negation of a position entails that position. Then, to affirm the negative formulation of a position after its logical negation is only to reaffirm the original position that one has just negated. The non-affirming negation forestalls this circularity.

On the other hand, with an implicative negation the opposite position is affirmed when the original position is refuted. In doing this the mutual dependency between a position and its opposite is lost sight of. A non-affirming negation of either a position or its logical opposite establishes the middle (non-positional) view in that it avoids affirming either the original position or its opposite. In other words, a non-affirming negation states a mere absence or vacuity of a position.

The *doctrinal* position of Middle Pathers who rely on paradoxes (*Prāsaṅgika Mādhyamikas*) is that their own negations are non-affirming. Candrakīrti states this quite clearly in the *Clear Words* [PP].[110] The point is also made in the *Commentary to the Introduction to the Middle Path* [MABh: 81] where Candrakīrti characterizes the negations (*ma yin*) involved in the refutation of intrinsically existent things through the production analysis as having no affirmative import because they mean a prohibition or exclusion (*dgag pa*). This means, for example, that when one negates the position of "birth from self" this does not imply that "things are born from another."

However, although Middle Path negations are theoretically non-affirming, in practice they are often not taken as such, and this is borne out by the fact that typically both the positive and negative formulations of a position are serially refuted in Middle Path texts. By a serial refutation I mean the *connected* refutation of a position and its negation, not the occurrence of refuting one position and then a subsequent but *unrelated* refutation of its negation.

In terms of Middle Path practice it seems that the Middle Pathers' negations are not always non-affirming, and that the non-affirming aspect of their negation is a statement of *intention* and not something intrinsic to their style of logic.[111] From this perspective, the mere intention by Middle Pathers that their refutation of a position doesn't affirm the opposite position need not preempt the possibility (even likelihood!) that an opponent may, subsequent to a convincing refutation of his native position, *slide* in his viewpoint so as to affirm, however moderately or tentatively, the negation of his initial position. In such a case the Middle Pathers—realizing that analysands may slide in their viewpoints, and wishing also to bring them to the point of rejecting all view-points—will frame their refutations to both the initial position *and* its negation. They are wise, in other words, to a tendency in their analysands (and within their own thought also) to construe their negations as implicative.[112] So when Middle Pathers cap their refutations with an affirmation of a negation they are vocal-izing and bringing to consciousness what they believe to be a conclusion in the thought of an analysand.

These two different types of negation, the implicative and non-affirming, respectively make for a conjunctive and disjunctive use of consequences. If negations are affirming, then both the affirma-tion and negation of a position must be refuted in order to exclude the possible views that can be adopted. If the negations are intended, and more important, are *taken* as non-affirming, then the middle view that precludes all viewpoints can be gained by the refutation of a single position in isolation from the refuta-tion of the opposite position, for in forsaking a position, the analysand does not take up the opposing position.

With respect to the confluting or coincidence of opposites that we talked about earlier, the conflutings take place naturally and as integral to analysis in the case of non-implicative negations. This is so because the basis for refuting a position is by the derivation of its negation or opposite. On the other hand, the confluting is artificial and a separate exercise to analysis itself in the case of affirming negations, as two contradictory conclusions are gener-ated *serially* within a mind-stream; these have to be temporally aligned as an act separate and subsequent to the derivation of those two appropriately juxtaposed consequences.

LOGICAL AND EXPERIENTIAL CONSEQUENCES

It should be clear now that the procedures of analysis produce not only a logical conclusion, or conclusion in reason, such as are expressed in the bi-negative disjunctions that summarize the conclusion to paradoxical analyses, but also produce an experiential result.

How is it then that the analytical processing of conceptuality can affect something more than a mere change in thought? How can conceptual analysis produce a radical and liberating transformation of an entire level of being? The transformative effects of analysis can be explained best by examining the meditative uses of analysis. Here experiential effects can be accounted for through two related factors: (1) through a perception of the ramifications of a concept on and within the reactive emotions, and (2) by a discernment of the deeper levels and infrastructures of the concepts that are analyzed.

The first factor involves a recognition of the structural role that any particular concept being analyzed plays in the arising and constellation of emotional reactions (*kleśa*) to cognitions. That is to say, when Middle Pathers are establishing the concept to be analyzed (i.e., ascertaining the object to be refuted [*dgag bya*] as in the first step of their analytical contemplations), they survey their affective mental states and tendencies with a view to ascertaining which moods, feelings, and emotions are dependent on the concept under analysis. They are concerned with the functional dependencies between concepts and different sets of emotions and explore the nexus in which concepts are placed with respect to other concepts. They become conscious of structural dependencies wherein negative emotions, moods, and feelings are dependent on misconceptions, and in so doing, they involve those emotions and moods in an analysis and bind these, in a sense, to the outcome of an analysis. Thus, when the misconceptions are reversed, this serves to undermine the structural basis of

85

the negative emotional responses.

So, although it is only a concept that is being analyzed, its influence within the psyche of an analyst is investigated prior to or rather as the first step in any analysis so as to ensure that an analysis has some effect in attenuating and countering affective responses, such as hatred, aggression, desire, lust, pride, etc. More specifically, as the conceptual bases to the afflictive emotions are destructured, this has an impact on the afflictive emotions that *corresponded in degree* to the dependencies that are ascertained at the beginning of any analysis. These dependencies become apparent to analysts only through deep contemplation and how much of an analyst's psyche is invested in an analysis depends on the thoroughness with which the dependencies are seen. In this way, for example, analysis of the view of individuality (*satkāya-dṛṣṭi*) would involve not only an ascertainment of the *concept* of a real self but also an appreciation of its influence on the formation of the personality and particularly on neuroses and stultifying emotions that develop on the basis of that view. These investigations of affective responses and their correlation with false modes of conceptuality have traditionally been facilitated by the Buddhist metapsychologies (*abhidharma*) and, for Tibetan philosophers, the mental typologies (*blo rigs*) literature.[113]

The second and partially overlaid way of explaining the experiential effects of analysis is to consider that the concepts themselves that are analyzed, exist and can be ascertained at varying degrees of depth and subtlety. This view is affirmed in the distinction drawn by Middle Pathers between intellectual (*pari-kalpita*) and innate (*sahaja*) concepts, in which intellectual conceptualizations are more superficial and less deeply ingrained and entrenched than innate ones.

While the surface aspects or components of conceptuality exist at the level of conscious experience (in fact, they are identified with conscious thought), the depth aspects exist at an unconscious level, at least for ordinary folk. Indeed, concepts must be so constituted for the Middle Path. This is apparent if we take the self-concept as an example, for were the self-concept merely the *conscious* thought of "I" or "me" it would mean that whenever the thought of "I" or "me" was absent within a stream of thought we would be realizing selflessness. We, for a great (and probably greater) part of our waking, and all of our deep sleep experience, would be realizing the selflessness that *only* the saints realize. So clearly the concept of a self is established by a mode of conceiving that operates at a subconscious level. Middle Pathers say this applies to other concepts as well. These subconscious, and hence, unmanifest modes of conceiving are probably more stable and continuous than the ever changing perturbations of conscious conceptuality.

In the meditative context when analysts are ascertaining the object to be negated, they are concerned with fathoming the deeper, more subtle and more entrenched modes of conceptuality; modes that could only be penetrated through deep and quiet meditation. And, given that there are deeper and structurally more significant modes of conceiving than conscious thought, and that an analyst can plum these and in fact take these as the concepts to be analyzed, then by realizing the openness of these structurally and effectively more significant aspects of conceptuality they can gain experiences that likewise have deeper effects than the mere manipulation of conscious thought. It seems, in fact, that openness can only be realized in dependence on an analyst knowing precisely and in detail what it is that he or she is analyzing. Thus, for example, the more fully and deeply that the errant view of a self, as permanent, intrinsically existent, etc. is ascertained, the fuller (and more freeing also) is the insight gained in realizing that *that* deeper and more entrenched self is open, in the sense that it doesn't have any intrinsic characteristics. Tibetan philosophers quote a line from Śāntideva's *Introduction to the Evolved Lifestyle* [BCA: 9.140a] in this regard which says that, "Without contacting the thing that is imagined there is no ascertainment of its non-[intrinsic] existence." The import of this line is that one must know the false cognition, the falsely established status of things, in order to be able to refute and negate it.

Thus analysts gain profound and existentially far-reaching results from their analyses by realizing the pervasive structure of conceptuality and its role in supporting the emotional reactions (*kleśa*) and by locating and analyzing the deeper flows and features of conceptuality. Exactly how experientially profound a paradoxical conclusion is would be dependent on how thoroughly the connections and dynamic dependencies between concepts and emotions are ascertained and to what extent the deeper levels of conceptuality are penetrated.

HABIT FORMATIONS IN THE ANALYST'S MIND-STREAM

Prior to concluding this chapter it is important to place the techniques of Middle Path analysis in a realistic context. On all accounts it would seem that we have described a highly refined and consciously used method for radically and swiftly transforming the cognitions and experience of a Middle Path practitioner. While this is true, the capacity to direct and sustain the type of thinking and emoting that truly transformational analysis requires is limited to the most highly trained practitioners. According to Middle Pathers, there are barriers to effective analysis. The barriers are "constraints on change" caused by the human propensity to repeat those patterns of behavior and experience with which we are most familiar. As humans we are conditioned by our past in ways and forms that limit our capacity for new, innovative action. More particularly, we are compelled or thrown to repeat those ways of thinking, feeling, and acting to which we have accustomed ourselves.

The full Middle Path explanation for how our thinking, feeling, and behavior is conditioned and limited by past individual experience is provided through the Buddhist theory of actions (*karma*) and their consequences (*vipaka*). In systemic terms karma is a self stabilizing influence that constrains a stream of consciousness by placing limits on what can be done, felt, and thought.

There are no great variations within Buddhism in explaining how we are conditioned, and so in general terms Middle Pathers have adopted what is a pan-Buddhist explanation of karma. Middle Pathers agree with the explanation of karma provided by the Buddhist meta-psychologists (Abhidharmists). They only add that the sense in which our experience is conditioned or caused by the past is merely nominal. Ultimately, we aren't conditioned by our past, but nor are we unconditioned by it. Karma is only an explanation. It doesn't actually describe anything going on out there or inside our minds. For Middle Pathers, karma has the status of a linguistic explanation. It is offered and used by Middle Pathers in order to design actions and a lifestyle that support the pursuit of realizing their own openness (*nairātmya*). Given that the Middle Pather believes that he or she is ultimately a fiction, the theory of karma provides guidelines for designing new (fictitious) experiences for an equally fictitious person.

According to the Buddhist metapsychologist Vasubandhu, karma is mental drive (*cetanā*).[114] Our experience is channeled in dependence on traces (*vāsanā, saṁskāra*) that are left in our psyche in virtue of having the experiences that we do. Experiencing leaves residues that serve to shape and delimit what we experience in the future. The so-called patterns of karma describe some basic constancies in how past and present actions (*karma*) produce specific types of consequences. Buddhist texts describe how the traces (*vāsanā*) left from our experiencing can be more and less influential in shaping our future. They describe how the level or weight of influence is determined by factors such as the presence or absence of emotional reactions (*kleśa*) such as desire or aversion, and by the motivation or intention (*aśāya*). They also describe how positive experiential outcomes are conditioned by authentic (*kuśala*) and truthful behavior while negative outcomes are conditioned by inauthentic and harmful actions.

In terms of analysis, we can see that karma places limits on the capacity of a practitioner to effectively analyze. Even if practitioners are genuine and well motivated in their intention to rigorously analyze their experience along Middle Path lines, still they will find themselves unable to sustain the level of coherence and concentration that effective analysis requires. They will become confused, wish they were doing something else, be distracted by memories from their past, and so on.

But, conversely, once a practitioner becomes accustomed to regular and disciplined analysis, her or his practice will be empowered and made easier through the very same conditioning principles that hindered effective analysis when first embarking on this particular discipline of self-development.

IS INSIGHT A NECESSARY RESULT OF CONSEQUENTIAL ANALYSIS?

In concluding this chapter we will briefly address the question of whether insight is contingently or necessarily related to analysis. Or posed in a more sharply focused form: Is the realization of a logical conclusion to a paradoxical analysis necessarily productive of some measure of insight into openness? Answering these questions involves determining the *extent* to which paradoxical analysis models deductive forms of reasoning, for if it can be shown that indeed the Middle Path *logic* is deductively valid then there are grounds for holding that insightful conclusions necessarily follow if analyses do conform to sound deductive thought-processes. The problem is complicated, though, for the logic of the Middle Path is not a pen-and-paper logic but a logic embedded in the *experience* of Middle Pathers. Hence, while logical necessities might function at a *formal level* in Middle Path analysis, the empirical contextualization of Middle Path logic weighs against the necessity of insight arising from analysis. That is to say, the grounding of Middle Path analysis in the experience of analysts introduces contingencies into the relationship between analysis and insight. The introduction of contingencies means that it wouldn't be imperative that insight arose from analysis. If they are contingently related, any logical compulsion is ameliorated and insight may or may not arise at the completion of any analysis.

First, we will talk about the types of contingencies that might exist in Middle Path analysis and then show that the procedures of Middle Path analysis are designed to preclude the entry of contingencies into the relationship between analysis and insight and in so doing point to an *ideal* form and structure of analysis in which insight necessarily follows from analysis.

The first contingency, though one may not really wish to call it such, is that an analysis fails to be followed to its logical completion and so stops at a non-conclusive and hence non-insightful conclusion. Even given that a conclusion is realized, other genuine contingencies would act to ameliorate the quality and strength of any insight gained. Two significant factors are: (1) changes to the identity criteria of the concept being analyzed, and (2) a failure to perceive the need for refuting *both* the positive and negative formulations of a position in order to exclude *all* views. As I'll explain in more detail, these two factors revoke the first and second steps respectively of the meditative contextualization of analysis into four steps, that has been referred to earlier. Contingencies such as the above could occur for any number of reasons, for example, being interrupted or being ignorant of or forgetting analytical procedures. The most interesting case—and one that throws light on the dynamic between analytical and non-analytical mentalities within a single continuum—is where the concept as originally specified, is modified in the course of an analysis so that it is not implicated in a conclusion. A likely occurrence in such a case is a diminution in what constitutes the concept. This would be caused by a relinquishing of the deep and subtle aspects of a concept and/or a failure to retain the emotional reactions that were originally implicated in an analysis. That is to say, the concept would be narrowed down through a spilling out of the deeper more entrenched levels of the concept so that only the more superficial aspects were retained within the conclusion. A more obvious revoking of identity criteria would occur where the identifying characteristics of a concept were changed partway through an analysis.

Even though various contingencies can and obviously would enter into an analyst's contemplations, the procedures and guidelines used in directing analytical contemplations appear to be designed to reduce the *occurrence, strength, and influence* of contingent factors. The procedures do this by (1) ensuring predicative coherence and consistency, (2) by acknowledging the principles of contradiction and joint exhaustion of a class or universal domain by logical opposites, and (3) by preempting a slide to an opposing viewpoint. Although some of these features of the

Middle Path analysis have been mentioned before, the context of discussion is different here.

The first step in the meditative contextualization of analysis appears to require not only a location of errant conceptions but their specification by a coherent and consistent predicate. Thus, the concept that is analyzed is *rigidly designated* in an effort to remove all referential opacity. An analyst gains a clear and distinct perception of the concept to be analyzed, and attempts to ensure that the very same concept is implicated in the conclusion. This structurally models and forms thought in terms of the principle of identity and ensures (1) that the same concept is analyzed throughout a contemplation, and (2) that the same concept is affirmed and denied in the conclusion. The first step is thus a commitment to the identity of a concept through characterizing it coherently and consistently.

The second step, as explained earlier, psychologically commits a saint to two jointly exhaustive and mutually exclusive possibilities that serve to prescribe two alternative and well-defined sequences of thought. This aligns his or her thought with the principles of the excluded middle and contradiction.

As argued earlier, paradoxical analysis aims, via *reductio ad absurdum* arguments, to bring the positive and negative formulations of positions into a co-spatial and co-temporal alignment which *necessitates* the destructuring of a concept. A psychological necessity flows from the fact of the logical impossibility of such a co-alignment. The co-spatial and co-temporal alignment of logical opposites constitutes the sufficient and necessary condition for the destructuring of a concept and hence, on the interpretation given earlier, for an insight into the openness of the concept. With respect to the third and fourth steps in the four-step format of meditation, these last two steps each follow up an argument that in essence constitutes a sequence of thoughts. When the negation implied in an analysis is implicative or affirmative (*parudāsa*) the third *and* fourth steps *together* preempt a slide in viewpoint and hence offset the establishment of a position or viewpoint (for example, that there *is* a transcendental or non-transcendental self) rather than an openness. The structure of non-affirming negations seems to guarantee a co-temporal affirmation of a position and its logical opposite through *either* of the last two steps. In this case the two options contained in the third and fourth steps serve to bridge the heuristic contingency that analysts may be inclined to different views of the self and other concepts.

Thus, there are certain structural features to the techniques of Middle Path analysis that serve to remove the entry of contingent factors into analysis and so increasingly ensure that appropriately insightful conclusions do follow from analysis. Middle Pathers consciously and gradually hone down and refine their analyses so that their conceptual trajectories, as specified by the analytical procedures, become integrated, controlled, specific, firm, focused, and stable. In this way they make their meditations more fruitful.

A SIMULATION MODEL
OF MIDDLE PATH ANALYSIS

INTRODUCTION

THIS CHAPTER CONSTRUCTS an *exploratory model* of paradoxical analysis that attempts to develop one step further the explanation given in chapter two. In particular the model extends the earlier explanation by (1) coordinating various aspects of the explanation advanced there, and (2) placing paradoxical analysis in a temporal context that in general terms accounts for the development of insight within a graduated process such as is envisaged in Middle Path literature. This literature describes a series of levels in which insight into openness is progressively enhanced.[115] The idea for the model arose in the course of my own thinking about the likely, or at least possible, course of events that takes place when Middle Path analysts engage in an intensive and active practice of debate and private analytical contemplations.

THE CONTEXTUAL VALIDITY OF A SYSTEM-CYBERNETICS
INTERPRETATION

Before embarking on the development of a system-cybernetics model of Middle Path analysis it is important to acknowledge that the interpretation we will develop is self-contradictory from a Middle Path perspective. This is unavoidable for the Middle Path reduces every interpretation of the world to absurdity. The interpretation we will develop has no *special* epistemological or hermeneutical status that shields it from the Middle Path critique. It too rests on assumptions that are *ultimately* indefensible.

It is worth exploring the aspect of "temporal interpretations" of the Middle Path just a little since a variety of such interpretations have been offered through both traditional and contemporary philosophers. By a "temporal interpretation" of the Middle Path we mean an interpretation that places the Middle Path analysis in the context of how an individual who follows such a path changes over time.

The first point to note is that traditional Middle Pathers have developed their own temporal interpretation of the Middle Path. It appears in the path-structure (*krama-mārga*) literature developed by philosophers such as Asaṅga in his *Ornament for the Realizations* (*Abhisamayālaṁkāra*).[116] According to this interpretation, insight into openness occurs as a radical event in the mind-stream of a practitioner who has been practicing serenity and discernment meditation for some time. Suddenly, in a moment of illumination, the meditator has a full-blown, direct insight into openness. The moment is of such significance that it heralds entry into what is called the Path of Vision (*darśana-mārga*). Interestingly, this path has no duration since the moment of insight occurs not gradually over time but in a single instant of illumination. If we are to subject this interpretation to a Middle Path analysis, it appears to be a case of "production from another," since the moment of insight has antecedent causes in the form of discernment meditation, yet it represents a mind-state that is totally different from those which preceded it. If this is the case, this interpretation suffers from the contradiction that if the moment of insight is intrinsically different from what has preceded it, then any prior mental state could equally produce insight. Getting drunk, standing on one's head, killing oneself, sleeping, etc. could equally produce insight. In other words, if the two states are radically discontinuous in terms of their defining characteristics, then no specific practice or discipline fosters the development of insight. Thus any practice, or no practice, could cause insight which makes nonsense of the concept of causation.

Some recent comparative philosophers interpret the Middle Path as a "leap philosophy."[117] According to this interpretation, spiritual insight occurs as a totally unpredictable event. It is *unrelated* to any antecedent causes. If and when it happens, it happens spontaneously and for no apparent reason. If we subject this interpretation to a Middle Path analysis, it appears to be a case of "production from no cause." If this is the case, it is not a causal account for the development of spiritual insight.

So what about the system-cybernetics interpretation we are developing in the study? In this interpretation we are first talking about "insight being caused by analysis." This, in large part, was our argument in the last chapter. So it is clear that, contrary to the "leap" interpretation, we interpret insight as being dependent on particular antecedent causes and conditions. Further, we are also developing an interpretation that will speak in terms of the "gradual development of the insight of openness over time." Thus, the form of production we are assuming in a system-cybernetics interpretation looks like a mixture of production from self and other. Analogically it is like the production of a sprout from a seed, since we want to say that a sprout is different from a seed, yet that there is a sense of continuity wherein the sprout emerges out of the seed. In the same way, we are saying that the fully developed insight into openness is a fundamentally different mode of cognition than cognition that is predicated by a lack of awareness (*avidyā*). And we also want to say that insight into openness emerges gradually as an individual practices Middle

Path methods of meditation and analysis.

But this interpretation can be taken apart by Middle Path analysis using Nāgārjuna's and Candrakīrti's refutations of production from self and another as outlined in the last chapter. The Middle Path invites us to be specific about whether insight into openness is an intrinsically different condition from lack of awareness. If it is, then Middle Pathers will analyze our model as a case of "production from another." If they aren't intrinsically different, they will interpret our model as an instance of "production from self." Either way, our interpretation can be shown to be self-contradictory. If we try to avoid the paradoxical consequences by saying that the system-cybernetics model is more complex and that it cannot be resolved into a simple case of "production from self" or "production from another," the Middle Path will invite us to clarify this complex process, for our own purposes as much as for theirs. As we clarify the process (i.e., get specific about it), our description will resolve again into one or another (or both) of the alternatives, and paradoxical consequences will be offered.

So what can we say in response to the Middle Path critique of the interpretation we are developing here? The first point to make is that in developing this system-cybernetics model we are not making any epistemological or ontological claims. The model doesn't describe any real process that happens independently of our interpretation. The model is a linguistic interpretation which is developed for the purpose offering a new and modern understanding of one particular method for addressing human pain and suffering. Beyond this purpose the model has no intrinsic value since, if the Middle Path is right, there is no *real* human pain, or *real* state of insight for that matter. Thus, the model shouldn't be viewed as attempting to show how things *actually* are or even what is *really* possible.

In the spirit of the Buddhist tradition of skillful means (*upāya*), both the system-cybernetics model developed in this chapter and the suggestions for a clinical application of Middle Path analysis in the next chapter, are simply devices for modifying the ultimately illusory phenomena of human suffering and ignorance by creating a contemporary (yet still fabricated) interpretation of how suffering and ignorance can be overcome.

We can do this because, in a sense, everything is up for grabs in the Middle Path. There is no *right* interpretation. As we have shown, even the "temporal interpretation" of the Middle Path developed by Middle Pathers is self-contradictory. Middle Pathers will be the first to point this out. The validity for developing a new and modern interpretation rests in specifying the purpose for which the interpretation is developed. Every interpretation has a purpose and is validated through fulfilling that purpose. Each interpretation is like a different story, the aim of which is to awaken different listeners to the fact that who they are—their pains, accomplishments, and possibilities—is just another story, and that even the *telling* of the interpretation is yet again another fictitious story.

The purpose of the original path-structure interpretations was to draw attention to the mystical and radically transforming nature of the insight into openness. The audience for this interpretation were meditators who were accomplished in the meditative arts. The purpose of the "leap" interpretation is to highlight the unconditional nature of spiritual insight. Our purpose in this study is to provide an interpretation that has specific value in the psychological and therapeutic domains. For this purpose we deem that a base-line model, in which the insight into openness is developed gradually over time and in dependence on specific causes and conditions, is appropriate. Our reason for this is that scientific disciplines are based on a notion of "causal continuity." Cybernetics, for example, is based on the presupposition that systems interact causally and cognitive therapies presuppose that cognitive inputs *produce* cognitive change in clients in a measured and partially predictable way.

THE SYSTEMIC PLACEMENT OF THE MIDDLE PATH

Prior to developing the simulation model we will discuss the general placement of the Middle Path in systems constructs and describe the specific relations between Laszlo's invariant properties of systems and those we have located in the Middle Path.

The three systemic levels that Laszlo isolates in the *System, Structure, and Experience* are homeostasis, sensory feedback, and meta-sensory activity.[118] The Middle Path is primarily concerned with meta-sensory activities. These are defined as systems or components of systems in which the "cognitive requirements *exceed* the potentials of sense-codes."[119] Such activities are motivated by the failure of living organisms to satisfy all their needs by the adaptation to and manipulation of sense-cognitive inputs. The failure to satisfy all needs at the sensory-cognitive level drives the human organism to create more sophisticated, meta-sensory activities for the fulfillment of desires, comprehension, and expression. Laszlo subdivides such meta-perceptual patterns of activity into experiential structures represented by rational, aesthetic, and religious constructs. Ontological and epistemological inquiry, whether for soteriological ends, or otherwise, is necessarily meta-sensory (even if ultimately experiential and non-conceptual). Hence, the Middle Path describes the structures, procedures, and results of an essentially cognitive practice focused at the level of meta-sensory processing.

The two other systemic levels that Laszlo has isolated center on homeostatic and sensory feedback processes. Homeostatic and sensory processes are concerned with the stabilization and modification of physiological, or motor activities, and sensory-inputs respectively. All three levels are continuous, interactive, and hierarchically structured, and together constitute an integrative framework. The Middle Path is also concerned with this supra-systemic, or integrative framework as it discusses motor, volitional, perceptual, and affective actions besides those that are strictly meta-perceptual. The Middle Path assumes that there are bi-directional information-flows between all these levels and a hierarchical structuration. Both of these, the information-flows and hierarchies, are variable within the diachronic structure of the Middle Path, as represented in its path-structure, but broadly, physiological and sensory activities are governed—increasingly so in the path-context—by meta-sensory activities. Motor activity, sensory inputs, and connative responses become relevant in terms of their bearing on intra- and inter-mental systems. More specifically, behavior modification and mood management (through living an ethical lifestyle and engaging in yogic exercises) are employed in order to support the mental development of practitioners and the information-flows between them that take place in a teaching or dialectical (debating) context.

Laszlo's Four Invariant Properties

As we have said, the paradigmatic contribution of Laszlo to the discipline of systemic organization is his specification of systems and their behavior by the device of "invariant properties." An "invariant property," or alternatively "organizational invariance," he defines as the "on-random regularity of the coactions" of systemic components.[120] Laszlo's rationale for defining systems in terms of their salient components or invariances is that:

101

> There can be no science of a phenomena in a constant state of flux: *some* parameters must remain constant, or invariant under transformation. These constancies and invariancies furnish the systemic elements in reference to which theoretical structures can be built, mapping the fluctuating phenomena under investigation.[121]

The discipline of systemic analysis, then, is to locate and describe systemic invariances that can be described by a selective screening of the observed data.[122] In the *Introduction to Systems Philosophy*, Laszlo has mapped a handful of such systems properties. Specifically he has located four invariants that are applicable to and descriptive of a wide range of systems.[123]

They are, that systems manifest (1) wholeness and order, (2) adaptive self-stabilization, (3) adaptive self-organization, and (4) intra- and inter-systemic hierarchies. Since we will be utilizing these invariances and correlating the Middle Path's own constancies of behavior with these invariants, it is appropriate that we briefly describe them here.[124]

Wholeness and order. The property of wholeness assumes that wholes are coordinated aggregations, or complexes of parts, that have properties and characteristics not possessed by the parts individually. Systemic organization advocates an *in situ* consideration and study of a system's components as cumulatively forming orders and coordinated wholes.[125]

Adaptive self-stabilization. This and the next invariance, adaptive self-organization, together express the diachronic features of systemic transformation; in other words, the behavior of systems through time.

Adaptive self-stabilization refers to the homeostatic, or self-maintaining properties of systems. In systems, energies are deployed and invested in maintaining (or attempting to maintain) their stationary or steady-states by compensating for changes in the ambient and effective environment. Were systems not to stabilize themselves, i.e., not to exert a counteractive influence to environmental forces, they would de-autonomize, disorganize, and ultimately collapse and decay.[126]

Stabilization is achieved by negative feedback circuits that eliminate, or at least reduce, externally introduced perturbations by directing that available energy returns a system to internally specified parameters or constraints. This may involve introducing permanent or interim modifications to the effective environment. Laszlo likens the process of compensating for or offsetting external influences, to a constant deployment of energies "poised for action [...] with forces available to activate all needed processes."[127]

In the case of cognitive systems, self-stabilization acts to maintain a constancy in cognitive organization, or ensure a correspondency with existing constructs by changing processing programs and/or modifying the environment so as to confirm and reinforce existing cognitive configurations.[128] Self-stabilization corresponds roughly with the Festinger's "cognitive dissonance theory" of cognition which says that impressions and constructs are rigidly maintained and that discrepant information (i.e., whatever does not confirm existing constructs) tends to be ignored in preference to making structural changes.[129]

Adaptive self-organization. Adaptive self-organization like adaptive self-stabilization specifies processes that issue from a dynamic relationship between the internal constraints of a system and its environment. Adaptive self-organization, though, exhibits processes quite different from self-stabilization. Rather than blanketing out environmental influences, adaptive self-stabilization involves the structural, functional, and creative evolution of systemic parameters. That is to say, in response to environmental inputs, systems will, via positive feedback, reorganize themselves internally—beyond what may be required for self-maintenance—so as to accommodate new and more inputs. Such accommodation involves a complexification of systemic structures and manifests as the development of organizational hierarchies, the production of new subsystems and routines, and an overall increase in informational content. Systems seek out rather than resist environmental influences and creatively generate new codes, mappings, and behaviors to assimilate, organize, and manipulate those influences. Adaptive self-organization, then, accounts for learning, progress, and evolution.

In the case of cognitive systems, self-organization is the seeking out and acquisition of new experiences, the integration of these into existing cognitive constructs and/or the evolution of finer and more specialized constructs to assimilate new modes of experience/or map existing ones more satisfactorily.[130] Cognitive systems tend to display behavior suggested by Kelley's "personal construct theory": that judgments change and adapt to new information as it becomes available.[131]

Intra- and inter-systemic hierarchies. Laszlo's last invariant says that systems manifesting both stabilization and organization will develop "in the direction of increasing structuration."[132] Such hierarchical structures, within and between systems, expedites adaptation and evolution and simplifies the organizational, managerial, and agential functions of systems by introducing levels of command, directions, and routes for information-flows, and dependencies and independencies appropriate to each level in a hierarchy.

These are the four invariants of Laszlo's "system-cybernetics philosophy."

FIVE PROPERTIES THAT CHARACTERIZE THE MIDDLE PATH

The Middle Path describes a psycho-philosophical and religious meta-system. The key features of this system are the acquisition of the liberative insight of openness, achieved by the dialectical purification of consciousness; the establishment and deconstruction of a series of worldviews on the path to realizing the open dimension of reality (*śūnyatā*). Within the Expansive Career (*Mahāyāna*) this also involves the growth and perfection of an active altruism that issues forth in the development of vast cognitive and expressive capacities. The systemic transformations occur within the experience of Middle Path analysts. The contextual environment of the path of experience is a community of basically like-minded practitioners who are at various stages of their psycho-philosophical and spiritual development.

In order to describe this system we have located five salient properties. Individually they seem to be very general properties but when spelled out and coordinated together they are a powerful heuristic means for organization and understanding. These five properties can be viewed as subsystems within the Middle Path. We have designated them thus:

(1) Inducement-analysis
(2) Expansion
(3) Ramification
(4) Engramming
(5) Randomness

Together these represent one possible way of viewing the meta-system that is the Middle Path. In this chapter they provide a

105

basic infrastructure around which to develop a systemic model.

With the exclusion of the last property,[133] these are all invariants, or constancies, in the systems philosophical sense, since they display a discernible presence and *regularity* of pattern and behavior.[134] Each of the first four properties is a mode or instantiation of one or more of Laszlo's four invariant properties. Each has its own constraints, parameters, functions, behavioral dynamic, etc.

At this point, we will briefly introduce these five properties and relate them to Laszlo's set of invariances and the Middle Path system.

Inducement-analysis. Inducement-analysis specifies the etiology and evolution of a path leading to personal freedom (*pratimokṣa*). This is the system based on the paradoxical analysis (*prasaṅga-vicāra*) we have described in the preceding chapter.

As the designation "inducement-analysis" implies, this system is concerned both with analysis per se and the methods and conditions for its inducement.

More specifically, "analysis" refers to the structural manipulation of thought in conformity with the patterns of reasoning (templates) that formalize the procedures of paradoxical analysis. Such analytical processing destructures, and if it is sufficiently precise and thorough, dissolves conceptual elaboration (*prapañca*) leaving the mind of an analyst clear or diaphanous. This result is coterminus with an unmediated cognition of reality (*tattva*) or openness. "Inducement" refers to the conditions and practices that promote and support analysis. It thus indicates conditions such as a quiet, non-distracting environment and the absence of strongly disorienting emotions. It also refers to practices such as serenity meditation (*śamatha*) and meditative integration (*samādhi*). It also includes the will, or intention to analyze, without which a person doesn't begin to analyze even though he or she is prepared for this practice.

This subsystem displays both self-organizing (i.e., evolutionary) and self-stabilizing (i.e., homeostatic) behavior. Meta-systemically "inducement-analysis" behaves adaptively for it involves the progressive modification of behavioral, cognitive, and conceptual structures in response to environmental influences.[135] It is evolutionary for it involves a reduction in dissatisfaction and an increase in happiness and freedom of behavioral response. It is also a stabilizing system as the insight into openness has the function of increasing and ultimately ensuring the full integrity and autonomy of individuals within their environment. This is achieved by freeing individuals from fixed and determined responses to their environments. That is to say, the Middle Path system stabilizes internal perturbations by effectively isolating individuals from their environments through the induction of a valuational and ontological neutrality with respect to all objects of cognition. Hence, analysts become increasingly resilient to environmental factors.[136]

Expansion. Expansion refers to a system of cognitive change that is invoked when the Middle Path is practiced within the Expansive Career (*Mahāyāna*) of Buddhism. Within the Expansive Career, analysts are motivated to continually expand the distinctions with which they can observe the world. Their motivation to constantly expand their awareness stems from their wish to interact more powerfully and usefully with others. In order to develop powerful, effective, and relevant relationships with others, they seek to know all perspectives of things (*sarvākārajñata*). They continually add new linguistic concepts to their repertoire of linguistic distinctions in order to better appreciate the perspectives and interpretations that other people bring to their experience.

107

They become empowered to "observe as others observe."

The traditional literature which outlines the Expansive Career describes its development as the acquisition of ever more comprehensive levels of social knowledge (*vyavahāra*) coupled with the capacity (*bāla*) to use such knowledge to produce constructive outcomes for others. This capacity is summed up in the Expansive Career idea that practitioners (*bodhisattva*) develop skillful means or superior pedagogical and therapeutic skills (*upāya-kauśalya*).

The subsystem that we are terming "expansion" thus displays what Laszlo calls "organization characteristics." It is an outwardly directed system that is not concerned with its own autonomy and survival (at least directly). This system seeks to increase its capacity to *interact* with the environment—particularly with other people. As a publicly oriented system it is increasingly *adaptive* to the interpretative systems that others use to organize their experience and lives. This system consciously self-modifies and moves to ever increasing states of complexity. It changes in order to accommodate and manipulate an increasing number of environmental factors. This system develops organizational hierarchies and multilevel representational structures. This system acts against contextual isolation and moves consistently toward an ever increasing pervasion of and participation with the environment.

These first two subsystems, "inducement-analysis" and "expansion," are intersystemically related in at least two ways. First, "expansion" is related to "inducement-analysis" since every new linguistic distinction that an Expansive Career analyst acquires is analytically processed and its openness (or lack of intrinsic identifiability) realized. Thus, the data of the "extensive system" *flows through* the "inducement-analysis system."

Second, "organizational properties" of the type that characterize the "expansive system" are, as Laszlo observes,[137] structurally unstable and prone to disorganization unless balanced by more thorough self-stabilizatory functions. "Expansion" is a system that seeks out new interactions with the environment, thus placing the meta-system in a vulnerable position vis-a-vis its integrity and autonomy. In the case of the relationship between these two systems, this means that "expansion" (the organizational system) is dependent on the realization of non-intrinsic-existence (a stabilizing force) in order to offset the instabilities produced in the meta-system by its information exchanges with the environment. Thus we see Expansive Career analysts developing their awareness of the open dimension of reality alongside the extension of their relationships with others through the expansion of a range of perspectives with which they can view the world. If Expansive Career analysts ceased to develop their appreciation of non-intrinsic identifiability they would become burdened and confused by the new environmental information they constantly seek out.

In the simulation model we will shortly develop the "expansive system" is not displayed.

Ramification. Ramification is a subsystem of both "inducement-analysis" and "expansion." It relates to the notion of interdependence or relational origination (*pratītyasamutpāda*) and says essentially that the behavior of individual elements occurs within a casual matrix such that the changes of any element within the meta-system influences the behavior of other elements. It is a statement of intra-systemic dependencies and will be subsequently interpreted in the context of analytical meditation.

Engramming. The term "engramming" denotes a subsystem of "inducement-analysis" that is designed to capture the notion of habituation as understood in the Buddhist theory of karma. It is a self-stabilizing system that acts to reify the analyst's stream of experience by change-reducing negative feedback. It attempts to maintain constancies and so acts in opposition to the evolutionary and transformational qualities of "inducement-analysis." In practice it is responsible for backsliding, the need for analysts to repeat their meditations, and the temporal elongation of their path.

Randomness. In the model we will introduce a stochastic factor which we will call "randomness." This refers to genuinely random-behavior and strictly represents random-flows within the meta-system. In fact, it is used as a general influence and used interpretatively to capture random movements and non-random—but for practical purposes—indeterminate subsystems. A level of random movement of concepts within the simulation model thus represents events such as the unpredictable movement of objects and thoughts into and out of awareness. It also includes changes in the objects and thoughts that an analyst chooses to be aware of.

The Middle Path suggests, for example, that advanced practitioners analyze different worldviews and ontologies as they progress through the various levels (*bhūmi*) to accomplishment.

These are the five subsystems we will use as a framework around which to organize the simulation model. Their contribution to the meta-system can be summarized in the following diagram (*Figure 3.1*). The arrows signify how subsystems influence each other within the meta-system.

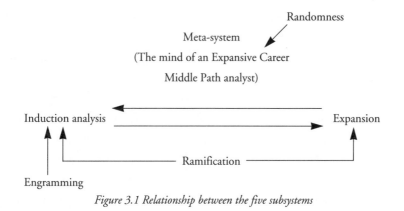

Figure 3.1 Relationship between the five subsystems

THE PLACE OF THE SIMULATION MODEL

The basic format followed in the remainder of this chapter is to describe, explain, and interpret the behavior of the Middle Path around a simulation model. The model is very basic and symbolically describes just the key and defining process(es) of each subsystem and coordinates their synthesized behavior as a meta-system. Details and features of the Middle Path system of meditation that are not directly modeled are linked to the structure of the model.

THE PROGRAMMED MODEL

The model will simulate some key features of the analytical processing of conceptuality by symbolically representing various events and processes that are at least consistent with the general framework of Middle Path analysis. Some of the features that are modeled are, I believe, *required* by the analytical practices developed by Middle Pathers. The model is a working or dynamic model as opposed to a static model. This means that it is not programmed to produce just one output, but rather is programmed so that it is possible to include and exclude various influences, and to change the *behavior* of certain of the influences that may be operative during paradoxical analysis. This is achieved by using a modular program. This allows different combinations of modules to be activated. Each module specifies a routine of behavior. Any set of modules are then coordinated so that they produce a *single* output. Some of the influences can be changed by changing the variables to certain input parameters. In this way a modular programmed model enables one to coordinate and display—and thus investigate—the dynamics of key inter-relationships between different factors that influence the changes that occur when someone is employing paradoxical consequences as a regular technique in their meditational practice.

The heuristic power of the model is significantly increased because of its working, or dynamic abilities, since one can analyze different outputs that can be obtained by using different combi-nations of modules, and varying the input values where these are provided. The heuristic features and subtleties of the model are best appreciated by working with the model. Still, even though it is not possible to demonstrate the full range of its behavior in the chapter of a book, it is possible to show some of its power and at least demonstrate its important features.

The model, to be sure, is artificially exact in the behavior and changes it describes. Still it would be very difficult to describe the same ideas and concepts at the same level of lucidity without recourse and reference to some form of model that gives a graph-ic display around which one can develop a verbal description. This is not only because the ideas themselves are far-reaching, but that they reach a level of *abstraction from thought* such that the written word may cease to be the best medium in which to express those ideas.

Two final points to emphasize are (1) that the model is hypothetical, indeed it is clearly speculative, and (2) the model gives a picture of just *one possible* way in which Middle Pathers could have conceived of the instrumental role that paradoxical analysis was thought to play in the acquisition of insight.

THE ASSUMPTIONS OF THE MODEL

A presupposition on which the model is constructed is that of a gradual as opposed to an instantaneous growth of insight (*prajñā*). Middle Path literature doesn't explicitly address the question of whether the realization of openness is supposed to be developed gradually, or all at once in a single, once-only insight. Generally the literature seems to presuppose a gradual development throughout an analyst's career, though the development is punctuated by certain significantly pronounced insights at the saintly (*ārya*) stage, i.e., on entering the first level (*bhūmi*), and at the sixth or seventh level where insight is completed.

With respect to the model, the instantaneous versus gradual development can be accommodated by a temporal compression of the processes that it models. It is only when the instantaneous theory means literally an insight that is entirely absent at one point in time and then fully developed in an adjacent moment that the model depicted loses its value. But I don't think such an interpretation is what Middle Pathers understand to be the case. And nor is such an understanding consonant with the Middle Path philosophy.[138] We will return to this question later when interpreting the model. Certainly without an assumption of a gradual development very little can be said about a *process* whereby insight is envisaged to arise in the mind-stream of an analyst.

It is instructive and important to see how the model is developed for once the symbolism is fully grasped the interpretation of the model becomes deceptively simple and its heuristic potential can be explored to the full in several illustrative event-graphs.

THE INITIAL CONDITIONS AND SYMBOLISM OF THE MODEL

The aim of the model is to symbolically describe some key features of the cognitive changes that may be thought to occur in an analyst's development as these are determined by the introduction and conscious and active deployment of paradoxical analysis as a means of processing concepts within the analyst's conceptual makeup. The model is concerned to depict the progressive eduction and genesis of a full insight into openness from its inchoate beginnings in a state prior to the employment of paradoxical analysis.

The model is thus focused on the evolution of an analyst's mental continuum (*saṁtāna*). The model symbolically represents this as events occurring on a directed-graph. The graph is placed on Cartesian coordinates thus (*Figure 3.2*).

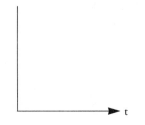

Figure 3.2 Stream of conceptuality

The vertical axis represents the conceptual makeup of an analyst at a particular time. It depicts the content and configuration of whatever concepts are present at any moment in time. Thus, the vertical axis should be thought of as representing the conceptual content of an analyst at any point in time.

What we are calling the initial conditions of the model are an interpretation of the symbolic entities that will figure in the model and a description of the conditions obtaining at the start of the model. The conditions obtaining at the start of the model and the symbolic data are represented thus in (*Figure 3.3*).

First, we will explain the symbolism. The concepts depicted in the model are each characterized by four features that we will call concept *type*, degree of *cathexis*, *sign*, and *placement* within a field of attention.

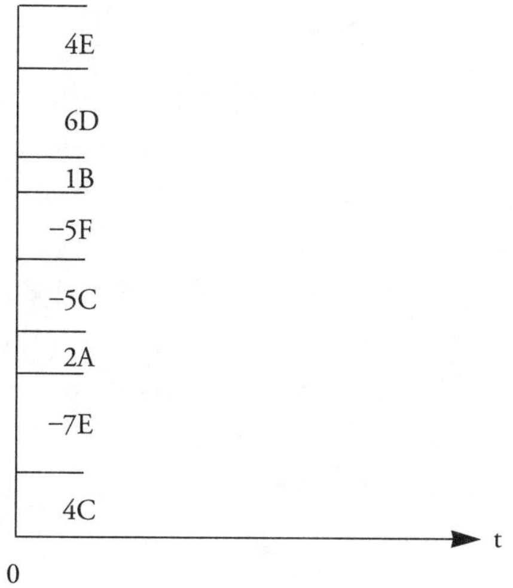

Figure 3.3 The symbolism and initial conditions

Concept *type* is designated by a *letter* (in the model between **A** and **F**).

Concept *cathexis* is designated by an *integer* between 1 and 9. In the model this is represented as a corresponding unit displacement.[139]

Sign, which indicates positive and negative cathexis is designated by a **+** and **−** *sign* respectively. The positive (+) sign is omitted in the graphs.

Placement within a field of attention is represented by a concept's *displacement* from the horizontal axis.

Thus, in Figure 3.3, the codings: 4C, −7E, 2A, etc. represent different *types* of concepts (C, E, A, etc.), each with its own degree of *cathexis* (4, 7, 2, etc.), which may be positive or negative (+, −, +, etc.). The concepts are also arranged on the vertical axis in a certain configuration. These four characteristics need to be explained separately.

By a concept's *type* is meant the label that identifies a concept by differentiating it from other concepts. A concept *type* is thus determined by what it refers to. This could be an object, event in the world, or an internal event, or phenomenon such as a feeling, thought, attitude, etc. The concepts thus represent a set of concepts that *structure* a worldview. As such they would include the concepts that identify feelings, thoughts, sense-perceptibles, inferred entities, relations, theory structures, etc. They account for the sensory and mental world as it is experienced by and in terms of a set of intentional, categorial, affective, and cognitive structures.

More specifically the types of concepts would be composed of innate and acquired conceptions. The acquired or intellectual concepts are philosophical in nature and differ in dependence on the philosophical persuasion and worldview of an analyst. For Middle Path analysts the meta-psychological (*abhidharma*)categories would figure as a prominent undercurrent throughout a flux of changing concepts. Similarly, for a Middle Path meditator typologies such as the twenty types of openness and other meditative schemas would likewise structure an analyst's thinking. Non-Buddhist analysts would analyze whatever concepts and categories make up their intellectual worldview. These intellectual concepts and conceptual categories would be augmented by innately given concepts that as such structure the natively experienced worldview. The innate concepts would include a common-sense conception of the self in which the self is identified with the psycho-physical organism, the concepts that structure the perception of an ambient environment, (this would include the psycho-physical person) and an inferential structure that habitually extrojects or externalizes sense data.[140] In point of fact, to the extent that native concepts are more trenchant than the philosophical ones the former are in all rights augmented by the latter. And as to which set would be prominent, it seems that the philosophical concepts would come to dominate a network of conceptuality as a meditator fully entered into his or her analyzing activity.

Although the number of different concept types is open ended, for the sake of visual manageability the model depicts just a handful of concepts. In the model we have not specified the concept types, i.e., correlated the letters with any real concepts. To do so would be a case of "misplaced particularization" if we can modify Whitehead's warning. Even so, presumably one of the concepts would be a conception of the self and another would probably be the conception of the psycho-physical organism, for these would surely undergird every set of concepts that make up a complete worldview.

CONCEPT CATHEXIS AND INTRINSIC EXISTENCE

The elements comprising a network of conceptuality are further specified by a value. The assignment of a value to all concepts is denoted by a *numerical value* (an integer between 0 and 9) and a *sign* (+ or −). This value represents a psycho-ontological attitude that is assumed, consciously or unconsciously, and freely or compulsively, by an analyst to the concepts she or he entertains.

The magnitude of the numerical value can be interpreted from either an ontological or psychological perspective.

117

The psychological framework. From a psychological viewpoint the value represents object cathexis. The higher the numerical value the more intense the *cathexis* of that element. We may think of a high numeral as signifying a fixation and a low numeral as a relatively mild emotional response. A positive sign indicates positive cathexis—i.e., an investment of energy, value, and judgment in a referent's ability to satisfy a desire. Negative or hostile cathexis is the adoption of an adverse reaction to an element. The former produces attachment and grasping and the latter aversion and hatred. This method of modeling the psychological valuation of elements accurately represents what happens in our experience. Drawing on the theorizing of Whitehead and the experimental work by Grastyan, the systems theorist Ervin Laszlo writes that:

> An entire continuum or wide range of emotional coloring may be given by the direction and intensity of the basic pro or contra attitudes. Both directions may have various levels of intensity, with the result that the full scale of feelings may be embraced by the hypothesis, ranging from unqualified and intense repulsion to similarly unqualified and intense attraction.[141]

As Laszlo also notes, these emotional reactions tend to accompany "recurrent types of stimulation."[142] Thus we would generally expect that compulsive, habitual, and ingrained reactions would have high cathexis value.

A zero numeral indicates an attitude of equanimity with respect to an element. The state of spiritual freedom (*nirvāṇa*) is characterized by a removal of all cathectic reactions.[143] It is represented by all concepts assuming a zero valuation.

The ontological framework. The ontological framework interprets the *magnitude* and *sign* assigned to a concept around the notion of the middle view (*madhyama-dṛṣṭi*). The middle view, as we have explained, is an ontologically neutral view that affirms neither intrinsic existence nor non-existence. This middle view is denoted by a zero value. Any deviations from that is an errant view of reality tending either toward the extreme of realism or nihilism. A nihilistic reification of cognition is assigned negative values and realist reifications are assigned positive values. (By a realistic reification we mean that which asserts intrinsic existence, not the philosophical position that the physical world exists independently of perceivers.)

The numerical assignments represent, if we can think of such, the *degree* or *intensity* with which nihilism and realism are grasped, or what amounts to the same thing, the degree to which and consistency with which phenomena are, to use terminology of the Tibetan Middle Pathers—under-negated (*khyab chung ba*) or over-negated (*khyab ches ba*). To deny that things exist conventionally is an over-extended negation in that it denies too broad an object, whereas the failure to negate an intrinsic nature does not go far enough and so is a case of under-negation. Under-negation is substantialistic while over-negation is nihilistic.[144]

The ontological interpretation as represented in the model is perhaps slightly contentious for Middle Path literature doesn't give explicit sanction to the idea that the conception of intrinsic existence (*svabhāva*) may permit of degrees or graduations. Nor does the traditional literature speak about variations within a composite conceptual network in terms of the extent to which individual concepts are conceived to intrinsically exist. We are suggesting (1) that an entire conceptual field may be conceived to be *more and less* intrinsically existent and (2) that individual concepts within that field may likewise be conceived as varyingly intrinsically existent, with some concepts conceived to be weakly intrinsically existent and others strongly so.

Such a variation could be thought of as a difference in the *degree* to which concepts are seen to be related to other concepts. The concepts that were more isolated and less relationally ramified, would be more intrinsically existent.

Such an interpretation seems to be reasonable and also consistent with the rest of the Middle Path assumptions. First, the idea that the concept of intrinsic existence has degrees is *compatible* with the fact that the reactive emotions (*kleśa*) vary in their intensity. Further, it may even be necessary that the intrinsic existence of things permits of degrees, for if it is a genuine feature of the emotional reactions that they have degrees (for example, we can be strongly or weakly attached to something), and that these emotional reactions are *functionally* dependent on the conception of intrinsic existence (which is the contention of Middle Pathers), then it may be that the *variation* in an emotional reaction can only be accounted for by some commensurate variation in the cognitive response of conceiving intrinsic existence. This would support the idea that individual concepts could be conceived to be more and less intrinsically existent, just as one may be strongly attached to some things and weakly to others, and that an entire conceptual field could be grasped with more and less intensity vis-a-vis its intrinsic existence.

Second, if the insight of openness is acquired by degrees, and this insight is the removal of the view of intrinsic existence, then the view of intrinsic existence must also permit of degrees. At the beginning of the path, when the insight into openness is weak, the conception of intrinsic existence is strong. And near the completion of the path, when the insight into openness is firm and intense, the conception of intrinsic existence would be weakly affirmed. Hence from this perspective there would be a gradual attrition of the concept of intrinsic existence throughout an analyst's career.

Finally, there is some sanction for this view in the stages of the path (*krama-mārga, sa lam*) literature, on which Tibetan scholars have developed a Middle Path account. In this account of the stages[145] the spiritually advanced practitioners (*bodhisattva*) progress by first eradicating the emotional reactions in their coarsest and crudest aspect, then in their middling form, and finally they remove the most subtle traces or manifestations of the reactive emotions. Included among these emotional afflictions are the cognitive ones of conceiving a self (*ātma*), which is understood by Middle Path philosophers in terms of conceiving intrinsic existence, and holding to the extreme views.

Thus, we can talk coherently about strong and weak conceptions of intrinsic existence and I regard this feature of the model as an innovation rather than an inaccuracy.

A combined interpretation. As to which framework of interpretation, the psychological or ontological, more accurately reflects Middle Path assumptions there is no clear answer. Middle Path literature doesn't make a formal distinction between the two frameworks. Even so, the ontological framework would seem to be the primary way of resolving the notion of concept cathexis as ignorance (*avidyā*) or confusion (*moha*) is considered to be the basic affliction (*mūla-kleśa*). More specifically, the view of intrinsic individuality (*satkāya-dṛṣṭi*), which is defined as the view which grasps the self as real,[146] is the affliction from which the other emotional responses such as desire and attachment arise. On this view the emotional reactions to conceptual referents are based on a cognitive impairment. That is to say, emotional reactions such as attachment and aversion are mental distortions that are thought to arise on the basis of an ignorance conceiving

intrinsic existences. The psychological framework on this interpretation would thus be a secondary resolution of the problem of
suffering. This theory, of a cognitive basis to emotions, is incidentally supported by the work of R.S. Lazarus, et al.[147] who
have proposed a "cognitive theory of emotions." This theory says
that emotions arise subsequently to, and on the basis of the
appraisal of information. Information (from inside and outside of
the body) is received and the emotions that arise depend on how
that information is evaluated and processed. The appraisal mechanisms and procedures are complex for they also take into
account habituations that have developed prior to the appraisal of
data. The mechanism also includes emotional reaction patterns,
and the projected consequences of behavior. The argument for
this cognitive basis is said to be supported by the phenomenon of
reappraisal. Cognitive information may be *re-* or differently
assessed, i.e., evaluated in a new light, with corresponding
changes in the emotions that the information arouses.

Even so, the psychological framework must also be thought of
as accurately describing the processes and causes impelling concept cathexis. This framework should not be underplayed, for we
recall that the formulation of the four saintly truths (*ārya-satya*)
cites grasping (*tṛṣṇā*) as the cause of suffering and the *Kindred
Discourses* (*Samyutta-nikāya* [III.190]) speaks of nirvāṇa as the
eradication of craving (*tanha*). Middle Path philosophers have
also defined insight as "being without attachment."[148]

There is clearly a relationship between the psychological and
ontological interpretations, and it is worthwhile exploring this
just a little, given that the model represents just one resolution.
It is one resolution which is intended to be interpreted in both
the psychological and ontological frameworks.

It seems that we can make out something of a correlation,

albeit quite a rough one, between under-negation (realism or essentialism) and positive emotional cathexis in that we frequently find that objects we desire are also over-estimated or over-stated in an ontological sense. And likewise, over-negation (nihilism) often correlates with negative or hostile emotional cathexis to the extent that aversion is, or is accompanied by, a psychological attempt and effort to ontologically negate the referent to an adverse reaction. Further, the more extreme and thorough an under- or over-negation the more intense may be the adversion-aversion that accompanies it. These are just indications of a correspondence. And it may be that this correspondence is more descriptive of innate conceptions in which reactions are typically compulsive and impulsive, rather than of acquired concepts where, for example, an individual can be attracted to nihilism.

Both the psychological and ontological interpretations are implied in the model, and it can be skewed to emphasize either one. Hence, what we have in mind is an integrative framework that assimilates both aspects yet bears in mind its breadth and possible resolution into either framework. The fact that Middle Path literature itself fails to formally make the psycho-ontological distinction perhaps means that a more generic framework, such as the model represents, is at least heuristically serviceable, even given that many anomalies between the two frameworks could be pointed to. In summary, then, the value denotes a psycho-ontological standpoint with respect to the concepts that structure a worldview.

On the model the numerical value is denoted in two ways: as an integer and by a unit displacement along the vertical axis commensurate with the assigned integer. Thus, a concept that is assigned a value of 1 displaces *one* vertical unit, one assigned 2, *two* units, etc.

Finally, we are not assigning any numerical values to specific concepts except to say that one would expect the concepts of a self and

123

a body-image to be highly valued. Also, the innate conceptions may tend to be more highly valued, even if only unconsciously so.

The fourth characteristic that is specified for each concept is its *placement* within a field of attention or awareness. This is represented by a concept's displacement along the vertical axis. The vertical axis thus represents an attention gradient and so the position of a concept on this axis is a measure of the intensity or degree to which it is being attended to. The level of attention is at a maximum at the intersection with the horizontal axis and progressively reduces as the displacement from the horizontal axis increases. Thus, a concept positioned at the horizontal axis is receiving a maximum degree of attention and the concepts most removed from the horizontal axis are at a peripheral level of awareness. Eliot Deutsch has defined a phrase "natural focuses of attention," which represents the parameter represented on the vertical axis. The natural foci of attention are "those events within an environmental context ("perceptual field") which, by virtue of their nature, tend to become the center of a perceiver's attentive energies . . . The 'natural focuses of attention' tend to elicit responses from a perceiver by forcing their way, as it were, into his consciousness."[149] It is basically the same notion as "a point of concentration" or "focus of awareness."

This idea of a focus of attention clearly relates (though not directly or isomorphically) to spatial location in the case of sense-referents where concepts tend to arise in dependence on the immediacy of sense-referents. Though, of course, one can be attentive to distant objects. In the case of concepts that have mental referents it expresses the imaginal notion that thoughts, ideas, feelings, etc. may be closer to or further away from the focus of attentive energy. Although Deutsch is right that foci of attention seem to force their way upon a consciousness, in the meditative context and with an analyst's development of his or her concentrative powers, one expects that he or she could exercise an increasing degree of control over the entry and removal of concepts from awareness. The analyst, one presumes, is better able to control where she or he directs her or his attention than worldly folk.

We can make some broad observations about the relationship between the *sign* assigned to concepts and the "attention gradient." Within her or his psychological capabilities an individual would remove from her or his attention, concepts and their referents that were negatively affectively cathected, and positively cathected ones would tend (again within an individual analyst's capacities) to assume positions at the focus of attention. Though, of course, in the practice of paradoxical analysis the analyst needs to induce both the positively and negatively valued concepts to the focus of his or her attention. Concepts would tend to be removed via removing their referents, rather than the other way around, given a native predisposition to view referents as intrinsically defining their conceptual identification. It is only with the insight of the non-intrinsic identifiability of conceptual referents that concepts could be modified or removed without removing their referents.

As to the degree of valuation, or *cathexis* (i.e., the numerical assignments), concepts throughout the range of values (from 1 to 9) are presumably distributed fairly evenly throughout a "gradient of attention." More will be said on this soon. A concept of the self would figure prominently throughout the lifespan of a continuum and would probably vacillate near and around the maximum focus of attention. Undiscerned or as yet uncreated concepts would be such that were they discerned, i.e., brought within a field of attention, they would be cathected in such and such a degree of intensity and so could be assigned a "potential value."

In summary, the model depicts a small and abstracted set of concepts and attitudes toward them. The elements represent conceptual discernments made with respect to a sense-mental manifold of experience. They form a subset or sample from what would be a much larger set of concepts within an analyst's mental makeup.

Because it is an evolving process that is being displayed, the concepts depicted at the beginning of the event-graphs undergo various changes with respect to their configuration, magnitude, and sign as a result of various influences. The most important influence is the analytical processing of concepts using paradoxical consequences as we have described it. Although there is a continuity of change in the real system (i.e., the analyst's stream of conceptuality) and in fact in the program that drives the model as well, for the purposes of display,[150] a series of snapshots are read from the output. These represent profiles of a conceptual network taken at equal time intervals. Various possible path-structures can be produced by the model by changing various input parameters that govern the length of time taken to achieve a destructuring of conceptuality, the effects of different degrees of concentration and the pervasiveness of concentration, the influences of habituation, options as to which concepts are most easily analyzed, etc. We have chosen to trace out just one event-graph (except where we show the phenomenon of "habituation"). It is a fairly typical one and contains all of the features we wish to describe. To do otherwise would be to get too complex for the purposes of a preliminary study. (Also, beyond a certain level of complexity the model fails to have any real reference to possible vicissitudes within an actual stream of conceptuality and ends up just describing the dynamics of the model.)

INTERPRETING THE MODEL

For the sake of simplicity and relevancy the model picks up the analyst's development at a point where she or he is beginning to analyze.

If we look again at the initial conditions (*Figure 3.4*), the profile of concepts represent the analyst's network of concepts at the beginning of the process we will now trace.

The most significant feature to note, with respect to the profile of concepts at the beginning, is that some concepts (**A, B, D, F**) appear only once, whereas others (**C, E**) appear twice, and always in these cases as a pair of concepts with opposite signs. This feature of the model represents the Middle Path assumption we have already explained in some depth, namely, that concepts *exist* in dependence on their logical opposite. Concept **A** exists in dependence on the conception of a negation of **A**, and vice versa, and so for all concepts. We should not be misled by the phrase "a pair of concepts" for a pair doesn't constitute two different concepts, rather it is the one concept being affirmed and negated.

The fact that some concepts are displayed singly, (i.e., as only affirmed *or* denied) without the corresponding opposite being present in the set of concepts displayed, signifies that the opposition structure is lost sight of with respect to those concepts and they are perceived to exist in their own right and completely independently of their logical opposite. At a pre-analytical stage this would be the usual situation. That is to say, *most* concepts would be present singly, for example, a self would be affirmed without any denial.[151] Even so, in these cases a logical opposite to the concepts displayed would exist somewhere, for Middle

127

Pathers hold that *all* concepts exist in dependence on their logical opposites. They would be outside of an analyst's awareness, though, and for that reason are not represented in the concepts displayed in the model. As we have explained earlier, one concept from a pair that are mutually defining becomes psychologically separated from the other, to the point where a consciousness is cognizant only of the affirmation *or* negation of the concept. The logical opposite exists at an unconscious or subliminal level.[152]

We have included affirmations and negations of *some* concepts, even at the beginning of the model, for reasons that are explained earlier; namely, that the paradoxical structure of concept formation and maintenance may *surface* as an unconscious toleration of a certain degree of predicative ambiguity. Also, a meditator, in the course of her or his philosophical investigations may be aware of concepts and their opposites, though keep them at different cognitive loci and so fail to see their mutually affirming nature.[153]

Another feature of the model displayed in *Figure 3.4* is that the degree of *cathexis* (or magnitude) of the affirmation and negation of a concept need not be equal (this is the case for concepts C and E in *Figure 3.4*). Even so, the principle of reciprocity says that the magnitudes of affirmations and negations must be matched. (A *hypothetical* corollary of this is that a concept could only be sustained to the degree instanced by the lesser of the two magnitudes if the affirmation and negation are not of an equal strength. Such an inequality in the magnitudes, though, is incompatible with Middle Path assumptions.) Thus, wherever a concept is affirmed and negated in unequal degrees *within* the display we must assume that the residuum required to balance or even out the magnitude lies outside of the threshold of attention and so isn't present within the concepts depicted. In this case the affirmation or negation of the concept has become bifurcated so that an analyst is aware of only some portion of what is required in order to balance the logical opposite. This is an important feature of the model for it allows us to incorporate the phenomena of analytical under- (*che ba*) and over-negation (*khyab chung ba*). It is also a necessary feature for if the affirmation and negation with respect to each object is not equal then it would never be possible for there to be a complete reversal of conceptuality.

Our task now is to map various influences that introduce changes into magnitudes, signs, and configurations of the concepts depicted in *Figure 3.4*.

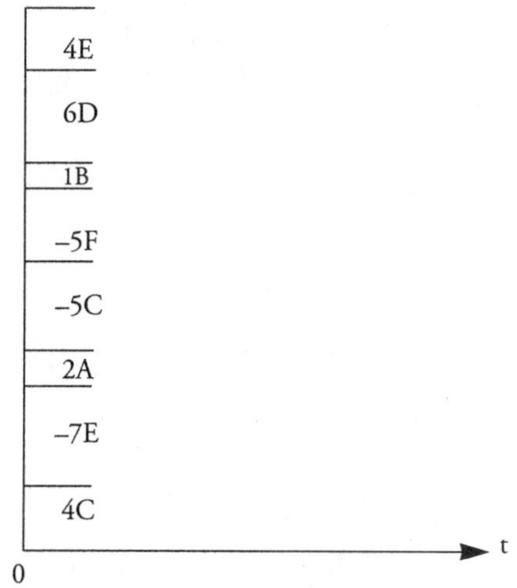

Figure 3.4 The symbolism and initial conditions

The first change introduced into the model is some random movement. This alters the configuration of the concepts. We interpret these changes as corresponding to alterations in an analyst's conceptual network that are caused by changes in the sense-mental manifold that arise due to changes in the manifold and movements of an analyst within his or her sense-mental world.

Also, there would be changes in conceptual structures tolerable within the parameters that define a worldview. Thus, although a worldview (i.e., set of concepts) is relatively stable and unchanging, there would be a certain amount of change as concepts change their arrangement and arise and dissipate. Some concepts would be displaced and other concepts would be introduced. That is, there would be changes in both the constitution as well as the configuration of a set of concepts. The model mimes only the changes in the arrangement or configuration of the concepts.[154]

Some of the random movement of the concepts is also interpretable as changes that are consciously introduced by meditators as they select and change the concepts toward which they direct their analytical energies. This, in fact, is not a random procedure but for want of avoiding any misplaced particularization can be adequately represented by some random movements in the configuration.

ANALYSIS

To recapitulate from chapter 2, the Middle Path method of analysis, which is based on generating paradoxical consequences, is a technique for gradually destructuring conceptuality (*kalpanā*). It does this by clarifying fundamental logical contradictions in the basis of concept formation. Analysis exposes the contradictory status of object identification and hence of concept formation by logical proofs that derive a substantive negation of a concept from its affirmation, or vice versa. This is done by drawing on the predicative structure of object identification wherein objects are defined by the presence of specified characteristics. Paradoxical analysis takes the definition of an object, or ascription of a characteristic to it, as a position (*pratijñā*), i.e., that **A** is **P**, and derives a logically opposite position. A thesis, or position, is thus seen to entail its negation. This serves to undermine the basis for concept formation, for the characteristic(s) on which identification is based are affirmed and denied at the same time with respect to the one object. The process whereby a position and its negation come to be simultaneously affirmed can be envisaged on a spatial analogy as the original position and its logical opposite being induced to coalesce at a common spatio-temporal locus. That is to say, the original position and its negation come to be affirmed at the same locus of consciousness. This produces a destructuring and dissolution of the concept specified by the characteristic(s), as Middle Path philosophers uphold the descriptive validity of the "principle of contradiction." The destructuring is also considered to be wholesale and leave no conceptual residue because they also uphold the "principle of the excluded middle."

In the model the process of analysis is represented by a coalescing of the affirmatively and negatively signed instances of a concept around a common spatio-temporal locus. The action of coalescing is induced by a paradoxical analysis. In the case of non-affirming (*prasajya*) analyses *either* the positive or negative instantiations of the concept (i.e., a position) is analyzed, but not both. In the case of affirming (*parudāsa*) analyses *both* instantiations are analyzed.

We should clarify a simplicity in the model at this stage. As we have explained earlier, the positive and negative instantiations do not represent two concepts, rather they represent one concept which is defined in terms of its mutual affirmation and negation. More precisely, the + and − signs represent the positive and negative ascription of a (defining) characteristic. (It is a *defining* characteristic if the concept in question is to be analyzed through a category restricted analysis, and *any* characteristic if it is to be analyzed through a category unrestricted analysis.) This predicative structure could be symbolized thus, "$A-y$" and "Ay" where

131

the lowercase letters would represent the characteristics or predicates in terms of which the concepts were analyzed. Using the formats of analysis suggested in Chapter Two this would mean that for concepts that were concepts of things (*dharma*), the lowercase letter would represent the characteristic of "being self-produced." Its negation, represented as "$-y$," would indicate the characteristic of "not being self-produced." For the concept of the person (*pudgala*) another letter, say z, could represent the characterization "is the psycho-physical organism." The lowercase letters would be much fewer in number than the uppercase letters which represent the concepts, for sets of concepts such as products and non-products seem to be analyzed in terms of the same characteristics or predicates. We haven't introduced this additional symbolism, though, as it would unnecessarily clutter up the already detailed event-graphs.

The process whereby the affirmation and negation of a concept coalesce around a common locus occurs for all the concepts represented in the model. If a logical opposite is already within the field of attention of an analyst it is drawn towards the affirmation or negation being analyzed. If it is not already within the purview of an analyst (as in the case of the opposites of concepts A, B, D, and F in the graph) it is analytically drawn into the field of awareness. It enters the graph at the top and is drawn toward the instances of a concept that is already present to an analyst, as the instance being analyzed. The instances are drawn together as the analysis proceeds, and they coalesce *as* the paradox is generated. As they coalesce around a common point or junction, the concept destructures for reasons explained in Chapter Two.[155] Although the conceptual movements implied here are figured spatially, the graphic movements signify a change in the attentive foci of concepts within a field of attention. The coalescing or confluting of the affirmation and negation of a concept signifies that these two come to assume the same locus of attention within a consciousness. The event of the affirmation and negation of a concept coalescing and destructuring can be observed in the next figure (*Figure 3.5*). The movements of just the first few analyses are tracked using different shadings.

At profile 1 the affirmation and negation of concept **E** begin to move toward each other indicating that an analysis is under way with respect to that concept. The same can be observed for concept **A** at profile 2 where the affirmation and negation are actually adjacent to each other. At profile 2 the affirmation and negation of concept **E** have coalesced and the concept has partially destructured. Likewise, concept **A** has partially destructured in profile 3. These last two events signify that a conclusion to an analysis has been realized. There are some differences in how the coalescing and destructuring may take place. For example, the two cases just described are cases of analyses that leave a residuum of the concept behind. These differences will be described shortly.

INDUCEMENT

The confluting of like-typed but oppositely signed instances of a concept is accomplished by a program routine called "inducement." When this routine is invoked it induces the negations and affirmations of concepts to be drawn towards each other. In the mind of an analyst inducement is propelled by initiating and pursuing a paradoxical analysis. The "inducement" routine is also tied to what we have called the "gradient of attention." The "gradient of attention," we recall, specifies that attention with respect to concepts is greatest at the focus of attention (represented by the horizontal axis) and that it decreases as the psychic distance from the focus of awareness increases. The "inducement" routine

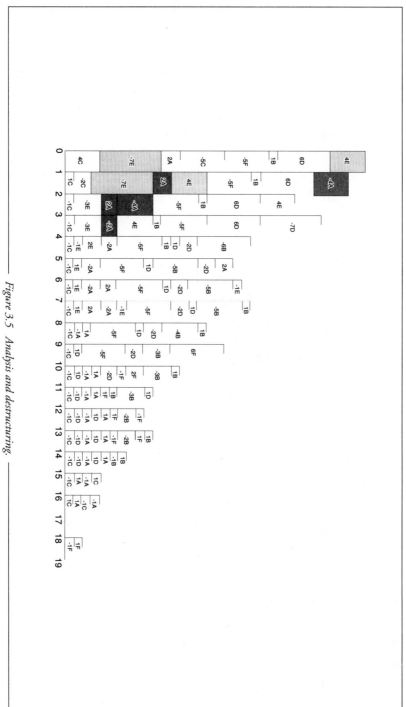

Figure 3.5 *Analysis and destructuring.*

is related to the "gradient of attention" in two ways.

First, the level of inducement is a variable in the model. That is to say, one can change the *rate* at which the negations and affirmations of concepts will move toward each other. The rate is increased by increasing an inducement *factor*. This factor is related to the "gradient of attention," for increasing the inducement factor serves to *extend the range* over which the affirmations and negations of concepts will be affected by the influence of inducement (= analysis). Thus, a low inducement factor will only influence (i.e., draw together) concepts that are in the near vicinity of the focus of attention, while a high inducement factor will command an influence over (i.e., be able to draw together) concepts that are more distant from the focus of attention and hence in many cases will be relatively farther apart.

The inducement *factor* is also a measure of the *range of concentration* of an analyst. The greater the range of concentration the easier and more probable it would be for an analyst to engage proximately distanced affirmations and negations into an analysis. The more narrow her or his concentration, the more likely it is that she or he would only analytically manipulate concepts that were within the field of concentration. The inverse proportion of the relation between inducement and the distance from the focus of attention also means that the *coincidence* of affirmations and negations of concepts tend to aggregate around the focus of attention, although as the inducement factor increases the coincidence *also* tends to occur farther away from the focus of attention.

The second way in which the inducement factor is related to the focus of attention is that the inducement factor automatically increases as the *net magnitude* decreases (i.e., as the acquisition of insight increases). The thought behind this is that as an analyst ceases—as a result of gaining insight—to invest his or her mental

135

energy and attention in emotional reactions to concepts, he or she can better deploy his or her mental energies toward meditation. Thus, we can expect that his or her concentration might *broaden* as well as become more intense. In other words, his or her powers of concentration might increasingly pervade the field of awareness.

Before looking at some finer details of the graph we will make some general observations about *Figure 3.5* which takes the analytical processing of concepts to its logical conclusion in the destructuring of all concepts at profile 19.

The first point to note is that the model, as it is set up, depicts a gradual development of the insight of openness. The net magnitude at each profile is a measure of the degree to which a Middle Path meditator has reified her or his experience on the basis of the postulates of existence and non-existence, and responses to these as desires and aversions. The line-graph that is scribed out by the *net* magnitude (i.e., the curve gained by connecting the overall magnitudes) thus represents a curve showing the acquisition of insight. The net magnitude is greatest at the beginning of the graph as positive and negative concept cathexes (i.e., realist and nihilist reifications) are at a maximum at that point. As analysis proceeds there is a *gradual* reduction in conceptual reification and at the completion of the graph the net magnitude is zero. The breaking up and removal of ontologizing thought takes place concept by concept rather than being distributed across all concepts at the same time. Thus, in a serial, and also overlapping process, concepts that are cathected in varying degrees, are ontologically neutralized by the paradoxical analysis. When the *last* concept is neutralized with respect to its being ontologically affirmed or negated, the net magnitude within a stream of conceptuality is zero. This final stage represents a *complete* reversal of concept cathexis and so signifies the realization of the Middle Path as a state where there is an

136

absence of all ontologizing conceptuality.

According to Middle Pathers, the absence of ontologizing means a removal of all reactive emotions as well. In other words, it is the achievement of a stasis (*nirodha*) with respect to all reifying conceptuality. On this interpretation, then, the analytical activity of an analyst is directly tied to the acquisition of insight. As Streng says, "the dialectical activity is reality-being-realized."[156] Hence, on this model it makes sense to talk about "degrees of freedom" and thus "degrees of bondage" too, for the level of insight is variable and the level or degree of insight is a direct measure of the extent to which a mind has freed itself from reifying conceptuality.

Some other points are also quite obvious. One point is that the rate of analysis would obviously influence the speed with which a consciousness would free itself of extreme conceptions. It stands to reason that the more active an analyst is in repeatedly analyzing her or his conceptual structures the quicker she or he would de-structure them. Also, at least in the model, it seems that the analytical activity of an analyst would slowly increase to a peak of activity and then drop off as he or she approached a complete cessation. Also, presumably, analysts would form some priorities, or at least have some procedures, for determining where, when, and for how long they would analyze different concepts. According to Candrakīrti, analysts would first gain an analytical familiarity with the concept of a self and presumably go on to analyze other concepts only after gaining some insight into the openness of the self.[157] Perhaps there are other criteria that we don't know about, which also determine the order in, and duration for, which different concepts are analyzed.[158] Perhaps, for example, partial insights are gained with some concepts and then the analysts move onto others. Or, full insights are gained for each concept prior to moving onto another.

This seems the right point to raise an ambiguity in the model that allows for two different methods of interpretation. The interpretative ambiguity turns on whether the event-graphs are taken as representing the development of insight that *leads up to* the first certified insight of openness that is gained, according to the structure of the spiritual path that is envisaged by Middle Pathers, at the path of intuition (*darśana*), *or* as representing a development spanning a stage at which analysis has begun, up to the *complete* development of insight in a continuous and all-embracing cognition of openness. The idea of a cognition that takes a certified or genuine object (*niyata-vastu, nges ngo*, lit. real thing) is to be distinguished from a cognition that knows only a facsimile object (*khyāti-vastu, snang ngo*, lit. a fancied thing). The difference here is that the former are immediate or unmediated cognitions of openness whereas the latter are mediated by a conceptual image (*sgra spyi*, lit. image [acquired through] audition) of what openness is.

In the first interpretation, the model would span a period from somewhere on the path of reaching (*prayoga*) up to the path of intuition, while in the second interpretation the model would span a period that began at the same point but finished at the sixth or seventh level (*bhūmi*) on the path of meditation (*bhāvana*), whichever level it is that the bodhisattva completes her or his perfection of insight. Thus, the first interpretation wouldn't display the path of meditation where the genuine insight is deepened, expanded, and consolidated.

The interpretative ambiguity is caused by a possible discrepancy between one feature in the model and Middle Path literature. In the model the insight into openness is had with respect to individual concepts, for insight is concomitant with the destructuring of a concept. (We will talk about a possible relationship between concepts later.) It is quite likely, though, that Middle Pathers hold that the first, and in fact all, genuine cognitions of openness have *all* concepts as the field of insight. (It is even possible that facsimile cognitions are thought to have all concepts as the field of cognition.) Candrakīrti doesn't express the view that all concepts are implicated in every insight of openness, but it is a well-known Middle Path view stemming from an oft quoted verse from Āryadeva[159] that says: "Whoever sees one thing is said to see all; the openness of one is exactly the openness of all." Candrakīrti quotes (MABh: 200.16–17) a similar verse from the *King of Concentration Scripture* (*Samādhiraja-sūtra*) that says: "If [one] has contemplated [just] one thing, all these will be meditated." However, this verse doesn't specify openness as the object of meditation.[160] (Whether Āryadeva and Middle Pathers who follow suit mean that it takes some time for all concepts to become the field of insight or whether this is instantaneous upon an insight made with respect to one object, is not clear. This is an important point, and we will take it up and make some suggestions soon when we discuss a process called the "ramification of insight.")

The upshot of the verse from Āryadeva with respect to the model is that only the final stage in the model—where all concepts have been analyzed without any residuum of conceptuality left—can be interpreted as a certified cognition of openness. The insights gained from analyses occurring prior to the final profile would produce facsimile cognitions, if we assume that facsimile cognitions need not exhaust the field of insight. So, if we follow Āryadeva, it is better to interpret the model as culminating at the path of intuition. Even so, we propose to interpret the model along the second line of interpretation. There are heuristic reasons for this and also several considerations that lend weight to a gradual acquisition of insight, not only in terms of increasingly prolonged insights, but also in terms of the pervasiveness or expansiveness of insight at any moment of time. Thus, if doctrinal consistency is any reason, the entities meant by "all" in verses such as the aforementioned from Āryadeva must be delimited in some way. Perhaps it means all entities that an analyst is normally aware of, or even just those that he or she is concentrating on. Further, if cognizing the openness of one entity automatically means that all were cognized as empty, it would make the many types of openness elaborated in Middle Path literature redundant, for analysts would only need to analyze one concept.[161] Presumably they would analyze the concept with which it was easiest to gain insight into openness. The most important of the heuristic reasons for adopting the second method of interpretation is that it lets us make some sense of what it means for cognitions of openness to become more expansive. It also facilitates an explanation of what facsimile cognitions might be and how they are different from, and related to, certified cognitions.

ANALYTICAL VARIATIONS

We will now focus on some details of the graphs and explain certain variations and subtleties in how concepts may be analyzed. In general, we can be fairly certain that most of the variations and refinements introduced into the model have an analog in the minds of Middle Path analysts.

COMPLETE ANALYSES

In the ideal case an analysis would have thoroughly destructured a concept without leaving any residuum behind. We call this a full, complete, or non-residual analysis. Such an analysis presupposes that the affirmations and negations of a concept that is implicated in an analysis are balanced, i.e., of an equal

magnitude, and that the analysis is brought to a complete conclusion in the simultaneous and co-spatial affirmation and
negation of the position or thesis that defines the concept in
question. Such a form of analysis shows a degree of finesse and
refinement and one would expect it to be found more often in
the advanced stages of analysis and less so at the beginning of
an analyst's meditations. We see this is the case in the graph
(*Figure 3.6*) where complete analyses occur at profiles 8, 14, 15,
17, and 19. Also, in the model a full analysis represents the last
moment of a concept's presence in the stream of conceptuality,
although two concepts (**A** and **F**) are *reintroduced* for reasons to
be explained shortly.

RESIDUAL ANALYSIS: UNDER- AND OVER-NEGATION

In contrast to complete analyses are residual analyses. In residual
analyses a conclusion to an analysis is realized but because the affirmation and negations implicated in the analysis are not balanced
(i.e., are of different magnitudes) a residuum of the concept being
analyzed remains after the conclusion to an analysis is realized. A
residual analysis relates to a process of under- and over-negation.
An under-negated analysis occurs when an analyst fails to implicate
a logical opposite that is of sufficient magnitude to destructure the
concept being analyzed. The result is that the original position,
which either affirmed or negated a concept (whichever the case
may be), is still the focal position at the conclusion to a paradoxical
argument, although the cathexis associated with it has decreased by
the measure of the magnitude of the opposite position. In the case
of an under-negation, an analyst has under-estimated the ontological commitment to be invested in the opposite position that was
required in order to completely de-structure a concept. An over-
negated analysis occurs when an analyst implicates a too heavily

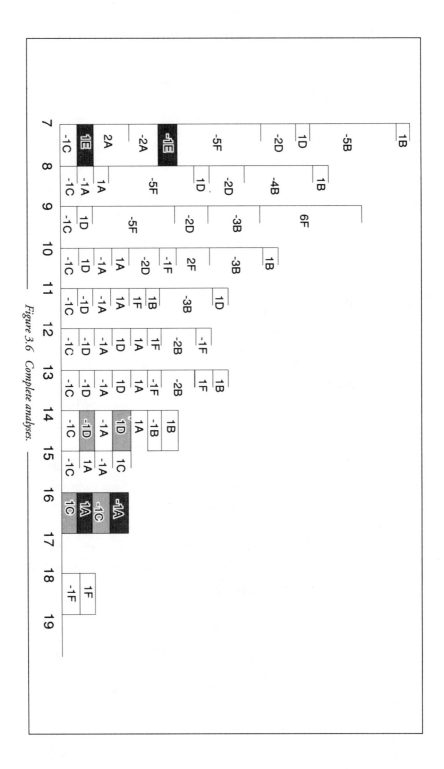

Figure 3.6 Complete analyses.

affirmed opposite position, which, being excessive in magnitude, not only neutralized a position but ends up being affirmed in its own right. This would be a case of an analyst over-estimating the strength with which she or he needs to affirm an opposite position. The result is that the opposing position *replaces* the original position in the focal attention of the analyst.

The notions of under-negation and over-negation are relative notions in this interpretation (in contradistinction to their use by Tibetan Middle Pathers[162]) for an under-negation needn't result in an affirmation, and likewise an over-negation needn't result in a negation. Rather, under-negation signifies that an affirmation *or* negation that is introduced into an analysis in order to neutralize the negation or affirmation of the concept under analysis, was *not* of sufficient magnitude to produce a completed or non-residual analysis. Conversely, over-negation signifies that the affirmation *or* negation drawn into an analysis was excessive in magnitude in comparison to the magnitude of the position being analyzed. The result again is that a residuum of a concept remains, only here there is also a change in sign. Some clear instances of under-negations occur in the graph (*Figure 3.7*) at profiles 1–2 (concept E) and 8–9 (concept B) and instances of over-negations occur at profiles 2–3 (concept A) and 4–5 (concept B).

The process depicted here doesn't relate to a difference between space- and illusion-like meditations on openness. According to Middle Path practice, an analyst is advised to break the practice of insight into formal meditation sessions in which he or she meditates on an openness that is like space, and post-session exercises in which he or she practices perceiving the sense world as illusory and dream-like. Such a process isn't displayed in the model.

Even so, we can speculate that there may be a danger of

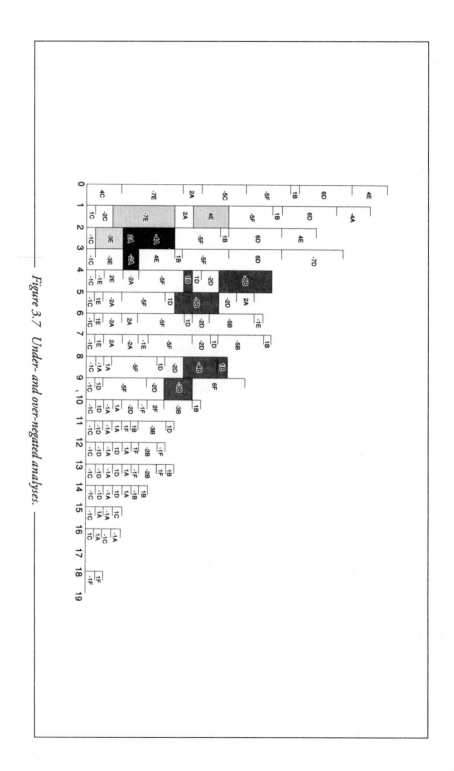

Figure 3.7 Under- and over-negated analyses.

space-like meditations on openness leading to over-negations in the Tibetan sense of leading to the nihilistic view of reality. Candrakīrti warns of this possibility.[163] Whereas complete or non-residual analyses display a balance and finesse on the part of an analyst in being able to accurately tune his or her analyses so that no conceptual residuum is left after realizing the conclusion, residual analyses are coarser.

We would expect residual analyses to occur more frequently at the beginning of analysis, and for the differences in the disparities between the magnitudes of the affirmations and negations of a concept to progressively reduce with time, for an analyst could be expected to learn from experience to gauge the degree of cathexis to be invested in an opposite position with more accuracy. In the model, this learning process—whereby grossly under- and over-negated analyses become converted into non-residual analyses—is simulated by a routine that ensures that the disparities between paired affirmations and negations progressively decrease. The first time the affirmation or negation of a concept is introduced to match one that is already present (so forming a pair) its magnitude is chosen randomly. From then on the difference in the magnitude between the affirmation and negation is always equal to or less than the disparity in the immediately preceding profile.

There is no exemplary example of this process in the event-graph. Still, one can see that whenever an affirmation or negation is introduced at the top of the graph, representing the exposing of the reciprocity of definition during an analysis, the affirmation and negation that is introduced is such that the *difference in magnitude* between it and the concept (negated or affirmed) that is being analyzed, is always less than or equal to the difference in the magnitude when compared with the next most recent occurrence.

A fair example can be seen in concept E (*Figure 3.8*). It begins

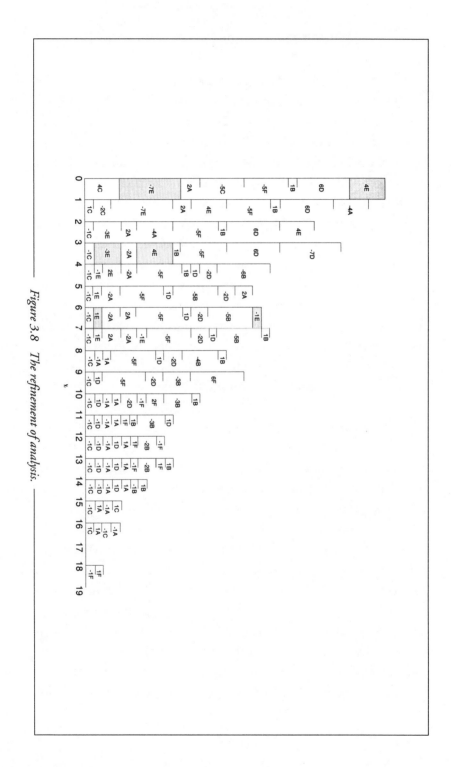

Figure 3.8 The refinement of analysis.

(profiles 0 and 1) with a disparity of 3, at profiles 2 the disparity is 1, and at profile 6 there is no disparity. The ideal case
would show a marked initial difference and a gradual reduction
in the disparity.

PARTIAL ANALYSIS

In the foregoing types of analysis a full conclusion is realized
within the possibilities determined by the magnitude of the affirmation and negation of a concept that are implicated in an analysis.
In a non-residual analysis no further conclusion could be realized
for a concept is completely removed from a mind-stream. In a
residual analysis a full conclusion is also realized to the extent
that a concept is destructured to the measure of the lesser of the
two magnitudes of the affirmation or negation of the concept.

It seems likely that analysis wouldn't always lead to a full conclusion and that only a *partial* conclusion may be realized. In this
case an analysis would fall short of reaching a full conclusion (or a
complete conclusion that can be made in an unbalanced analysis)
though *some* destructuring would take place. That is to say, only
some part of a concept that is originally implicated in an analysis
would turn out to be analyzed and in consequence only a portion
of the concept would be destructured in the conclusion. One likely
reason for this would be that an analyst is pulled out of an analysis
prior to reaching a full conclusion, perhaps because of a counteractive, or more accurately counter-analytical, commitment to the
reality of the concept being analyzed, the existence of which an
analysis would threaten. That is to say, the existential commitment
to an analysis could not overcome the commitment to an investment of intrinsic value in the concept being analyzed. Analysis
would make some ground in countering an extreme view, but in
turn the extreme view would exert a force that makes analysis peter

147

out due to a non-analytical mentality that consciously (or even unconsciously) considers that the loss of effective response that would be entailed by following an analysis through to a complete conclusion would be too expensive. Not only might this occur unconsciously, it may even go against the conscious wishes of an analyst who finds her- or himself compelled to forsake her or his analytical mentality due to habits which she or he cannot overcome. In these cases a *balance or equilibrium* between the opposing influences of the analytical and non-analytical mentality is arrived at. The result would be a partial conclusion with a partial destructuring of a concept. Partial analyses may continue through to residual or complete analyses, or lapse from an analytical posture for some period of time before the concept is analyzed further. An example of the latter can be seen in *Figure 3.9* with concept **D** between profiles 3 to 5. An example of a partial analysis leading to a full analysis can be seen with concept **A** at profiles 7 to 9, and an example of a partial analysis leading to a residual conclusion is seen for concept **E** at profiles 3 to 5. Other partial analysis occur at profiles 1(**C**), 8(**A**), and 10(**F**).

COARSE AND REFINED ANALYSIS

While on the discussion of different forms of analysis we can note that it is likely that analysis could begin at rudimentary or advanced levels. At the beginning of an analyst's career, when a pair of concepts are at some distance from each other (i.e., at quite different foci of attention), the analysis may involve, in fact require, hard-nosed dialectics in order to generate the awareness that concepts arise in the context of their logical opposites. On the other hand, at advanced stages of analysis, when an analyst is already familiar with analysis and acquainted with the realization of the principle of reciprocity, analysis may be more refined in the sense

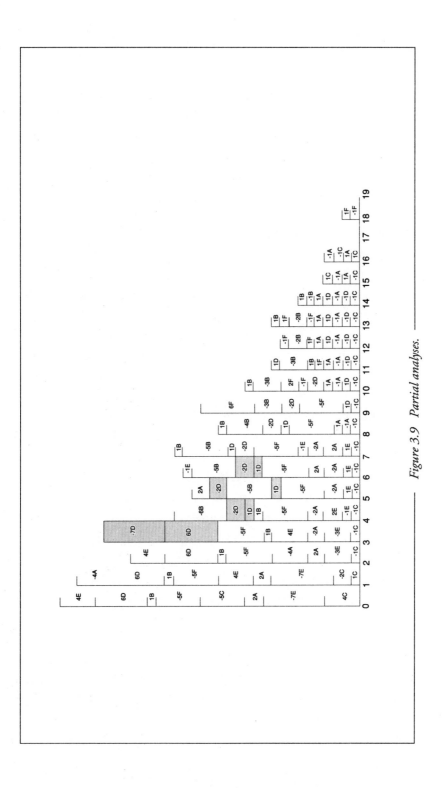

Figure 3.9 Partial analyses.

that an awareness of logical opposites as mutually defining each other would be at the level of consciousness and perhaps at the forefront of an analyst's awareness. The former situation, where dialectics is hard-nosed, is represented by the affirmation and negation of a concept being distant from each other. The latter situation, where an analyst is aware of a definitional reciprocity between the affirmation and negation of a concept, and hence is able to easily analyze and destructure a concept, is represented by the affirmation and negation of a concept being proximately close to each other i.e., both within the same general area or level of awareness. The closer they are to each other, the easier it would be for an analyst to realize a paradoxical conclusion. The process whereby analyses become more subtle can be observed on the graph. At the beginning, the affirmations and negations of each concept tend to be at a maximum separation, and as analysis proceeds the separation is progressively reduced. Another way of explaining the more subtle form of analysis that occurs as the analyst gains experience with analysis and a recognition of the principles involved is to say that analysis can *begin in the advanced stages.*

An advanced form of analysis would presuppose an intellectual appreciation of openness and certain preliminary stages that are necessary at the beginning of an analyst's career. For example, the hackwork involved in determining what is to be analyzed and the task of becoming aware of, and assenting to the logical principles assumed in analysis, could probably be dispensed with, and the paradoxical nature of designation could be easily brought to mind. In these cases less mental energy would be required to conjoin conceptual opposites, and analysis would be more subtle for that reason. An analyst can, in fact, be constantly aware of the oppositional structure in which concepts arise and easily, or at least more easily, be able to analytically dissolve that structure.

Perhaps it is understood that an analyst doesn't even work through all the steps and procedures normally required in analysis but can begin at or quite near the conclusion.

A question arises at this point concerning the procedures and structural dynamics of analysis: namely, which concepts are the easier to analyze, those with high or low values, i.e., those which are weakly or strongly cathected? Intuitively one would think that the more extreme the grasping to a concept the more difficult it would be to successfully, i.e., fruitfully, analyze it. The concepts that were less highly valued could be more easily committed to an analysis, knowing or sensing that an analysis would ontologically and affectively devalue a concept. Candrakīrti's suggestion that analysts first analyze the self, though, seems to run against this if we assume (1) that the self is more highly valued in comparison with most other concepts, and (2) that he suggests for beginners whatever is the easiest concept to analyze. Both these assumptions seem likely. One possible response in support of Candrakīrti's implied position is that the coarse grasping at the self may be easier to recognize than coarse grasping at things, and thus if the coarse aspects of the reactive emotions (*kleśa*) are removed before the subtle aspects, as the path-structure literatures suggest,[164] then although self-grasping may be very trenchant, its coarser aspects would be easier to remove than the coarse aspects of grasping to phenomena, just because they are easier to recognize. (Incidentally, the model is programmed so that one can specify either that higher or lower valued concepts are more easily analyzed. The event-graph used here assumes that the higher the summed value of an affirmation and negation, the easier it is to analyze a concept. If one specifies that the lower the summed value, the more easily a concept is analyzed, then the graph takes about thirty percent longer to reach a zero net magnitude. Although nothing can be held by this, it would suggest that it is more economical for analysts to put their efforts into analyzing the concepts that they most highly value.[165]

MEDIATED AND CERTIFIED COGNITIONS OF OPENNESS

Mention has been made early on of a distinction between so-called facsimile cognitions of openness that are mediated by an image and genuine cognitions that cognize openness directly. Also, we have said that interpreting the model on the extended path lets us give some sense to the difference that might be intended between these two types of cognition. A mediated or inferential cognition can be seen as an intellectual foreshadowing of the possibility of the future destructuring of a concept, and perhaps also, some appreciation of the spiritually freeing effects of a destructuring of conceptuality. The process whereby the perceived possibility for a destructuring and hence insight into the openness of a concept would become an actuality could be paralleled by the conceptual image of openness thinning out, as it were, so that an unmediated cognition came to replace the cognition that was mediated by an image. Thus, mediated and genuine cognitions wouldn't be two discreet modes of cognition, rather mediated cognitions would permit of degrees. As cognitions became less mediated they would acquire the epistemological and phenomenological characteristics of genuine cognitions. When the conceptual image was washed out entirely the cognition would be genuine.

In the event-graph this process would occur as the affirmation and negation of a concept *approach each other*. As the affirmation and negation approach each other through the force of a paradoxical argument an analyst perhaps sees that *taken further* such a movement would result in a coincidence of opposites and conceptual destructuring. The coincidence that is foreshadowed would be a genuine cognition for it would *actually* destructure a concept, while the perception of its possibility as a harbinger of the real event would be an inferential or mediated cognition. Thus, as the negation and affirmation of a concept approach each other, and to the extent that an analyst foreshadows a continuation of the same process, a mediated cognition would become clarified and finally transform into a genuine cognition.

INNATE AND INTELLECTUAL CONCEPTIONS

The so-called innate (*sahaja*) and intellectual (*parikalpita*) conceptions, that are mentioned earlier, can also be assimilated into the model. We recall that intellectual conceptions are more superficial and more easily removed than innate conceptions. In the levels of the path (*krama-mārga*) literature, the errant intellectual conceptions are removed first. In fact, apparently only the errant intellectual conceptions are thought to be removed up to the path of intuition while the innate conceptions are removed on the path of meditation. (This is interesting for it lends added weight to the idea that the insight of openness as the removal of the view of intrinsic existence can be deepened on the path of meditation as the innate conceptions are gradually whittled away.)

As innate conceptions are more ingrained and deep-rooted, by and large we must assume that they are more highly valued, and hence that the highly valued concepts are innately held concepts. This is a general rule. While some intellectual concepts do not seem to have an innate counterpart, others do seem to have both an intellectual and innate aspect to them, for example, the view of intrinsic existence (*svabhāva*). Thus, on the model, some of the more highly valued concepts would be comprised of two facets, an intellect facet and an innate facet.

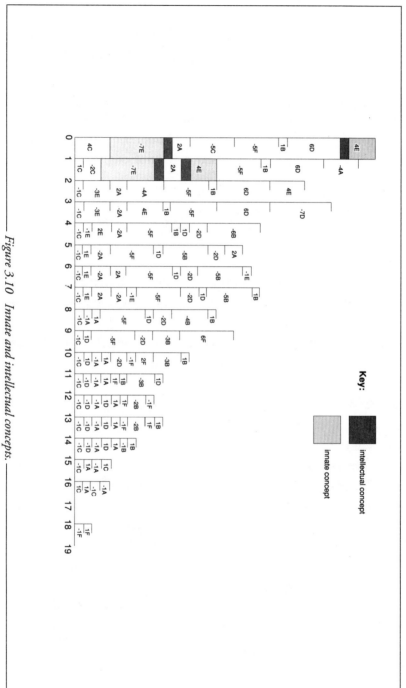

Figure 3.10 Innate and intellectual concepts.

Now, if the intellectually held concepts are removed first, then the lower the value of a concept the more likely it would be to be removed first. In the case where the one concept has both an innate and an intellectual facet to it, the intellectual facet would be the first part of the concept to be engaged in an analysis. Thus, in the model, where a concept has these two aspects, the parts of the negation and affirmation of the concept that *first* came into contact with each other would represent the intellectual aspect. This is shown in *Figure 3.10* for concept E. The shaded portion would be the intellectual aspect.

Referring back to the phenomenon of partial analyses, at least in some cases perhaps it is only the intellectual component of a concept that is being engaged in an analysis, the innate facet being uncommitted.

RAMIFICATION

We will now return to some implications of the verse quoted earlier from Āryadeva. Although it seems doctrinally problematic to claim that all cognitions of openness must have all concepts as the basis for the openness, it does make sense, and is consistent with the doctrine of relational origination (*pratītyasamutpāda*), that an insight that is gained with respect to one concept in a conceptual network, would ramify throughout the entire conceptual network. More specifically, it makes sense that an insight gained with respect to any one concept would reduce the cathexis for concepts that were *functionally related* to the concepts being analyzed. If concepts do exist in a matrix of causal relations, dependencies, and information flows, then the devaluation of any one concept would act to devalue other concepts that were related to it. Concepts that were strongly related to the concept being analyzed (and especially those whose existence and function were dependent on it) would be devalued to a significant degree. Those concepts that are only weakly related to the concept being analyzed would perhaps be only marginally destructured. In other words and broadly speaking, related concepts would be destructured to a degree that is commensurate with the degree to which they were functionally related to the concept that was successfully analyzed. The result would be that analytical meditations would produce *pockets of openness* within a matrix of conceptuality that centered around the concept being analyzed. In fact, this general assumption seems to be behind Āryadeva's position also, except that his position is radical in the extreme for it assumes (1) that the process of ramification occurs instantaneously, (2) that it occurs equally for all concepts, and (3) that there is no loss of insight as the information ramifies throughout the conceptual matrix.

It seems reasonable to suppose that the insight cognizing the openness of the self-concept would probably ramify very extensively, perhaps influencing *all* other concepts in virtue of the relational structure of all cognition in which all cognizables depend on a cognizer and all feeling, emotions, and memories depend on an experiencer.

It is difficult to speculate on the temporal effect of ramification. On the one hand, the ramification of insight throughout all or part of a conceptual matrix would tend to accelerate the gaining of insight, although, on the other hand, the fact that concepts are embedded in a matrix of dependencies and causal relationships may mean that they are more highly reified than if they weren't, and hence that they are harder to analyze for they can't be analyzed in isolation from (some) other concepts.

HABITUATION

In completing the interpretation of the model an explanation for

156

the *reappearances* of concepts is required. In the graph it is concepts
A and **F** that reappear. If we ignore those two reappearances for a
minute, the graph depicts a situation where once a concept is successfully analyzed it destructures and is removed forever from the
stream of conceptuality. This assumes that once an analyst cognizes
the openness of a concept that insight is retained with him or her
and is never lost. In other words, there wouldn't be a relapse to the
situation that obtained before she or he had successfully analyzed
the concept, i.e., when it was ontologically affirmed or denied.
Middle Path Buddhism understands that this isn't the case, though,
and that insights can degenerate due to their being overridden by
habits that maintain and sustain a non-analytical posture with
respect to experience. Hence there is thought to be a need to
repeatedly analyze concepts in order to gradually counteract and
weaken the habits that natively affirm the existence and non-existence of things. The *Introduction to the Evolved Lifestyle* [BCA] says,
for example, that:

> By consolidating the imprint (*vāsanā*) of openness, the
> imprints of things will be abandoned, and through repeti-
> tion (*abhyāśa*), [the view] that "nothing at all exists," will
> also come to be abandoned.[166]

(The reference to abandoning the view that nothing at all exists
means forsaking the view that openness is a phenomenon.)
Habituation of this sort acts to reify the stream of conceptuality by
a *change-reducing* negative feedback. Habituation thus acts in
opposition to analysis and attempts to return the stream of conceptuality to earlier states. It is a counter evolutionary force. It is thus
responsible for backsliding and, as said before, accounts for the
need by analysts to repeat their analyses many, many times. It also,
of course, elongates the analysts' path.

In the model this form of habituation is simulated by a routine called "engramming." This routine keeps a record of all the behavioral states of the model as they are created. In other words, it keeps a history of prior behavior (as *vāsanās* keep a history of and encode actions!). The prior states of the model then bear on the reintroduction of a concept after it has been destructured. The reappearance and strength (i.e., magnitude) and duration of a reappearance are determined by the presence, magnitude, and duration of the concept *prior* to its removal. The influence that a concept has in determining its reappearance drops off in direct proportion to its temporal distance from the present state of the model. Thus, the immediately preceding state of the model is the most influential in determining the next state vis-a-vis the reappearance, magnitude, and configuration of objects, and this influence progressively decreases as one works back through the earlier states.

In the model, the habituating function also serves to create a *temporary* cessation to *all* conceptuality. An instance of this in the graph we have been using occurs where a net magnitude of zero is reached at profile 17 but lost at profile 18 with the reappearance of concept **F** before being regained at profile 19. A more extended example can be seen in *Figure 3.11* in which the engramming function is much stronger.

If a cessation of conceptuality is identical with nirvāṇa, then the model displays a process whereby nirvāṇa is first gained for short durations which are progressively extended until, presumably, there is a never-ending nirvāṇa. Also, the relapses to conceptual elaboration become less significant and less pronounced.

The form of habituation referred to above only takes into account habituations that exert a counter-evolutionary influence on the acquisition of insight. To be sure though, analysts would also become habituated to engaging in analysis and this would accelerate their evolution through in that they would become

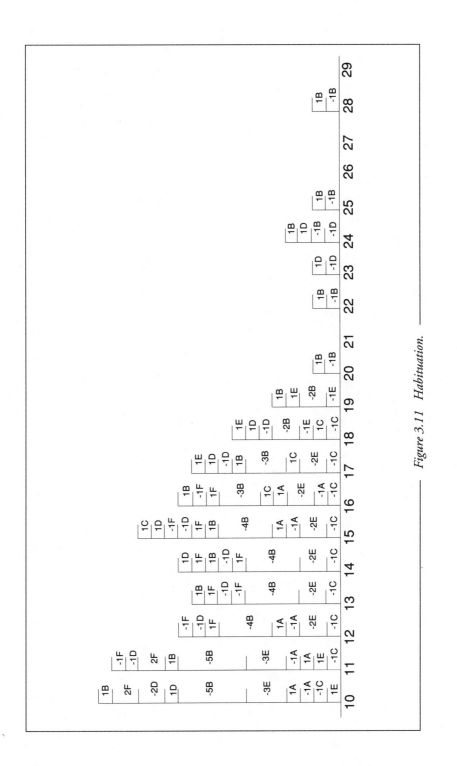

Figure 3.11 Habituation.

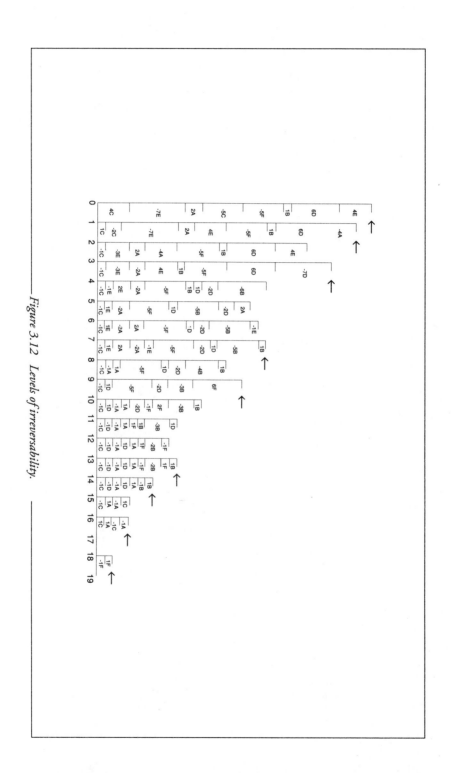

Figure 3.12 Levels of irreversability.

more familiar and comfortable with an analytical mentality, and this would make them more prone to analyze concepts. This is also simulated in the model by another optional routine, which can be given a varying level of influence. This variable specifies that the greater the number of times that a concept is successfully analyzed the more liable it will be to be analyzed in the future. It is a case where "successful sub-routines of activity become more likely to be tried again while unsuccessful ones become less frequently assayed."[167]

Finally, the idea of so-called stages of irreversibility (*anivartana-cārya*) is also roughly represented in the graph. If a level of irreversibility is defined as achieving a level of insight below which a saint will not drop in the future then several such levels occur in *Figure 3.12* which are indicated by arrows.

This definition of irreversibilities in terms of the criterion of levels of insight accords with a path-structure criterion used by Middle Path philosophers in defining the *second* stage of irreversibility that occurs at the seventh level (*bhūmi*).[168] This is the stage when an advanced practitioner (*bodhisattva*) cannot lose his or her insight. The graph specifies several intermediate levels and this is consonant with the model's gradual path assumptions.

4

A THERAPEUTIC APPLICATION
OF MIDDLE PATH ANALYSIS

INTRODUCTION

IN THE PRECEDING CHAPTER we developed a systems-based model that describes the changes that occur when paradoxical analysis is used in a rigorous and disciplined way by meditators who have prepared themselves over many years through the practice of serenity meditation and the development of focused and powerful concentration (*samādhi*).

The model and outline of the methods of paradoxical analysis that were developed in Chapter Two, will now serve as a reference point from which we can explore contemporary therapeutic possibilities for Middle Path paradoxical analysis. We have given an *ideal representation* of Middle Path analysis, which is to say, we have given an abstract and generalized description of the principles of paradoxical analysis and modeled the changes that would occur if analysis is used in an *ideal environment*. And now we are in a position to venture beyond the ideal environment for we have a grid or reference system to which we can always refer. We can now begin to explore the possible therapeutic use of Middle Path analysis in a Western urban setting.

CONTEXTUAL DIFFERENCES

Buddhist Middle Path analysis has traditionally been used in a monastic setting by Buddhist monks and nuns as a technique of mental training designed to bring about a more accurate and satisfying appreciation of reality. In its traditional context the technique of paradoxical analysis is used in both the public arena in the debating forums of monastic colleges and privately in the meditational exercises that Middle Pathers employ as a part of their meditational training.

There are a number of major differences between a traditional Asian and Western urban environment. These differences compel us to introduce some important changes in using paradoxical consequences if this method of therapeutic intervention is to be successfully employed in Western clinical settings.

The first and obvious difference is that in the traditional Buddhist context the goal or outcome that is sought through the use of paradoxical consequences is the radical transformation of the very core of a person's existence, since ultimately the Buddhist Middle Pather is seeking unconditional freedom (*nirvāṇa*). Conversely, in a Western urban context the outcomes that are sought in therapy are usually quite specific and concrete. Typically, therapists aim at resolving problems that arise in particular environmental contexts (e.g., at home or at work), with particular people (e.g., with partners, children, parents, colleagues). The problems occur in the context of relationships and take the form of debilitating moods and emotions such as depression, anxiety, rage, fear, grief, etc. The removal of such emotional problems becomes the goal of therapy. At one extreme a therapist may have to deal with the panic, anxiety, and profound resignation that accompanies a suicidal personality or manage the rage and aggression of homicidal impulses. At the other extreme therapists provide counsel in life-enhancement—what we often call "self-development."

Another major divergence between the traditional Asian and

modern Western setting lies in the differences between the level of mental preparedness of a client and those of a monk or nun. In particular, the Buddhist has received training in serenity (*śamatha*) and mental integration (*samādhi*). The development of serenity produces a mood or atmosphere in which analysis can occur and the development of mental integration gives intentionality and direction to the analytical process. Thus, his or her meditational analyses can be expected to be more powerful and sustained, and hence more effective, than those of an urban client who generally lacks the ability to sit with sustained concentration on one topic of analysis for some minutes or even an hour. This is an important difference as we will see later, for among other factors, the effectiveness of Buddhist paradoxical analysis is dependent on a person's capacity to pursue a well-defined pattern with a minimum of distracting thoughts. This factor is important since there are often very understandable reasons from the client's point of view for becoming distracted. In fact the very notion of "a distraction" needs to be rethought since it presupposes that someone would be better served by thinking about something different from what they are in fact thinking about. Analysis can threaten a client's self concept and have ramifications concerning lifestyle and interpersonal relations. A quite natural reaction is to defend old patterns of thought and behavior and this can result in conscious or unconscious tactics to avoid a genuine therapeutic encounter.

A third difference between the traditional Asian and modern Western setting is that the emotional problems that a Buddhist meditator is working with will usually have less urgency about them. Only rarely does a person who is skilled and accomplished in meditation become frenetic to remove a problem. Their practice of serenity tempers the moods of panic and urgency that often appear in urban clients. And finally, and related to the foregoing point, the urban client may well come equipped with more expectations than the Buddhist analyst who with hindsight has come to expect small results, and even these only after a prolonged and intensive application of analytical techniques.

The conclusions or consequence that Buddhist monks and nuns arrived at after a series of logically connected thought processes are surprising for they point to the fact that disturbing thought patterns and their corresponding emotional reactions are baseless or without a solid foundation. An awareness of the baselessness, or lack of any foundation, to these problems is then said to render the problems themselves impotent or incapable of drawing mental attention and energy since the problems are viewed as groundless and without any point. Emotional problems can thus be dissipated and neurotic energy can be freed for deployment in more creative and less self-centered activities and concerns. The aim for the Buddhist, naturally, is to be freed from all emotional problems; in other words, to liberate all emotionally constricted energy and vitality.

However, even given these differences Middle Path analysis lends itself to a Western urban application, since unlike other Buddhist techniques such as mindfulness meditation it doesn't require a meditational practice. Thus, it can theoretically be extended to clients who are unwilling or unable to employ techniques based on meditation. However, if a client can also use other practices such as training in serenity (*samatha*) and mental integration (*samādhi*) we expect that his or her therapy would be strengthened.

Before suggesting some techniques and procedures of a clinical Middle Path we will briefly explore some parallels and affinities between Buddhist assumptions about the causes of emotional disturbance and some current theories in mainstream Western psychology. This comparison will show that the foundations of Buddhist psychology, and in particular the Middle Path interpretation of Buddhist psychology provide, a workable basis for therapy *within* the accepted parameters of Western psychotherapy.

Cognitive theories of the emotions in Buddhism and Western psychology

In this section we will compare Buddhist theories of emotions with "cognitive theories of emotions" that have been developed in contemporary Western psychology.[169] More specifically we will map the intersections and differences between Buddhist and Western cognitive theories of the emotions, since the parallels and differences between the theoretical foundations of Buddhist Middle Pathers and contemporary cognitive theories of emotions also determine similarities and differences in the development and utilization of therapeutic techniques based on their respective theories. Cognitive theories of emotions are one theory about the cause of emotions that are subscribed to in Western psychology. As a psychological platform, cognitive theories of emotions are gaining increased acceptance among theoretical psychologists and therapists. It is also the theoretical model that has by far the greatest affinities to Buddhist theories of the emotions. It is, as we will see, entirely accurate to say that all schools of Buddhism subscribe to a cognitive theory of emotions.

Cognitive therapies are typically defended on the basis of being linked to cognitive theories of emotions. Albert Ellis,[170] the originator of Rational Emotive therapy, when writing in 1973 cited fifty-one studies that support the cognitive mediation of emotional responses.

Although a large number of theorists have advanced cognitive

167

models of varying complexity and linked in varying degrees to experimental data, we will here restrict ourselves to the theories of Richard Lazarus and Albert Ellis. Lazarus[171] is a leading contemporary exponent and defender of cognitive theories of emotions. Ellis's theory is particularly useful since it is explicitly used to support a popular and respected form of psychotherapy called rational-emotive therapy (RET). Prior to outlining these Western theories of emotions and making the comparisons with Buddhist theories I will briefly detail the Buddhist theory of emotions.

BUDDHIST THEORIES OF EMOTIONS

Theories that explain the arising of problematic emotions and moods have been expounded in all schools of Buddhism. The explanations all use the same basic framework although they interpret the key terms that occur in the model differently. In general terms the Middle Pathers adopt the basic *structure* of the model that was developed in the phenomenological tradition of Vaibhashika Buddhism, but give their own interpretations to some of the key concepts. This model is described by four key concepts, namely:

(1) reactive emotions and moods (*kleśa*);
(2) ontological blindness (*avidyā*);
(3) confusion (*moha*); and
(4) a fixed view about who we are (*satkāyadṛṣṭi*).

These concepts figure in Buddhist phenomenological literature, what is termed *abhidharma*, and also in Middle Path texts. While the meaning of some of the terms have been described in earlier chapters we will briefly explain our understanding of these terms.

In Buddhist phenomenological psychology the phrase "reactive moods and emotions (*kleśa*)" stands for a class of mental events (*caitta*) that precipitate ill-directed actions (*karma*).[172] The *Collection on Phenomenology* [AK] of Vasubandhu [5.1cd] further distinguishes six principal types of reactive moods and emotions. Vasubandhu in fact speaks of these as predispositions (*anuśaya*).[173] More specifically the emotional predispositions are the reactive moods and emotions in their dormant or latent condition. Vasubandhu lists the six root emotional predispositions as: desire (*rāga*), anger (*pratigha*), arrogant pride (*mana*), ontological blindness (*avidyā*), opinions (*dṛṣṭi*) and doubt (*vicikitsā*). These emotional predispositions are also called [AK: 4.36cd] biases (*āsrava*) and are divided into the biases for desire, for existence, and for ontological blindness.[174] In their developed state the emotional predispositions develop into a number of debilitating moods and attitudes (*pāryavasthana*). Vasubandhu [AK:5.47–48a] lists these as: lacking the capacity to feel shame, lacking the capacity to experience embarrassment, jealousy, miserliness, excitement, guilt, lethargy, languor, anger and concealment.[175] These moods and attitudes together with deceit, dishonesty, arrogance, spite, resentment, and aggression, are referred to as the sixteen subsidiary or derivative reactive moods and emotions.[176]

In translating *kleśa* by the phrase "reactive moods and emotions" we may note that the basic emotions that are recognized as problematic in Western psychology also appear in the Buddhist lists. Thus, we find: desire, anger, jealousy, excitement, guilt, resentment, and aggression. The Buddhist lists, though, also include mental events that we might call wishes or motivations, such as concealment, spite, and dishonesty. They also include certain reactions that Western psychology would see as the results of powerful emotions, though not as emotions themselves, such as: lethargy and languor. The lists also include events that are less emotive and more cognitive and intentional, such as: doubt, views, concealment, and deceit. We see from these lists that Buddhists consider a greater range of affective and cognitive states to be problematic than does Western psychology. Some of the *kleśas* such as doubt, non-shame, non-embarrassment, concealment, and some limited forms of desire and attachment, can be viewed by Western theories of personality and psychotherapies as, if not healthy mental postures, then at least not attitudes that Western psychotherapy would see as representing personality defects or indicative of mental problems. These differences reflect different cultural norms and ideals in traditional Eastern and modern Western societies. They demonstrate differences in how cultures *declare* some moods to be positive and others negative. These declarations in turn derive from the goals and aspirations that different societies value since different moods and emotions open and close different possibilities for people and cultures.

From a traditional Buddhist and Middle Path perspective all the moods and emotions we have mentioned above are forms of mental disturbance. Thus, they are all types of mental events that a spiritual praxis would address.

The next concept to define is "ontological blindness (*avidyā*)." In many ways this is the most crucial term to "get right" in comparing Buddhist with Western cognitive theories of emotions since moods and emotions (*kleśa*) are constituted by "ontological blindness (*avidyā*)." What is "ontological blindness," and how does it relate to the types or modes of cognitions that are thought to underlie or generate emotional responses in Western cognitive theories of emotions, such as the theory developed by Lazarus? The first point to note is that "ontological blindness" does not stand outside the list of primary "reactive moods and emotions": it is listed by Vasubandhu as the fourth reactive mood and emotion.

170

It is, though, distinguished from the other reactive moods and emotions in terms of its concomitant presence with all the other reactive moods and emotions. This is made clear by Vasubandhu (1980) when he is explaining the Buddhist theory of relational origination (*pratītyasamutpāda*). In that context he explains that "ontological blindness" is selected from the full list of reactive moods and emotions. This is confirmed elsewhere by Vasubandhu, where he identifies "ontological blindness" with confusion (*moha*). He claims that confusion is necessarily present whenever someone is experiencing a reactive mood or emotion. Also, in the discussion of the biases (*āsrava*), Vasubandhu [5.36cd] states that "ontological blindness" is the foundation (*mula*) of all the biases.[177] "Ontological blindness" is listed as the universal foundation of the reactive moods and emotions (*klesamahabhūmika*). The term "*avidyā*" has been rendered into English differently by different scholars. The most commonly used term is "ignorance." Herbert Guenther and Leslie Kawamuru use the phrase "lack of intrinsic awareness."[178] Bimal Matilal, who has made a detailed study of the concept as it is used by Vasubandhu writes that:

> In a general context, *avidyā* may stand for false beliefs or a false belief system which we all grow up with in the worldly environment. But in Buddhism it obtains a specialized meaning.... It is the inherent misconception, a beginningless, *cosmic*, confusion in all of us, which perpetuates our painful existence.[179]

This definition concurs with the usual translations of *moha* as "confusion" or "bewilderment." Matilal summarizes that *avidyā* signifies "false beliefs, misconceptions and wrong convictions."[180] My own feeling is that a better equivalent is found in the phrase "ontological blindness." This phrase captures the idea that *avidyā* denotes an impoverished set of distinctions with which to deal with our lives in a wholesome and integrated way. It also captures the notion that *avidyā* signifies a blindness or lack of insight into the very nature of being, an ignorance about the nature of existence. As Matilal rightly says *avidyā* indicates a "cosmic confusion" in the sense of a fundamental and pervasive ignorance about the ontological status of things. According to Buddhism, we are blind to the fact that we are blind in this fundamental sense. We do not see that the very *fabric and substance* of our discernment, our language, and our cognition may radically distort our experience of ourselves and the world.

As we have mentioned at the beginning of this section, the Middle Pathers gave their own interpretations to some of the concepts in this Buddhist model of moods and emotions. In particular the Middle Pathers specifically link the concept of "ontological blindness" to the notion of conceiving things to have an intrinsic or essential existence (*svabhāva*). Thus, the eighth century Middle Path philosopher Śāntideva states that the generation of feelings (*vedana*) in terms of the perception of the essential existence of feelings and the one who feels.[181] The Middle Pathers also identified "ontological blindness" with the mistaken opinion that there is a real individual. Thus, we see Candrakīrti writing that all of the reactive moods and emotions (*kleśa*) such as desire and attachment and the problems of existence (*dosa*), arise from the wrong view of the individual (*satkāyadṛṣṭi*), which he defines as an emotionally contaminated cognition (*shes rab nyon mongs*) that entertains the thought of "I" and "mine."[182]

LAZARUS'S THEORY

We should note at the outset that the phrase "cognitive aspect of emotions" is sometimes used to indicate the "idea" or meaning of an emotion. In this sense it denotes the signal function of emotions or the message or information they contain. It is, for example, the cognitive aspect in this sense that psychoanalysis attempts to uncover. This, though, is not the sense in which cognitive theorists speak of the cognitive aspect to emotions.

The cognitive theory of emotions, as stated by Richard Lazarus, is that "emotions are products of cognitive processes."[183] He elaborates that emotions are elicited "by a complex cognitive appraisal of the significance of events for one's well-being."[184] Thus, according to his theory, cognition is a causal antecedent of emotional reactions such that in the absence of cognitive activity there would be no emotional reactions. The role of cognitive appraisal is to "mediate the relationship between the person and the environment. The appraisal process gives rise to a particular emotion with greater or lesser intensity depending on how the relationship is evaluated with respect to the person's well-being."[185] For Lazarus an appraisal or evaluative perception "can operated at all levels of complexity, from the most primitive and inborn to the most symbolic and experience-based."[186] Further, in Lazarus's view there are very likely no exceptions: all emotional states have an underlying cognitive component, barring perhaps certain instinctual fear-and-fight reactions, and even these most probably have a cognitive component too.[187] He writes that, "cognitive appraisal is *always* involved in emotion, even in creatures phylogenetically far more primitive than humans."[188] According to Lazarus, belief is also implicated in the positively toned emotions and gentle emotions.[189]

In general, Lazarus's theory squares very well with the Buddhist theory, although there are some significant points of divergence. First, I'll point out the convergences and in a later section I will note the differences.

There is a clear concurrence between Lazarus and the Buddhist psychologists who, as previously mentioned, are of the opinion that all reactive moods and emotions, including instinctive responses, are structurally dependent on our blindness to our being (*avidyā*).

The Buddhists and Lazarus also agree on a number of more subtle points of theory. Lazarus writes, for example, in parallel with Buddhist psychology that "the full experience of emotion normally includes three fused components: thoughts, action impulses, and somatic disturbances."[190] The parallel with Buddhist psychology is, to say the least, striking, for there is agreement not only at a categorical level, but also at a *process level*, since Lazarus is stating that the emotional reactions arise only when these components are associated. His theory is thus in correspondence with the Buddhist theory of conditionality. And in even closer parallel with the Middle Path psychology, Lazarus considers that cognition, emotion, and motivation are interdependent entities.[191]

Further, and again in complete agreement with Buddhist theories, cognitive activity of the type that supports emotional reactions can, in Lazarus's view, function at a pre-reflective and even on an unconscious and subliminal level. He writes: "The cognitive activity in appraisal does not imply anything about deliberate reflection, rationality or awareness."[192]

And we have already noted his view that cognitive evaluation can occur in animals. In Middle Path Buddhism these instinctive and pre-reflective levels of cognition are the innate (*sahaja*) conceptions that we referred to earlier. These are distinguished from the intellectual (*parikalpita*) cognitions which are socially acquired.

To recap, the innate (*sahaja*) affects and conceptions are

biologically or genetically determined. They are transcultural and inherited from an individual's past-life thought and action. The intellectual (*parikalpita*) affects and cognitions, on the other hand, are comparatively more superficial, less trenchant and more subject to influence and change by prevailing cultural, ideological, and philosophical climes than are the inherited predispositions and cognitions. Very loosely the culturally acquired affective propensities and cognitions have their analog with the Freudian "superego" and the biologically determined propensities and cognitions with the "id." The Freudian "ego" would, in the Buddhist view, be constituted by a mixture of deeply rooted and socially acquired conceptions. Still, in Buddhist psychology there is not the degree of conflict and tension between the biologically and culturally acquired conceptions that there is between the "id" and the "superego" in Freudian theory, since for Buddhist psychologists the biologically conditioned affects and conceptions are simply the result of a prolonged and repeated activation, over innumerable lives, of what would otherwise be more superficial drives and impulses.

ELLIS'S THEORY

Ellis's cognitive theory is not as precisely formulated as Lazarus's. It is relevant in this context, however, as his cognitive theory of emotions is integrated with a form of therapy that will provide a reference for later discussion.

The first point to note is that Ellis doesn't claim originality for his theory. He traces its origins to the Stoic philosophers and cites Alfred Adlers's *Individual Psychology* as its most recent precursor.[193] He also mentions the Taoist and Buddhist philosophies. Further, Ellis acknowledges that what he calls "general or inelegant rational-emotive therapy" is virtually synonymous with cognitive-behavior therapy.[194] As his form of therapy becomes more "elegant" the behavioral angle becomes more secondary and the manipulation of cognitions becomes more central.

Ellis bases his rational-emotive theory on a so-called ABC theory of disturbance and personality change.[195] This model holds that when an emotional consequence (C) follows an activating event (A), A does not cause C. Rather, the emotional consequences are largely created by an individual's belief system. The component of the model that is significant from the viewpoint of cognitive theory and therapy is "B" or "belief" system. Ellis also writes that: "The 'real' cause of his emotional upsets, therefore, is *himself*, and not *what happens* to him (even though the experiences of his life obviously have *some* influence on what he thinks and feels)."[196] A clear parallel can be seen here with the Buddhist concepts of primary and secondary causation (*sahakāri-pratyaya*). Primary causes necessarily reside *within* an individual. They are, in fact, an individual's mental and behavioral predispositions and latent propensities. Secondary causes on the other hand, are located in the environment. The inner mental causes are primary in the sense that even if the relevant configuration of secondary causes are present as environmental conditions, without internal mental predispositions no emotional reactions can precipitate. In some Buddhist traditions, notably the Phenomenalist, or Vijñānavāda system, there is also a sense in which the primary causes create the secondary causes.

Even though Ellis mentions some very basic and foundational forms of conceptualization, in the course of therapy he focuses on unrealistic beliefs. That is to say, in practice he tends to assume that emotions are conditioned by conscious or readily accessible beliefs. And in this he departs from both Lazarus's and the Buddhist theory of emotions. As I will have occasion to comment on this difference later I would now like to look at the important differences between the Buddhist and Western theories.

Differences between the Buddhist and Western Theories

The first point of difference to note between Buddhist and Western theories is that according to Buddhist psychology, it is ontological blindness (*avidyā*) that conditions moods and emotional reactions. Ontological clarity (*vidyā*) does not condition moods and emotions, rather ontological clarity conditions the attenuation of reactive moods and emotions. For Lazarus, on the other hand, the evaluations that condition emotions need not be errant. He writes that: "The cognitive appraisals that shape our emotional reactions can distort reality as well as reflect it realistically."[197] Thus, the major difference between the theories is that in Buddhism all cognitive activity which supports reactive emotions is discordant with reality.

In rational-emotive therapy and Beck's cognitive therapy[198] some stipulation is made: emotional reactions tend to be conditioned by unrealistic evaluations, that is, by judgments and evaluations that do not accord with reality. Cognitions that don't condition emotional reactions would thus be, or be based on realistic evaluations. However, the hedonistic tenor of Ellis's overall philosophy indicates that on his theory, realistic cognitions could condition what he would label "positive emotions," such as, conjugal love and self pride. Moreover, with respect to Ellis's theory, and his understanding of the term "realistic," we can point out that realistic perceptions need not always be expected to preclude emotional responses. If one realistically perceives that one's life or well-being is *genuinely* threatened this may very well condition an emotional response. Ellis himself, in one sense goes further than this when he writes that: "Even negative emotions, such as sorrow, regret, annoyance, and irritation, stem largely from rational sentences."[199] The implication is that rational beliefs can condition emotional disturbances. This signals a possible difference between rational-emotive therapy and Buddhist concepts to which we will return shortly.

In rational-emotive therapy it is also theoretically possible that someone could have an irrational worldview but still be happy and contented. It is possible, in other words, to hold an irrational belief which does not cause a person to be disturbed. If such a situation were to obtain, though, the person's happiness would be contingent on certain particular environmental circumstances. The conditions for the happiness of the individual would not reside with the person. Buddhist psychology would agree with this as a possibility. However, Buddhist observations about the impermanence and changeability of all phenomena would render it a highly contingent and unstable form of happiness that is the very antithesis of the *unconditional* happiness that Buddhists seek in the realization of selflessness.

Rational-emotive therapy does link different types of beliefs to different types of emotional responses. In particular rational-emotive therapy distinguishes between beliefs that describe wants and desires, and beliefs that constitute demands. According to rational-emotive therapy theory, beliefs that articulate wants or needs can result in disappointment, frustration, and sadness, if the desires or needs are unfulfilled. Beliefs that are premised on demands condition emotional responses such as anger. Now, according to rational-emotive therapy, it is only the latter type of emotional responses that constitute emotional disturbances. In rational-emotive therapy the former responses, such as disappointment and the frustration of desires, are not emotional disturbances. In fact they can be life-enhancing if they motivate and energize people to more creative actions for achieving long term goals. This part of rational-emotive therapy theory is based on the assumption that it is the demand that a desire be realized rather than the desire itself which causes an emotional disturbance. Desires that are not accompanied by a demand that they be realized are thought not to condition emotional disturbances. And it is for this reason that desires can be rational in rational-emotive therapy theory. Ellis writes:

> I think that almost all wants, desires, or preferences are appropriate, and very much help to make life worthwhile. Only the escalation of such wants into "needs" is inappropriate and had better be surrendered.[200]

It is only when humans believe that they *must* have what they want that they irrationally create unrealistic "needs." Thus, Ellis advises that clients should retain their wants and surrender only their needs. A consequence of this aspect of rational-emotive theory is that rational-emotive therapy deals only with the emotional disturbances and not with the emotional responses that arise due to frustrated needs and desires.

On this issue there is a major and fundamental departure between rational-emotive therapy and Buddhism. This difference appears on two accounts. First, Buddhist psychology disputes that the emotional responses that are conditioned by desires and wants are *not* disturbances. According to Buddhism the emotional responses conditioned by desires are a problem for people. This is confirmed by the centrality of desire in the formation of emotional problems. In the Buddha's very first address after his enlightenment, the *Putting the Cycle of the Philosophy in Motion Sermon* (*Dhammacakkappavattana-sutta*), grasping (*tṛṣṇā*) is cited as the cause of all human problems (*duḥkha*). Second, as a form of therapy Buddhism does address the emotional precipitates to unfilled desires and wishes. The third and fourth "facticities of the saint (*ārya-satya*)" are that the problems that are conditioned by grasping can be removed by the saint's path that eradicates desire.

There are other significant differences between rational-emotive therapy and Buddhist psychology. Rational-emotive therapy distinguishes between long-term and short-term goals. Long-term goals concern survival and the enhancement of life. Short-term goals focus on immediate comfort. Rational-emotive therapy observes that long-term life enhancing goals are often forsaken for short-term goals, and advocates that people should tolerate and accept short-term discomforts en route to achieving long-term goals. This attitude is, of course, not unlike the Buddhist concept of transforming painful circumstances into the path of achieving longer-term aims. However, in Buddhism the aims are much more long-term and distant, and include an achievement of meditational accomplishments and ultimately the unconditional freedom of nirvāṇa. The differential between the present circumstances of people and the focus on such long-term aims as achieving nirvāṇa or enlightenment also means that Buddhism advocates a higher degree of resolve and endurance (*ksanti*) in the present than does rational-emotive therapy. Consequently Buddhism appears as a philosophy of renunciation while, at least in comparison to Buddhism, rational-emotive therapy appears to be a philosophy of cultivated hedonism.

It is, in fact, fair to observe that rational-emotive therapy advocates a basically self-centered and individualistic attitude to life. Ellis writes: "The frank and honest goal of RET [rational-emotive therapy] is quite hedonistic: longer life and greater enjoyment."[201] In this, his therapeutic philosophy is radically different from the Expansive Career (*Mahāyāna*) in Buddhism in which the

Middle Path system is situated, in which egolessness is conjoined with a philosophy of unbounded altruism. Still, it is important to note that the hedonistic tenor of rational-emotive therapy is not determined by its cognitive basis or its *method* of confrontation and refutation. The individualistic and self-centered thrust of rational-emotive therapy is defined by the particular set of beliefs that Ellis and rational-emotive therapists deem to be irrational and which they refute in the course of rational-emotive therapy. More particularly, the self-centered flavor of rational-emotive therapy is determined by regarding certain nominally altruistic beliefs as irrational; such as, that people should get upset over other people's problems and disturbances, and that people should help all those who are in need of help. Incidentally, in giving this self-centered directionality to rational-emotive therapy Ellis has moved significantly away from Adler's individualistic psychology which is laudable among contemporary systems of therapy for its emphasis on "social concern." And for this reason Adler's system is much closer to the social and humanistic values embodied in the Expansive Career in Buddhism.

Having said that the self-centered thrust of Ellis's therapy is not linked to the cognitive basis of his therapy I will just briefly raise the question of the "positive emotions" in Buddhism and their relationship to cognition. As already noted, for Lazarus, the positively toned and gentle emotions (which he doesn't list) depend on beliefs. Certainly there are the positive empathies and active motivations (*apramāṇa*) such as compassion, love, and impartiality. These are quite explicitly not reactive moods or emotions (*kleśa*). Nor are they the positive emotions of Western psychology such as conjugal love and feelings of self-worth. From Buddhist doctrine we can infer that the empathies such as love, compassion, and even-mindedness are based on accurate cognition

181

and would be impeded or restricted by errant cognitions. However, it is not the case that accurate cognition necessarily conditions the empathies since insight (*prajñā*) can be developed without their cultivation. One value of the translation of *kleśa* as "reactive moods and emotions" is that it signifies the reactive quality of the *kleśas* while the empathetic responses are controlled and well intentioned responses to the accurate perception of suffering in the world. Now whether the positive emotions of Western psychology and therapy are emotional reactions or empathetic responses is a question for internal analysis by Western psychologists.

We should also note that Vasubandhu [AK: 2.25] and other Abhidharmists recognize a class of mental events that are positive or wholesome (*kuśala*), within which are attitudes that might be regarded as emotions or affects, such as, serenity, humility, and regret.[202] Vasubandhu and the Abhidharmists also recognize a class of emotional responses that can be viewed as either positive or negative depending on whether they enhance or hinder progress on the Buddhist path to unconditional freedom.[203] This class of undetermined (*aniyata*) emotional responses includes responses such as regret, languor, anger, desire, and pride. From a comparative viewpoint the question is: can any of these emotional responses be viewed as positive or wholesome in Buddhism outside of the context of motivating a person in Buddhist mental development?

Beyond this all the theories are fairly ill-defined. Buddhist psychology indirectly draws some connections between different types of errant cognitions and the different types of emotional reactions that are conditioned by them. The sixth chapter of Vasubandhu's *Collection on Phenomenology* [AK], for example, describes how different sets of behavioral predisposition (*anuśaya*) are conditioned by a failure to discern one or more of the four facts or realities expounded in Buddhism, viz., the fact of pain, its cause, its cessation, and the means to its cessation. Also *within* the emotional reactions, species-generic relations are made between the subsidiary and primary emotional reactions. Even so, there is no indication in terms of specific forms of ontological blindness of how say hatred, as opposed to pride, is conditioned. The Western theorists elaborate even less on which cognitions are errant and which are accurate, and make no attempt to specify the range of emotions that they can respectively condition.

COGNITIVE THERAPIES AND MIDDLE PATH ANALYSIS

A number of forms of psychotherapy have been developed that are based on cognitive theories of emotions. These are included in the standard handbooks of psychotherapy under rubrics such as cognitive, rational, and attitudinal forms of therapy. Falling in with these categories are therapies that have been developed by Alder,[204] Kelly,[205] Ellis,[206] Raimy,[207] Williamson,[208] Beck,[209] and Meichenbaum.[210] What cognitive therapies have in common is that therapeutic intervention is directed toward bringing about the inhibition and attenuation of emotional reactions through inducing alteration in the cognitive matrix of the client. In Ellis's ABC model of emotional disturbance, for example, the point of therapeutic intervention occurs at "B," the belief system of the client.

To this extent cognitive therapies are thus distinct from the other major forms of therapy such as psychoanalysis, behavior therapy, and neuro-chemical therapies. Although these latter therapies may provide therapeutic interventions at a cognitive level, it is not their primary focus of intervention. What cognitive therapies have in common is that they advocate the intrapsychic self-regulation of emotions as opposed to direct-action coping procedures. They are more concerned with the direct control of emotional responses rather than with manipulating either the environment or the neurophysiological constitution of the individual.

We may note that although in cognitive therapies the channel of input or intervention operates at a cognitive level, such therapies have direct implications for behavior since emotional arousals stimulate and motivate behavior. Thus a number of theorists have developed models for the cognitive control of behavior. The Buddhist analogs to such cognitive theories of behavior are to be extracted from the Buddhist excursus on the dependency and conditioning relationship between *karma* and *kleśa*. There is no need to elaborate on either the Buddhist or Western models here except to note that cognitive therapies can be directly linked to normative goals that require the modification of behavior.

RATIONAL-EMOTIVE THERAPY

How I plan to proceed from here is to use the form of therapy developed in the 1950s by Albert Ellis, which he has termed rational-emotive therapy, as a structure, guide, and benchmark for developing a Buddhist Middle Path form of therapy.

There are three reasons for doing this. First, it is pedagogically useful and instructive to describe a clinical Middle Path in terms of its similarities to and differences from a well-known, respected, and widely employed form of counseling and psychotherapy. Second, rational-emotive therapy is probably the most cognitive and rational of the "cognitive therapies." And third, and most important, Ellis's rational-emotive therapy is a tested, and it seems sound and positive, form of therapy. Hence it seems prudent to develop a therapy and counseling directives that can be viewed as a variation to a sound therapy, rather than to develop a therapy that doesn't intersect at all with a tried and tested therapy.

The form of rational-emotive therapy that has the closest alignment with a therapeutic version of the Middle Path is Ellis's elegant or preferential rational-emotive therapy. This version of rational-emotive therapy is more refined and, as was mentioned earlier, it emphasizes the cognitive dimension of rational-emotive therapy to a greater extent than does the earlier general or inelegant version. It employs quite distinctive logico-empirical, problem-solving techniques.

The elegant version of rational-emotive therapy "stresses the achievement of a profound cognitive or philosophical change in clients' basic assumptions, especially their absolutistic, demanding, musturbatory, irrational ways of viewing themselves, others, and the world."[211] The elegant method differs from the general version by disputing the demandingness and absolutization of beliefs. It does not specifically refute the content of a belief but aims, rather, at removing the absolutization of the beliefs being disputed. The less elegant method is to dispute the assumptions of an irrational belief. Such a disputation results in a client forsaking the form and content of the belief that is being disputed. The elegant method of disputation is said to be more valuable as it gives a client a tool that can be generalized to different situations. In other words, elegant rational-emotional therapy not only reduces an existing disturbance, it also equips a client with a resource for coping with future emotional problems. The therapist tries to change a client's fundamental disturbance-creating philosophies so that the client is henceforward equipped "to deal fairly comfortably, unneurotically, and non-self-downingly with *any* present or future difficulty that might arise."[212]

Like a prospective Middle Path therapy, rational-emotive therapy is an active, directive, challenging, and educative form of cognitive therapy. Rational-emotive therapy is also like Middle Path analysis in that it operates at a conscious and volitional level. Ellis writes that change occurs "through self-consciousness, willing, determination, deciding, planning, self-control, and self-acceptance."[213] Middle Path techniques and rational-emotive therapy both require hard work on the part of a client since the environment can no longer be blamed for a client's disturbance. Both forms of therapy are premised on the use of an active, thoughtful, repetitious, and forceful disputation of specific beliefs. And in both systems the disputation can be self-directed through the private presentation of arguments and reasons, or prompted by a second party (the therapist in rational-emotive therapy and the disputant in traditional Middle Path debates).

Ellis's therapy is guided by ten or so rational beliefs. These rational beliefs and their irrational counterparts provide an infrastructure which guide a therapist's clinical and counseling work. Very simply, the irrational beliefs serve to define a distorted worldview, and it is precisely these beliefs that a therapist attempts to have the client reject. These are then replaced with their rational counterpart. That is, the therapist attempts to refute the irrational beliefs and replace them with rational beliefs. Irrational beliefs are those which tend toward exaggeration, generalization, absolutization, globalization, and trivialization. Irrational beliefs also include thoughts governed by notions of unconditional rights and needs, infallibility, perfectionism, and worthlessness. Ellis has formalized these into a set of irrational beliefs. To some extent these provide a typology of irrational beliefs. The list includes the beliefs that:

1. It is essential that a person be loved or approved by virtually everyone in the community.

2. A person must be perfectly competent, adequate, and achieving to be considered worthwhile.

3. Some people are bad, wicked, or villainous and therefore should be blamed and punished.

4. It is a terrible catastrophe when things are not as a person wants them to be.

5. Unhappiness is caused by outside circumstance, and a person has no control over this.

6. Dangerous or fearsome things are cause for great concern, and their possibility must be continually dwelt upon.

7. It is easier to avoid certain difficulties and self-responsibilities than to face them.

8. A person should be dependent on others and should have someone stronger on whom to rely.

9. Past experiences and events are the determinants of present behavior; the influence of the past cannot be eradicated.

10. A person should be quite upset over other people's problems and disturbances.

11. There is always a right or perfect solution to every problem, and it must be found or the results will be catastrophic.

Although, as we will see, a clinical Middle Path can be applied with a degree of *partiality* that allows one to quite methodically and systematically *re-* rather than *de-*structure a worldview or cognitive appraisal.

For a Middle Path, the fact that a belief is realistic in Ellis's sense (i.e., corresponds to reasonable expectations concerning the vicissitudes of human life) need not entail that it doesn't condition emotional disturbances. (Ellis himself acknowledges this, as we have previously noted.) In the Middle Path, the view of realism, in the sense of a positive affirmation and evaluation of the sense world, is itself a cause for emotional disturbances. The Middle Path treads a "middle path" between realism and nihilism. I don't want to pursue this point any further since in a therapeutic context such a discussion is irrelevant. Nāgārjuna and Candrakīrti both explicitly say that of the two erroneous views of realism and nihilism, it is safer to fall to the extreme of realism. To err to the extreme of nihilism is to court disaster. It is thus absolutely clear that clients with emotional problems should have a realistic view of the world affirmed.

From a Buddhist perspective, rational-emotive therapy seems to downplay a possible discordance between what a person is "telling him or herself" and their behavior. It is quite possible that a person "tells himself not to do something or react in a certain way" while responding in just the opposite way. A clinical Middle Path psychology would attempt to cover this by eliciting deeper cognitive structures, that is, the biologically determined conceptions, and these may not correspond directly to surface forms of thought can be at variance with more congenital forms of conceptuality.

Having said that a clinical Middle Path would attempt to elicit deeper cognitive structures than those which rational-emotive therapy attends to, we will now attempt to formalize a set of cognitive structures that in some sense serves the same function as Ellis's dozen or so irrational beliefs. Of course, the fact that we are here formalizing a particularly Buddhist set of cognitive structure is not meant to indicate that this is the only set of beliefs or cognitive perspectives that can be linked to a Middle Path form of refutation. In terms of a clinical Middle Path, a therapist could, for example, frame her or his therapy around analyzing any of several different schemata of purportedly errant beliefs. Were a rational-emotive therapist to employ Middle Path logical paradoxes, he or she could focus on Ellis's set of irrational beliefs. A Middle Path therapist, on the other hand, could derive a therapeutically relevant set of beliefs from the traditional Middle Path literature since in philosophical Middle Path literature the beliefs are a mixture of philosophical and metaphysical beliefs some of which have clear psychological import. Nāgārjuna, for example, analyses beliefs in an ego, defining characteristics (*svalakṣaṇa*), causation, a supreme person (*tathāgata*), the phenomenon of suffering (*duḥkha*), desire (*rāga*), impulses (*saṁskāra*), and views or opinions (*dṛṣṭi*). Alternatively, the clinical application of Middle Path analysis could be directed by the afflicted cognitive structures (*dṛṣṭi*) that are tabulated in the typologies of Buddhist phenomenology (*abhidharma*). In each of these three cases the cognitive structures that a therapist would attempt to elicit from the client, and then refute, would be the beliefs that underscore the surface representations which take the form of consciously accessible and recognizable beliefs. In other words, in Middle Path analysis a therapist would attempt to elicit deep rather than superficial cognitive structures.

I would like to elaborate on the third of these three alternatives since the Buddhist phenomenological (*abhidharma*) lists provide a therapeutic focus that aligns a clinical application of the Middle Path with the more general psychological perceptions in Buddhism. Another reason for choosing the *abhidharma* structures is that they display some interesting parallels with Ellis's set of irrational beliefs. There are some significant differences, too.

THE BUDDHIST PHENOMENOLOGICAL ERRANT COGNITIVE
STRUCTURES AND THEIR THERAPEUTIC INTERPRETATION

The Buddhist phenomenological literature traditionally uses a schema of five afflicted cognitive structures or views *(dṛṣṭi)*. The *Collection on Phenomenology* [AK: 5.3 and 5.7] of Vasubandhu gives the five as:[214]

1. The view of an irreducible personality *(satkāya-dṛṣṭi)*. This is defined as the apprehension of a self and its possessions *(ātmātmiyagrāha)*. Middle Pathers stipulate that this is the apprehension of an intrinsically existent self and its possessions.

2. The view that clings to extremes *(antagrāhadṛṣṭi)*.

3. The tendency to absolutize opinions *(dṛṣṭiparāmarśa)*.

4. The tendency to absolutize codes of morality *(śilavrataparadṛṣṭi)*.

5. False views *(mithyādṛṣṭi)*.

The fifth category is further divided into four wrong views. The first two involve the Buddhist theory of karma, i.e., the cause-effect next as specified in Buddhist theories of action. The four wrong views are:

1. The view that there is no discrimination to be made between positive and negative forms of behavior.

2. The view that denies that positive and negative actions have consequences.

3. The view that former and future lives do not exist, that is, there is no cyclic existence *(saṁsāra)*.

4. The view that denies the empirically obvious. In

190

Buddhism this includes denying phenomena such as the achievements of saints *(arhats).*

A belief in a creator god *(īśvara)* is included as a fifth mistaken view in some *abhidharma*s. If these five conceptual structures are to have an urban therapeutic relevance some additional interpretation is needed. In fact, they have a very significant and immediate relevance in their traditional form. This relevance can, however, be highlighted by extending the scope of the traditional definition of these views. I would suggest the following interpretation which specifies six basic points of view. These are the views that would first be elicited within the cognitive and valuation matrix of an individual and then analytically investigated and refuted.

1. The first false view is divided into two types:

(a) The first type is the view that a person is completely autonomous. I would include this to overcome people's perception that they should be completely unmoved and unaffected by their environment.

(b) The second view is that people are completely conditioned by their environment. This is spelled out to cover the view that people's well-being is entirely at the mercy of their environment. This view conditions a very wide range of problems in which people feel threatened by their environment. (On the other hand, the same view can condition problems that arise from sensual engagement with the environment. This would be countered by the view that the self need not be conditioned by the environment, i.e., by arguing for increased personal autonomy. This two-pronged resolution of beliefs allows for a flexibility of intervention that will be referred to later in this work.)

The correct view under this interpretation would be that people are neither completely autonomous nor completely conditioned by extra-personal factors, such as their dermal and extra-dermal environments. Thus, we would reject the view that the self is totally conditioned by the environment, since this doesn't allow that one's own qualities and mental states may be conditioning factors. We also reject the view that the self is totally conditioned by the environment. By separating out the two extreme opinions, a therapist can recognize whichever one is operative in a client and work at refuting that belief. Although we cannot find support for such a specification of ātmagraha in the Abhidharma nor a rejection of complete conditionality in the Middle Path, it does tread a middle view. (In fact there is no contradiction here with Middle Path thought since the "absolute conditionality" mentioned here doesn't include the self-conditioning feature of things.)

> 2. The second cognitive structure that conditions emotional reactions is the view that hypostatizes phenomena as being either permanent or non-existent. It can readily be seen that this structure conditions a manifold complex of emotional disturbances since it attempts to control and manipulate the environment by seeking to eternalize desirable objects and annihilate undesirable objects. Such an exercise is naturally impossible, save for the very limited degrees of manipulation people can affect in the world and on their experience, and so it is fraught with disappointment and upset. Of particular significance in a therapeutic context is the view that the environment is composed of objects that can be experienced as though their qualities, attributes, etc. were independent of one's perception of them. The qualities that are particularly

relevant in a therapeutic context are those that condition unpleasant emotional responses such as
desire, aversion, hatred, and jealousy.

3. The third cognitive structure is very like a number
of Ellis's beliefs, viz., that everything should be
absolutely perfect and that if not, then things are
disastrous.

4. The fourth view is that the forms of conduct and
self-restraint that are relevant to people are
absolute, in the sense that the same levels of self-
discipline and self-restraint are appropriate for all
people. In other words, the optimum degree of
control over behavior is not relative to a person
and her or his environmental situation.

5. The fifth view that conditions emotional disturbances is divided into four with the most important mistaken view being a rejection of karma and
samsara. I would interpret this as a rejection of
the view that people's behavior doesn't condition
their thoughts, and emotions. In other words,
that there is no nexus between behavior, thought
and emotions. A corollary of this is that disturbing emotions and thoughts can be removed without any modification of behavior. Broadly this
view suggests the need for physical and mental
discipline in the control of emotional disturbances. This is also the view of behavior-modifi-
cation therapies and cognitive therapies such as
rational-emotive therapy.

We may note that views 4 and 5 dictate flexibility and control of
behavior respectively, and allow for directing a client to healthy

degrees of control and flexibility, as that might be determined by a person's mental, physical, and environmental condition.

The next task is to determine the connection between the Abhidharma beliefs that underscore the emotional reactions and the beliefs that are destructured by Middle Path analysis. The first question is: can these five mistaken opinions be refuted by uncovering logical contradictions in their form, and if they can, then which analytical format or formats from within the corpus of Middle Path texts should be applied to each of these beliefs? This is a complex question to answer satisfactorily since in some cases a number of traditional formats could be applied satisfactorily since in some cases a number of traditional formats could be applied to just one belief. And further, each format may not be equally effective or as easily induced in a counseling context. To determine the relative merits of each format would require some experimentation.

At this stage I only want to suggest that most of these beliefs can be refuted using Middle Path paradoxes. The first two errant views can quite clearly be refuted using logical paradoxes and I will be concentrating on the first of these in developing clinical Middle Path refutations in the next section. The third view, that is, a tendency to absolutize opinions, can also be refuted with Middle Path paradoxes. The fourth view most probably cannot be refuted with a Middle Path paradox since it involves value judgments. The fifth view, namely, that there are *no* patterns of correspondence or linear forms of conditioning between actions, thoughts and emotions, can be refuted by a selective application of the first and fourth positions in the Middle Path four-sectioned refutation of causation. It is worth noting, though, that traditionally this belief would not be countered by a selective application of Middle Path paradoxes, but rather by the various empirical and syllogistic arguments that Buddhism advances in support of the doctrine of *karma*.

The traditional specification of Middle Path analysis and its extension into the therapeutic context

In this section I propose to modify some traditional Middle Path analyses. The analyses are chosen from within the corpus of formats to be found in Middle Path literature. The modifications we will make are related to our reinterpretation of the first afflicted view (*dṛṣṭi*) that occurs in the Buddhist Phenomenological traditions, namely, grasping at [two extreme modes of] a self concept (*ātmagrāha*). We can recall that Candrakīrti says that it is this view which is the cause of all the reactive emotions and moods and problems of life. In developing this analysis we will draw on two popular analytical formats. We will mention their traditional presentation and then suggest how they can be extended into a contemporary Western and urban therapeutic context. There will be eight steps in the analysis. The first two steps precede *all* paradoxical analyses, and in a sense they set up the necessary conditions within which an analysis can be effective. The traditional account and logical implications of these first two steps have been described in Chapter Two. Here we are concerned with their therapeutic relevance.

Setting the mood for analysis

In a traditional Buddhist context Middle Path meditators precede their practice of analysis with the development of serenity (*samatha*) and mental integration (*samādhi*). These preliminary practices bring meditators to a level of unagitated focus wherein they can direct and focus their thought to a degree that is unusual and rare in a therapeutic seeking. Still, to some extent a therapist must create a level of peace and focused attention if a client is to process a concern of problem within a paradoxical form of analysis. Thus, before beginning to guide a client's thought in terms of anyone of the formats of analysis provided by the Middle Path the therapist needs to set a mood of peace and attention through appropriate conversations with a client.

STEP ONE: ASCERTAINING THE OBJECT TO BE NEGATED

Traditionally this is defined as fathoming the concept of an intrinsic or essential existence (*svabhāva*), since it is the concept of things having an essential existence that is said to condition all the reactive moods and emotions (*kleśa*). In the therapeutic context this first step is reinterpreted as *locating* the emotional problem or problems. The task at this initial stage is to focus attention on feelings or emotional problems, for example, anger, fear, anxiety, with a view to finding the feeling itself. One needs to obtain some *definition* on the emotional problem in terms of its fundamental and disturbing qualities. If one doesn't succeed in doing this one can very easily lose sight of the emotional problem in the course of an analysis. If this happens one fails to destructure the cognitive structure that supports the emotional disturbance.

Ontological blindness (*avidyā*), which supports the emotional reactions (*kleśa*) is, as we have said, unconscious and hence may require some preliminary analysis, perhaps even of a psychoanalytic form, in order to both bring its structure to consciousness and to expose the structure or matrix in which this blindness subsists. One needs to expose the particular constellation of emotional reactions that any particular structure supports. This would be particularly true of biologically conditioned affects, which like the Freudian "id," are much more deeply embedded in the psyche and thus are much more difficult both to consciously detect in the first place and then to remove. Therapy would tend, at lease in the absence of deep investigative work, to deal with the intellectual and consciously cognitive features of the emotional reactions. We can see already that a therapeutic form of the Middle Path is not linked so closely to *conscious beliefs* as is rational-emotive therapy.

STEP TWO: ASCERTAINING THE PERVASION

In the traditional context this second step commits a client to the validity of the principles of non-contradiction and the excluded middle. (A commitment to the first of the three Aristotelian forms of thought, that is, the principle of identity, is gained in the first step of the analysis.) In the therapeutic context it would generally be out of place to raise the question of suggesting that a client commits his or her thought to specific logical principles. Rather, one would be suggesting to a client the idea that if something exists and functions in a specified way, then this would be confirmed by a careful investigation of the phenomenon in question. And further, one would suggest that in the case of emotional problems one is not looking for sense phenomena, and thus one must be guided by conversational consistency and coherence. One would thus tell a client that his or her problem needs to be looked at very carefully. As we have observed, these first two steps preface all Middle Path paradoxical analyses.

Now we will suggest an analysis based on the production analysis that Middle Pathers typically use when analyzing phenomena (*dharma*). This analysis was first used by Nāgārjuna in the opening chapter of his most famous work, the *Fundamental Stanzas on the Middle Way* [MK].[215] It is interesting and supportive to note that Nāgārjuna uses this analysis based on production when investigating pain or suffering and showing the impossibility for suffering to arise.[216] We will then graft onto this the ingenious analysis developed by Candrakīrti in his *Introduction to the Middle Way* [MA] that we have detailed in Chapter Two. The aim in the analysis is to clearly and irrefutably show that the problem and its attendant circumstances cannot be located; in other words, to show that they are analytically unfindable. More specifically, the aim is to show that the perceived *source* or *origin* of a problem cannot in fact function as a cause of the problem, and moreover that nothing could act as a cause or condition for the arising of emotional problems.

A GENETIC ANALYSIS OF EMOTIONAL DISTURBANCES

In specifying a *process* of paradoxical analysis it is useful to introduce some steps or divisions. On the one hand the divisions are not at all arbitrary but at the same time it is important to appreciate that one is dealing with a process.

STEP THREE: ASCERTAINING THE CONDITIONS UNDER WHICH AN EMOTIONAL PROBLEM ARISES AND SUBSISTS

This is elicited by asking questions such as: Is the feeling (of anxiety, for example) constant, or does it arise and subside? In other words, does it change or fluctuate in either intensity or quality? Agreement would be elicited that it does arise and subside. In the extreme case the client will agree that he or she wasn't born experiencing the problem and thus, that it does arise and subside. The response or responses would then be channeled into one of two possibilities. The two possibilities are that the problem conditions *itself,* or that it is conditioned by *outside influences,* that is, by other things. If the response is ambiguous in the sense that it cannot be clearly resolved into just one of these possibilities then the therapy must in theory proceed in two stages. (It is important to bear in mind that when we are talking about clarity, first and foremost it is clarity for the client. If a client cannot clearly observe how his or her conversation is developing throughout an analysis, then one cannot expect a fruitful outcome.) First, the therapist must determine and separate out the self-conditioning from the environmental conditionings of the emotional problem. Once these have been isolated they are each analyzed in turn. One might begin with whichever one the client appeared to favor in his or her interpretation of the sources behind the problem. The next two steps seriously consider these two possibilities. If the factors that condition a client's emotional disturbance can be easily and genuinely resolved (that is, without a perception of distortion or deformation of the part of the client) into just one of the possibilities, then only one of the next two steps in theory would be used. In practice, though, and for reasons that will become apparent, both possibilities would generally have to be analyzed.

STEP FOUR: THE EMOTIONAL PROBLEM IS THE CONDITION FOR ITS OWN ARISING AND CONTINUANCE

This possibility is ascertained by receiving positive responses to questions such as: Does the problem appear to arise under its own steam independently of other conditions? Given a positive response to such a question the therapist would then have the client explore the consequences of his or her problem *not* being linked to any environmental factors. The primary paradoxical consequence of an emotional reaction being self-conditioned in that the emotional response would remain the same in intensity, quality, and tone no matter where the client was or whose company he or she was in. As Nāgārjuna writes: "If [...suffering] were produced by itself, it would not exist dependent on something else."[217] The therapist or

199

counselor would explore the work, home and family environments of the client to see if this was the case. Quite obviously, anger, fear, anxiety, etc., do well up and subside in relation to and in dependence on environmental conditions. Some correlations can be made. And so it would appear not to be self-conditioning, at least not in its entirety.

The therapist might well proceed slowly and gently at this stage. He or she might want to draw an interim conclusion; namely, that at least *some* of the quality and/or intensity of the emotional disturbance is conditioned by other factors. (These would then be analyzed in the next step.) The value in drawing an interim conclusion is that the therapist can fall back on that conclusion if the analysis in fact becomes regressive. Having drawn an interim conclusion the therapist or counselor would then proceed by saying: "Well, let us look further at the qualities of the emotional disturbance which you still feel are *not* conditioned by other factors." At this point the therapist might want to consolidate the analysis by working through the first two steps again, that is, by *locating* self-conditioned features of the disturbance and committing the client to the investigation. Slowly, perhaps through a number of cycles, the self-conditioned features would be seen *not* to be self-conditioned. While it would be nice and convenient for a client not to then conclude that these features are conditioned by *other* factors, this is probably the conclusion that a client would reach. Hence the necessity for proceeding to the next step. It is worth noting that the converse would very likely happen if one had begun by resolving the disturbance into the second possibility, viz., that it *is* conditioned by environmental factors. When one refutes this possibility the client would, in all likelihood, conclude that the problem was self-conditioning.

Thus, after exploring this to some depth, one can then turn

attention to whether problematic emotional reactions are caused by or conditioned by something else, as would seem to be implied by the first half of this analysis.

STEP FIVE: THE EMOTIONAL PROBLEM IS CONDITIONED BY ENVIRON-MENTAL FACTORS

The possibility that is being investigated here is that an emotional disturbance is conditioned by factors or influences that lie outside of the disturbance itself, that is, by factors that are different from the emotion itself. Thus, when we are using the term "environmental factors," we are not restricting the field of possible influences to just the extra-dermal environment of a person. We understand the environment to *include* the physical and mental condition of an individual. In other words, it covers the entire constellation of things and events that are different from the emotional disturbance itself.

Given this field of possible influences one would then ask the client: "What things, conditions, or events do you feel cause the problem?" We expect that the client would come back with one or, more likely, a list of things and events. Some of these might relate to the physical and general mental condition of the client, and other terms in the list might refer to objects and influences encountered in the work, school, and family environments.

If the client comes up with a list of factors, each one would initially be analyzed separately. The therapist would argue that if factor A is the cause then whenever A is present the emotional disturbance would arise, since it is not possible for factor A to be a *cause* without it producing an effect. If it doesn't produce an effect it is not a cause. If the client persists in believing that factor A *is the cause* but that it needn't give rise to the effect (i.e., the mental disturbance) then one would go into the notions of cause and effect and point out that they are reciprocally dependent on each other.

Given agreement on the valid usage of the terms "cause" and "condition" one would ask if it has *ever* occurred that the emotional disturbance has not arisen? It only needs one counter instance from within a person's life history in which the putative cause has been present but the effect hasn't, to show that factor A was not the cause of the emotional problem. The counselor would then invite the client to select another factor. This would then be analyzed in the same way, and one would work through the list until it has been exhausted. (It is clearly very important that a counselor keeps handwritten notes on the factors and influences that a client mentions during a counseling session, in order that the counselor can return to these in the event that the client forgets them.) There is little doubt that the client would remember the forgotten events once outside of a counseling session.

Having concluded that none of the factors that are mentioned can be the source or origin of the problem, the therapist or counselor would offer the client an opportunity to suggest any other candidates. The openness to re-formulations or new perceptions and perspectives on the problem and the factors which appear to condition it, would in fact, characterize all phases of an analysis. Thus, at a number of points a client would be given an opportunity—in fact, asked—to think of any further factors or events which might be thought to condition his or her problem.

STEP SIX: THE EMOTIONAL DISTURBANCE IS CONDITIONED BY A PARTICULAR CONFIGURATION OF CAUSES AND CONDITIONING FACTORS

The counselor could then offer the suggestion (if it had not formed or was not already forming in the client's mind) that the emotional disturbance comes when all or some of these conditions come together at the same time. The causes are individually necessary but not sufficient in isolation, or in their own right, to cause the emotional problem. It is only when the individual causes come together that they provide *sufficient conditions* for the problem to manifest. One would then look at the idea of a "complex". In particular one would then carefully investigate whether the complex of conditions or events was either the same as the components or different from the components. It is at this point that one can graft on an analysis utilized by Candrakīrti in analyzing the relationship between a parts-possessor and the parts-possessed.[218]

The analysis at this point becomes quite complex and sophisticated, and some (perhaps most) clients would find it difficult to keep abreast of the conversational and logical moves being suggested in the analysis. For clients who were reluctant to pursue this part of the analysis one could suggest that if the *individual factors* cannot cause or condition the problem, then their occurrence together cannot condition the problem since a collection of factors is *nothing more than* its individual constituents. One might want to assert this dogmatically in order to elicit the response that a collection or configuration of factors *is* more than the individual constituents of the collection.

If one can elicit this response one would then inquire what it was about the configuration of the influences that existed in excess, or in addition, to the influences when considered individually. We can make the analysis concrete by considering a hypothetical but very plausible example. Let us say that the client claims that his or her problem is one of "getting angry" and that the anger arises whenever the client is (a) in a home environment, (b) feeling under pressure from his or her boss, and (c) already feeling an undercurrent of annoyance. Thus, if the client was feeling annoyed, but was not at home, or being pressured by the boss then he or she would not be openly angry. Or, alternatively, if the client was at home and feeling pressured by the boss, but wasn't already feeling annoyed then again the anger would not surface.

In this situation the counselor could ask how precisely it was that none of the influences could individually trigger the reaction of "getting angry," yet together they seemed to. The counselor would stimulate analysis by arguing that there can be no *cumulative effect* beyond the *summation* of the effects of the individual influences. It was *not* an effect of each one individually that caused the emotion to arise and hence if one adds the effects together the aggregate of the individual influences is still unable to produce an emotional disturbance. It is only if the configuration represents something *more than* the simple aggregation of the individual effects that it could possibly cause an emotional disturbance. One would then investigate what more the configuration could be, beyond the arrangement of the individual factors. If the configuration is anything more, it could only be the fact that the influences are arranged in a particular configuration. Hence, it is the fact of being arranged or configured that makes the configuration different from the individual influence.

The question now is: Is the configuration entirely different from its constituent parts or only partially different from the constituent parts? If it is entirely different from its constituent parts then the configuration of parts could exist quite independently of constituent parts. This clearly is impossible, the arising of anger in the example cited earlier depends on the presence of each individual condition, that is, being at home, feeling pressured, and the presence of an undercurrent of annoyance. The only option left is that the configuration is identical with the individual conditions yet different from them at the same time. This needs to be resolved one step further since the suggestion that the configuration and individual conditions are identical *and* different can be understood in either of two ways. One possibility is that configuration as one entity is both different from, and identical to, the individual conditions. This is straightforwardly contradictory and hence must be rejected given our initial commitment to the canons of clear thought and straight reasoning. The other possibility is that one feature of the configuration is the same as the individual conditions and that another feature of it is different from the individual condition. An initial suggestion that might appear to have some plausibility is that the content of the configuration is identical with the individual conditions but that the form or structure of the configuration is different from the individual conditions. This possibility, however, can be resolved into the two previous options of identity and difference. To very briefly recapitulate: If the content of the configuration is identical with the individual conditions, then the content of the configuration can be found when the parts are dispersed. It is, however, contradictory to speak of the individual parts as being the content of a configuration. If the form or structure of the configuration is different from the individual constituents, then this form or structure can be discovered by referring to the individual conditions. This is impossible.

The conclusion, then, is that the configuration or constellation of the conditions cannot be anything different from the individual conditions. Thus, if the individual conditions cannot cause the emotional reaction, then no configuration of these conditions can cause it either.

MAINTAINING FOCUS AND LOGICAL COHERENCE

A major challenge for a therapist using this form of analysis is to maintain analytical coherence and a sense of logical development when using paradoxical consequences in nebulous and ill-defined therapeutic conversations. A primary skill is to first develop and then sustain an analytical structure when the therapeutic conversation is circuitous and lacking direction. On the one hand, it is vital that the therapeutic conversation constantly engages the background thoughts and unconscious feelings of the client yet on the other hand it is critical that the client's thinking become structured and doesn't just drift aimlessly in one direction and then another. The appropriate balance between formality and free association will be a key therapeutic skill and the capacity for a therapist to "collect" a client's thinking and incorporate it into an analytical structure will depend in part on a therapist acquiring a solid and automatic familiarity with a range of analytical formats.

STEP SEVEN: A CONCLUSION

A conclusion would be reached that there was no reason or cause for the client to feel anxious, angry, jealous, and the like. This would not deny that the client gets anxious and so on, but it would show in a very powerful way that there is no reason, cause of necessity for the client reacting emotionally to some set of circumstances. We have seen that there is, in fact, nothing to make the client anxious.

The therapist would then explain that the reason people get anxious, angry, frustrated, depressed, and so on is because they act in the belief that there is a real cause and reason for their emotional problems. In other words, even though one cannot locate a cause or reason, people operate with an unconscious assumption that there is a cause.

STEP EIGHT: POST-CLINICAL PRACTICE

In rational-emotive therapy clients are encouraged to make

audio-tapes of their counseling sessions and to play these over to themselves as an aid in the process of replacing their irrational beliefs with rational ones. The counselor provides the recording facilities and the client provides the tape. Thus, at the beginning of a counseling session the counselor would suggest to the client that he or she make an audio-tape of the session and listen to it in order to try and find both the logical flaws with the analysis and to come up with empirical circumstances that are not covered in the investigation. The client would be specifically directed to do this. Any perceived logical flaws or logical omissions would then be taken up for analysis and investigation in the next counseling session.

APPENDIX:

A FORMAL DESCRIPTION OF THE SIMULATION

THE SYSTEM TO BE SIMULATED consists of an infinite set of **objects** with a subset of these under simulation. These **objects** are arranged along a line unidirectionally from a fixed point called the **center of consciousness (c of c)**. Each object has a number of attributes:

(A) TYPE: object types are denoted by alpha symbols.

(B) MAGNITUDE: each object has a magnitude denoted numerically as an integer between 0 and 9.

(C) SIGN: each object with a non-zero magnitude has a sign. Either + or −. Objects with zero magnitude have no sign.

Objects shall be denoted in the output as: sign, magnitude, type e.g., **+5A, −2D, OX**.

This denotation is translatable into a cartographic representation. **Objects** can have their magnitude depicted in either of two ways:

(i) Each **object**, irrespective of magnitude, occupies the same number of lines. **Magnitude** is signified by a code. The addition and removal of objects in conformity with (4) below is given by a separate line plot, or

(ii) Each **object** occupies an interval on the line proportional to its **magnitude**. Then, **+9X, −9F, +9A** will all occupy intervals of nine units, while **OB**, will occupy no line units having only position on the line.

The **objects** are packed together on the line without intervening separation, unindirectionally outwards from the **c of c**. It is a section of this array of **objects** from the **c of c** out to some distance that will be simulated, with a small portion of these from the **c of c** outwards being displayed in the output. The size of that portion is dictated by the physical width of the output.

The **objects** in the array move about and change according to a number of influences:

(1) **RANDOM MOVEMENT**: The objects move toward and away from the **c of c** in a random way, with the restriction that the greater the **magnitude** of an **object** the less likely it is to move. If and when **an object** moves to a new **position** then all **objects** between the old and new **positions** are displaced to retain the packing. Thus, an **object** can only move in discreet jumps of a size determined by the **objects** adjacent to it. Two input parameters determine the average size of jumps and their average frequency.

(2) **INDUCED MOVEMENT**: The **c of c** has thus far been introduced only as the closed end of the array **objects**. That **c of c** is now considered as the center of a field of **influence**. The **influence** on an **object** is dependent upon three factors:

(a) The **position** of the **object**.

(b) An input parameter **range of influence**. (The relationship used here is variable (2.c). The mean of that relationship is uncertain but likely approximate to the inverse-square relationship, viz., **influence** = **range of influence/object-position** displacement from **c of c**.

(c) The net magnitude of objects within the purview of the consciousness, viz., the array of objects being simulated. Increases in the **net magnitude** have the effect of proportionately decreasing the **range of influence**. Decreases in the **net magnitude** have the effect of proportionally increasing the **range of influence**. (This relationship is again unspecified except to say that when the **net magnitude** is zero the **range of influence** is no longer inversely proportional but is equi-influential at all **object-positions** from the **c of c**. This is to indicate that the **c of c** as the focus of **influence** has become equally spread or distributed over all **objects** under simulation. Further, **objects** as they become increasingly within the **range of influence** of the **c of c** become less susceptible to the **random movement** as specified in (1). (It is likely, though, that there is always some random movement.)

Any object with non-zero **magnitude** which is the closest of its **type** to the **c of c** will induce the closest **object** of the same **type** but **opposite sign** to move inwards towards it. The strength of this **inducement** is dependent upon four factors:

(a') The amount of **influence** on the first **object**.

(b') The amount of **influence** on the second **object**.

(c') The **sum** of the **magnitudes** of the two **objects**.

(d') Prior instances of the first and second **objects** having occupied adjacent **positions**.

The greater the **influence** the greater the **inducement**.

The greater the **sum** of the **magnitudes** the smaller the **inducement**.

The greater the number of previous adjacently paired **positions** the greater the **inducement**. The relative contributions of (a'), (b'), (c'), and (d') are input parameters.

(3) **ANALYSIS**: This is an event which occurs when two **objects** of the same **type** but **opposite signs** are adjacent to one another in the array. If and when **analysis** occurs the two **objects** are replaced by one **object** of the same **type**. The **magnitude** and **sign** of the new **object** is determined by the sum of the two **signed magnitudes**.

E.g., +4A −8A becomes −4A

−3B +4B becomes +1B

−5C +5C becomes OC

This event is delimited by the stipulation that the difference between **magnitudes**, i.e., + and − for any **object** cannot increase for subsequent **analyses** involving that **object**.

(4) **EXPANSION**: The **number** of **objects** under simulation within the **range of influence** is a function of the net magnitude of the **objects**. New **objects** come within the **range of influence** when there is a reduction in the **net magnitude**. (Initially, any object of magnitude X can enter the field of consciousness when there is a net magnitude

reduction matching X.) Increases in the net magnitude have the effect of removing objects.

(5) **RAMIFICATION**: An indicator of the interdependence between **objects** is specified by a function called **ramification**. This function relates all **objects** to all other **objects** in terms of their **degree of relatedness**. Objects having a high **degree of relatedness** means that they will be behaviorally **influential** on each other. A lower **degree of relatedness** means that they will be proportionately less behaviorally influential on each other.

Ramification, then, has the effect of making related **objects** display similar behavior. (In practice it will be sufficient to specify for each **object** its relation to five other **objects** and its **degree of relatedness** via the integers 1 to 5, the higher the integer the more closely **related** are the objects. For any object, all objects other than those five are assigned a zero **degree of relationship**.)

(6) **ENGRAMMING**: The system stores its own state history. The influence of **engramming** has the effect of returning the system to its prior states. The influence of prior states on present states is determined by three factors:

(a) The immediately preceding state is the most dominant **influence** with prior states becoming less influential in proportion to their distance from present states. (Perhaps the inverse square relationship is suitable.)

(b) **Objects** are more likely to remain or reappear in the display in direct proportion to their **magnitude** (irrespective of their **sign**).

(c) **Objects** are more inclined to remain or reappear in (direct) proportion to the number (or) duration of prior occurrences.

The Display

The program begins with a randomly generated array of **objects**. The program displays a section of the line as a series of snapshots. Variables are to be inserted such that the limiting and separate influences of each of the factors can be displayed. The program prints out until the system has stabilized to a net **magnitude** of zero.

212

BIBLIOGRAPHY

PRIMARY SOURCES

Āryadeva. Tib. trs. as *bsTan bcos bzhi brgya pa zhes bya bai tshig leʼur byas pa* in D.T. Suzuki (ed.). *Tibetan Tripitaka, op. cit.* vol. 95, pp. 131–140.

Asaṅga. *Mahāyānasūtrālaṁkāra.* Ed. by Dr S. Bagchi (Sanskrit text) Buddhist Sanskrit texts, no. 13. Darbhanga: The Mithila Institute, 1970.

_____. *Mahāyānasūtrālaṁkāra.* Tr. by S. Levi *Mahāyānasūtrālaṁkāra.* Paris: 1911.

Candrakīrti. *Madhyamakāvatāra-bhāṣya.* Ed. by Louis de la Vallee Poussin. *Madhyamakāvatāra Par Candrakīrti.* Traduction Tibetaine,1907. Osnabruck: Biblo Verlag (reprint), 1970.

_____. *Prasannapada.* Tr. by Mervyn Sprung (of selected chapters) as *Lucid Exposition of the Middle Way.* Boulder, Colorado: Prajñā Press, 1979.

dGe ʼdun grub (First Dalai Lama). *dBu ma la ʼjug pai bstan bcos kyi dgongs pa rab tu gsal bai me long* in *The Collected Works (gSung bum) of dGe ʼdun grub pa.* Sikkim, Gangtok: Dondrup Lama, Deorali Chorten, 1978.

Kon mchog ʼjig med dbang po. *Grub pa mthai rnam par bzag pa rin po chei phreng ba.* Tr. by Geshe L. Sopa and Jeffrey Hopkins as the *Precious Garland of Tenets* in *Cutting Through Appearances.* Ithaca, NY: Snow Lion, 1989, pp. 109–322.

Nāgārjuna. *Mūlamadhyamakakārikā.* Tr. by F.J. Streng as *Fundamentals of the Middle Way* in *Emptiness, A Study in Religious Meaning* (Appendix A). Nashville, N.Y.: Abingdon Press, 1967.

_____. Tr. by K.K. Inada in *Nāgārjuna: A Translation of his Mūlamadhyamakakārikā.* Tokyo: The Hokuseido Press, 1970.

_____. *Suhrllekha.* Tr. by Leslie Kawamura (with a Tibetan commentary by Mi pham) as the *Golden Zephyr.* Emeryville, Calif.: Dharma Publishing, 1975.

Pañcaviṁśatisāhaśrikā-prajñāpāramitā-sūtra. Tr. by E. Conze (with some rearrangement) as *The Large Sūtra on Perfect Wisdom* with the divisions of the *Abhisamayalankara.* Berkeley: University of California Press, 1975.

Śāntideva. *Bodhicaryāvatāra.* Ed. by V. Bhattachārya (Sanskrit and Tibetan texts). Calcutta: Asiatic Society, 1960.

_____. Tr. by M.J. Sweet (of ch. 9) in "Śāntideva and the Mādhyamika: The *Prajñāpāramitā-pariccheda* of the *Bodhicaryāvatāra.*" Unpub. Ph.D. diss., University of Wisconsin–Madison, 1972.

_____. (ed.) *Tibetan Tripitaka.* Tokyo–Kyoto: Suzuki Research Foundation, 1955.

bsTan pai nyi ma (Fourth Panchen Lama). *gSung rab kun gyi snying po lam gyi gtso bo rnam pa gsum gyi khrid yig gzhan phan snying po* (being a guide to Tsong kha pa's *Lam gyi gtso bo rnam pa gsum*). Tr. by Geshe L. Sopa and Jeffrey Hopkins as *Instruction on the Three Principal Aspects of the Path of Highest Enlightenment, Essence of All the Scriptures, Quintessence of Helping Others* in *Cutting Through Appearances, op. cit.* pp. 1–107.

Tsong khapa. *Drang nges rnam 'byed legs bshad snying po.* Tr. by Robert A.F. Thurman in *Tsong Khapa's Speech of Gold in the Essence of True Eloquence: Reason and Enlightenment in the Central Philosophy of Tibet.* Princeton: Princeton University Press, 1983.

_____. *Lam rim chen mo.* Tr. by Alex Wayman (of the *śamatha* and *vipaśyanā* sections) in *Calming the Mind and Discerning the Real: Buddhist Meditation and Middle View.* New York: Columbia

University Press, 1978.

Vasubandhu. *Abhidharmakośa*. Tr. by Louis de la Vallee Poussin as *L'Abhidharmakośa de Vasubandhu*. Bruxelles: Melanges Chinois et Bouddhiques (reprint), 1980.

SECONDARY SOURCES

Adler, Alfred. *Understanding Human Nature*. New York: Greenberg, 1927.

_____. *The Science of Living*. New York: Greenberg, 1929.

Armstrong, David M. *Belief, Truth and Knowledge*. Cambridge: Cambridge University Press, 1973.

Balasooriya, S. et al (eds.) *Buddhist Studies in Honour of Walpola Rahula*. London: Gordon Frazer, 1980.

Bass, Ludvik. "The Mind of Wigner's Friend." *Hermathena*, 112 (1971), 52–68.

Bastian, Edward. *Mahāyāna Buddhist Religious Practice and the Perfection of Wisdom according to the Abhisamayālamkāra and the Pañcaviṁśatisāhaśrikā-prajñā-pāramitā*. Unpub. Ph.D. diss., University of Wisconsin–Madison, 1980.

Beck, Aaron T. *Cognitive Therapy and the Emotional Disorders*. New York: International Universities Press, 1974.

Bilimoria, P. and Fenner, P. (eds.). *Religions and Comparative Thought: Essays in Honor of the Late Dr. Ian Kesarcodi-Watson*. Delhi: Sri Satguru Publications, 1988.

Bimal K. Matilal. "A Critique of Buddhist Idealism." In L. Cousins et al. (eds.). *Buddhist Studies in Honor of I.B. Horner. op. cit.*, pp. 139–169.

Boguslaw, Robert. *The New Utopians: A Study of System Design and Social Change*. Englewood Cliffs, NJ: Prentice Hall, 1965.

Boorstein, Seymore (1982) "Troubled relationships: transpersonal and psychoanalytic approaches." In *Buddhism in Psychotherapy*, Kandy: Buddhist Publication Society.

Browning, Ronald W. (1979) *Therapeutic Change East and West: Buddhist Psychological Paradigms of Change with Reference to Psychoanalysis*. California School of Professional Psychology Dissertation.

Carr, Anne (ed.) *Academic Study of Religion: 1974 Proceedings*. American Academy of Religion, Annual Meeting.

Corsini, Raymond (ed.) *Current Psychotherapies*. Itasca, Illinois: F.E. Peacock. Pub, 1973.

Corsini, Raymond (ed.)(1973) *Current Psychotherapies*. Itasca, Illinois: F.E. Peacock Pub.

Cousins, L. et al. (eds.). *Buddhist Studies in Honor of I.B. Horner*. Dordrecht, Holland: D. Reidel Pub. Co., 1974.

Croake, James W. (1980) "The theories of Adler and Zen." *Journal of Individual Psychology*, 36.2, 219–226.

Cua, Antonio S. "Opposites and complements: Reflections on the significance of Tao." *Philosophy East and West*, 31.2 (April 1981), 123–140.

De Silva, Padmasiri. *Twin Peaks: Compassion and Insight (Emotions and the "Self" in Buddhist and Western Thought)*. Singapore: The Buddhist Research Society, 1991.

Deatherage, Gary (1975) "The clinical use of 'mindfulness' meditation techniques in short-term psychotherapy." *Journal of Transpersonal Psychology*, 7.2, 133–143.

Deutsch, Eliot. *Humanity and Divinity: An Essay in Comparative Metaphysics*. Honolulu: University of Hawaii Press, 1970.

Ellis, Albert. "Rational-Emotive Therapy." In Raymond Corsini (ed.). *op. cit.,* pp. 167–206.

_____. "Rejoinder: elegant and inelegant RET." *Counseling Psychologist*,

216

7.1 (1977), 73–82.

_____. *Reason and Emotion in Psychotherapy.* Secaucus, New Jersey: Citadel Press, 1979.

Fenner, Peter. "Asian Wisdom and Contemporary Psychology: a poly-methodic approach to the study of meditation texts." In R.A. Hutch and P. Fenner (eds.) *op. cit.* pp. 163–186.

_____. "A Therapeutic Contextualization of Buddhist Mādhyamika Consequential Analysis." In P. Bilimoria and P. Fenner (eds.). *op. cit.* pp. 319–352.

_____. *The Ontology of the Middle Way.* Dordrecht, Holland: Kluwer Pub. Co., 1991.

_____. (with Penny Fenner). *Intrinsic Freedom: the Art of Stress-Free Living.* Sydney: Millennium Press, 1994.

Festinger, L. *A Theory of Cognitive Dissonance.* Stanford, Calif.: Stanford University Press, 1957.

Fujinawa, Akira (1978) "Morita-therapy: Concerning a form of Japanese psychotherapy." *Psychologia: An International Journal of Psychology in the Orient,* 21.3, 113–123.

Gangedean, Ashok K. "Formal Ontology and Dialectical Transformation of Consciousness." *Philosophy East and West,* 29.1 (Jan. 1979), 21–48.

Gilandas, Alex J. (1974) "Morita Therapy: An Asian approach to behavior change." *Catalogue of Selected Documents of Psychology,* 4, 17.

Gregory, Peter N. *Sudden and Gradual: Approaches to enlightenment in Chinese thought* (Studies in East Asian Buddhism 5). Honolulu: University of Hawaii Press, 1987.

Guenther, Herbert V. and Kawamura, Leslie S. *Mind in Buddhist Psychology—A Translation of Ye shes rgyal mtshan's "The Necklace of Clear Understanding."* Emeryville, California: Dharma Press, 1975.

Guenther, Herbert V. *Matrix of Mystery: Scientific and Humanistic Aspects of rDzogs-chen Thought.* Boulder and London: Shambhala, 1984.

Hariman, J. (1983) "Wisdom meditation: a modified 'zen koan method' for ordinary people." *Journal of Eclectic Psychotherapy,* 2.1, 59–62.

Hopkins, Jeffrey. *Meditation on Emptiness.* Boston: Wisdom Publications, 1983.

Hutch, Richard A. and Fenner, Peter. *Under the Coolibah Tree: Australian Studies in Consciousness.* Lanham: University Press of America, 1984.

Ichimura, Shohei. "A Study on the Mādhyamika Method of Refutation and Its Influence on Buddhist Logic." *Journal of the International Association of Buddhist Studies,* 4.1 (1981), 87–95.

Inada, Kenneth K. *Nāgārjuna: A Translation of His* Mūlamadhyamaka-kārikā, *with Introductory Essay.* Tokyo: The Hokuseido Press, 1970.

Iwai, Hiroshi (1970) "Morita psychotherapy: the views from the West." *American Journal of Psychiatry,* 126.7, 1031–1036.

Kawamura, L. and Scott, K. (eds.). *Buddhist Thought in Asian Civilization.* Emeryville, Calif.: Dharma Press, 1977.

Kelly, G. A. *The Psychology of Personal Constructs.* New York: Norton, 1955.

Klein, Anne. *Knowledge and Liberation: Tibetan Buddhist Epistemology in Support of Transformative Religious Experience.* Ithaca, New York: Snow Lion, 1986.

Komito, David R. "Tibetan Buddhism and Psychotherapy: A Conversation with the Dalai Lama." *Journal of Transpersonal Psychology,* 16.1 (1984), 1–24.

Komito, David Ross (1984) "Tibetan Buddhism and Psychotherapy: Further conversations with the Dalai Lama." *Journal of Transpersonal Psychology,* 16.1, 1–24.

Laforgue, Rene (1968) "Personality structure and pathological symptoms." *Revista de Psicoanalisis, Psiquiatria y Psicologia*, 8, 90–102.

Lamotte, E. "Passions and Impregnations of the Passions in Buddhism." in L. Cousins et al, (eds.). *op. cit.* pp. 91–104.

Laszlo, Ervin. *System, Structure and Experience: Towards a Scientific Theory of Mind.* New York: Gordon and Breach Science Publishers, 1969.

_____. *The Systems View of the World.* New York: George Braziller, 1972.

_____. *Introduction to Systems Philosophy: Towards a New Paradigm of Contemporary Thought.* New York: Harper & Row, 1973.

Lazarus, Richard S. "Thoughts on the relations between emotion and cognition." *American Psychologist*, 37.9 (1982), 1019–1024.

Macy, Joanna. "Systems Philosophy as a Hermeneutic for Buddhist Teaching." *Philosophy East and West*, 26.1 (Jan 1976), 21–32.

_____. *Mutual Causality in Buddhism and General Systems Theory—The Dharma of Natural Systems.* Albany, N.Y.: State University of New York Press, 1991.

Matilal, Bimal Krishna. "Ignorance or misconception? A note on avidyā in Buddhism." In S. Balasooriya, et al (eds.) *op. cit.*, pp. 154–164.

Matsubara, Taro (1973) Japanese psychotherapy (Morita therapy) and its relationship to Zen Buddhism. *Journal of the National Association of Private Psychiatric Hospitals*, 5.1, 9–14.

Maupin, Edward W. (19) Meditation. In H. A. Otto and J. Mann (eds.) *Ways of Growth: Approaches to Expanding Awareness.* pp. 189–198.

Meichenbaum, D. *Cognitive-behavior Modification.* New York: Plenum, 1977.

Mihram, G. A. "Simulation Methodology." *Theory and Decision*, 7 (1976), 67–94.

Mikulas, William L. (1977) "Four noble truths of Buddhism related to behavior therapy." *Psychological Record*, 28.1, 59–67.

219

Mikulas, William L. (1981) "Buddhism and behavior modification." *Psychological Record*, 31.3, 331–342.

Perdue, Daniel. *Practice and Theory of Philosophical Debate in Tibetan Buddhist Education.* Ann Arbor: University Microfilms, 1983.

Pfeiffer, Wolfgang (1967) "Concentration-relaxation exercises." *Psychotherapy and Psychosomatics*, 15.1, 53.

Pleszewski, Zbigniew (1980) "Naikan: Japanese method of psychotherapy." *Przeglad Psychologiczny*, 23.1, 135–142.

Potter, Karl H. *Presuppositions of India's Philosophies.* New Delhi: Prentice-Hall of India (Private) Ltd., 1965.

Radford, John (1976) "What can we learn from Zen? A review and some speculations." *Psychologia: An International Journal of Psychology in the Orient*, 19.2, 57–66.

Raimy, V. *Misunderstandings of the Self.* San Francisco: Jossey-Bass, 1975.

Robinson, R. H. *Early Mādhyamika in India and China.* Delhi: Motilal Barnasidass (reprint), 1976.

Roccasalvo, J.F. (1980) "The Thai practice of psychiatry and doctrine of anatta." *Review of Existential Psychotherapy and Psychiatry.* 17.2–3, 153–168.

Roubiczek, Paul. *Thinking in Opposites: an investigation of the nature of man as revealed by the nature of thinking.* London: Routledge & Kegan Paul, 1952.

Ruegg, D. Seyfort. *The Literature of the Madhyamaka School of Philosophy in India.* Wiesbaden: Otto Harrassowitz, 1981.

_____. *Buddha-nature, Mind and the Problem of Gradualism in a Comparative Perspective: On the Transmission and Reception of Buddhism in India and Tibet.* London: School of Oriental and African Studies, 1989.

Schoen, Stephen (1978) "Gestalt therapy and the teachings of Buddhism." *Gestalt Journal*, 1.1, 103–115.

Shapiro, Deane H. (1978) "Instructions for a training package combining formal and informal Zen meditation with behavioral self-control strategies." *Psychologia: An International Journal of Psychology in the Orient,* 21.2, 70–76.

Sharrin, Ronald M. (1977) *Some Steps Towards a Conceptual Framework for Therapy Based on Buddhism.* California School of Professional Psychology Dissertation.

Sloman, Aaron. *The Computer Revolution in Philosophy: Philosophy, Science and Models of Mind.* Sussex: Harvester Press, 1978.

Smith, Edward W. (1976) *The Growing Edge of Gestalt therapy.* New York: Brunner/Mazel.

Smith, Kendra (1981) Observations on Morita therapy and culture-specific interpretations. *Journal of Transpersonal Psychology,* 13.1, 59–69.

Sopa, Geshe. "Some Comments on Tsong kha pa's *Lam rim chen mo* and Professor Wayman's *Calming the Mind and Discerning the Real" Journal of the International Association of Buddhist Studies,* 3.1 (1980), 68–92.

Speeth, Kathleen (1982) On psychotherapeutic attention. *Journal of Transpersonal Psychology.* 14.2, 141–160.

Sprung, Mervyn. "Non-cognitive Language in Mādhyamika Buddhism." In L. Kawamura and K. Scott (eds.). *op. cit.* pp. 241–253.

Streng, Frederick J. *Emptiness: A Study in Religious Meaning.* Nashville, N.Y.: Abingdon Press, 1967.

_____. "Religious Studies: processes of transformation." In A. Carr. *op. cit.*

von Bertalanffy, Ludwig. *General System Theory: Foundations, Development, Applications.* New York: George Braziller, 1968.

Wayman, Alex. "The Rules of Debate According to Asanga." *Journal of the American Oriental Society,* 78 (1958), 29–40.

Welwood, John (1982) Vulnerability and power in the therapeutic process: existential and Buddhist perspectives. *Journal of Transpersonal Psychology.* 14.2, 125–139.

Whorf, Benjamin. *Collected Papers of Metalinguistics.* Washington Foreign Service Institute, Department of State, 1952.

Williams, Paul M. "Some Aspects of Language and Construction in the Madhyamaka." *Journal of Indian Philosophy,* 8 (1980), 1–45.

Williamson, E. G. *How to counsel students: a manual of teachniques for clinical counselors.* New York: McGraw-Hill, 1939.

Wilson, Joe. *Candrakīrti's Sevenfold Reasoning: Meditation on the Selflessness of Persons.* Dharamsala: Library of Tibetan Works and Archives, 1980.

Wittgenstein, L. *Philosophical Investigations* (tr. G.E.M. Anscombe). Oxford: Basil Blackwell, 1974.

Wright, A.F. "Buddhism and Chinese Culture: phases of interaction." *Journal of Asian Studies* 17 (1957–8), 17–42.

NOTES

CHAPTER ONE: *Systemic Modeling and the Middle Path*

1.   In India the Middle Path (*Mādhyamika*) was formulated and
       developed in the large colleges (*vihāra*) in Bihar State such as
       Nālandā, Vikramaśilā and Odantapuri up until the twelfth cen-
       tury when these institutions were destroyed by Muslim invaders.
       The Middle Path tradition was brought to China around 400
       A.D. by Kumarajiva where it developed into the San-lun Tsung
       (Three Treatise School). See R. H. Robinson, *Early Mādhyamika
       in India and China*, Delhi: Motilal Banarsidass (reprint), 1976.
       Its influence in China waned in favor of the Phenomenalist
       (*Yogācāra*) tradition from the eighth century. The Middle Path
       took root in Tibet in the eighth century where it was studied
       and practiced in the central colleges and provincial monasteries
       throughout Tibet. The Mādhyamika was studied as the ortho-
       dox and mainstream philosophical system (*siddanta*) in the large
       central colleges around Lhasa (*hLa sa*) such as Sera (*Se ra*),
       Drepung (*'Bras spungs*) and Ganden (*dGa' ldan*) until the
       Chinese takeover in 1959. It continues to be studied and prac-
       ticed in the Tibetan colleges that have been re-established in
       Karnataka State, South India. The Middle Way was also prac-
       ticed in Korea (from the sixth and fifteenth centuries) and Japan
       (from the seventh to twelfth centuries).

2.   David R. Komito, "Tibetan Buddhism and Psychotherapy: A
       conversation with the Dalai Lama," *Journal of Transpersonal
       Psychology*, 1984, 16.1, pp. 22–23.

3.   Peter Fenner, *The Ontology of the Middle Way.* Dordrecht, Holland: Kluwer Pub. Co., 1991.

4.   E. Laszlo uses this term in a more technical sense that refers only to physical events. For mind events he used the term "cognitive system." Our usage is wider, with "cognitive systems" forming a subset within "natural systems." See ISP, pp. 30 and 144. For Laszlo's definition of a "natural system" see SVW, p. 37, and ISP, pp. 30–31.

    G. A. Mihram, "Simulation Methodology," *Theory and Decision* 7 (1976), uses the term in the technical sense of that which can be modeled. In systemic terminology it is synonymous with *simuland.*

    Our usage of this term clearly does not preclude that man-created systems are natural, nor even that textual descriptions are instances of "natural systems."

5.   If one were to suppose that descriptive literatures do not refer to anything outside of themselves, in other words that terms have no reference, one can reasonably query, contra Wittgenstein, that all bases for description, i.e., discernments of differentiation and comparison, are removed, for the reason that discernment, and hence meaning, requires a medium or mark which permits terminological comparisons. Such a medium or mark cannot be the descriptions themselves. If it were, language would be private in a most radical sense, to the point where it was private *from* oneself. Even so, that description describes things we are regarding as a presupposition.

6.   This difference may be merely definitional and the study, as such, does not have a built-in commitment to any one of the various mind-matter and psycho-neural theses, such as the identity theory, central-state materialism, double-aspect theories, epiphenomenalism, etc. With systems philosophy,

though, we will assume that mental and physical systems can be related and partake of some isomorphic characteristics. See ISP, pp. 120ff.

7.   This view, that textual materials describe systems of thought and matter, accords also with how Buddhist scholars understand their texts. With respect to the Middle Path philosophy and Perfect Insight system (*Prajñā-pāramitā*) Tibetan Middle Pathers have made a fourfold distinction as to the meaning of those terms. One of the meanings of Middle Path and Prajñā-pāramitā refers to the texts (*gzhung*). These are the *Prajñā-pāramitā-sūtras*, *Madhyamakāvatāra*, etc. The three other meanings, namely the nature (*svabhāva, rang bzhin*), path (*mārga, lam*), and goal (*phala, 'bras*) refer to the system the texts describe.

For the connotations of the "perfect insight" (*sher phyin*) see Edward Bastian, "Mahāyāna Buddhist Religious Practice and the Perfection of Wisdom" (unpub. Ph.D. diss., University of Wisconsin–Madison, 1980), pp. ix–x.

8.   ISP, p. 19.

9.   ISP, p. 199.

10.   It is not necessary that *all* cognitive categories and cognitive processing is conditioned for perspectivism to hold. Perspectivism stands to whatever degree cognition is conditioned. Reconstruction may be relevant to the degree it is conditioned.

11.   Individual researchers can overstate the case for their own discipline being the only or at least the primary influence. Whorf is an example. We assume that all are influential though in varying degrees, and further, that the predominancies with respect to the different influences again become conditioned, by themselves and as determined by cognitive contents. It is

this incestuous conditioning that research needs to be wary of.

12. Benjamin Whorf, *Collected Papers on Metalinguistics* (Washington Foreign Service Institute, Dept. of State, 1952), p.21, quoted in Ludwig von Bertalanffy, *General Systems Theory* (New York: George Braziller, 1968), p.223. The Whorf-Sapir hypothesis posits a uni-directional influence with language structures and linguistic patterns determining cognitive and perceptual processes. From our viewpoint it is more likely that they mutually influence each other.

13. Some of the above people rightly fit into two categories. Cognitive psychologists, like Piaget, often have a foot in a number of disciplines. The magnitudes of the respective differences, one supposes, are commensurable.

14. The process of reconstruction can occur at varying levels of discipline and awareness. The conscious and intentional reconstruction of some body of information presupposes an awareness of perspectivism and insight into the workings of contextualization. For the most part the reconstruction of religious, philosophical, and scientific worldviews operates self-consciously, whereas mythic and symbolic contextualization often functions unconsciously.

15. For a detailed characterization of the debate *genre* of literature see A. Wayman, "The Rules of debate According to Asaṅga," *Journal of the American Oriental Society*, 78 (1958): 29–40. See also Daniel Perdue, *Practice and Theory of Philosophical Debate in Tibetan Buddhist Education* (Ann Arbor: University Microfilms, 1983).

16. The tenets literature became a facilitator for monastic debate and can be viewed as an extraction of the tenets of various schools as implied in the disputational positions in texts like those of Bhāvaviveka, Buddhapālita, Candrakīrti and Śāntideva.

Though flowering in, and often thought to be indigenous to Tibet, its origins are in Indian texts such as the *Madhyama-kālaṁkāra* of Śāntarakṣita and the *Tarkajvālā* of Bhāvaviveka.

17.   Briefly, cognitive discourse assumes the integrity of cognition and is therefore based on locutions framed around the distinctions of cognizers, cognitions, and cognizables. Non-cognitive discourse, on the other hand, assumes there is not real cognition and refrains, within the limits allowed by language, from grounding itself in those distinctions. With respect to describing emptiness, these two modes can be broadly correlated with affirmative and negative assertions respectively. In turn these are often thought to imply respectively dualist and non-dualistic metaphysical assumptions.

This issue of cognitive and non-cognitive language has a significant relevance in the contemporary exposition of Middle Path philosophy. For the moment scholars appear to have polarized into two camps: those who espouse cognitive language and those who rely on the non-cognitive. Non-cognitivists feel that to talk about emptiness as being a cognizable is to phenomenalize it, that is, to reduce it to an appearance, or at least not sufficiently demarcate it from appearances. Mervyn Sprung espouses this position. Personal communication and his "Non-Cognitive Language in Middle Path Buddhism" in *Essays in Honor of H.V. Guenther* (Emeryville, Calif.: Dharma Pub.), pp. 241–53. Cognitive language is typically used by those who are versed in Tibetan expositions of the Mādhyamika, particularly those coming from the Ge lugs school.

18.   For an analogous description of influences at work in the Chinese contextualization of Indian Buddhism, see A.F. Wright, "Buddhism and Chinese Culture: Phases of Interaction," *Journal of Asian Studies* 17 (1957–8): 17–42.

19. In Anne Carr (ed.), *Academic Study of Religion: 1974 Proceedings*, American Academy of Religion, Annual Meeting.

20. *Ibid.*, p. 118.

21. *Ibid.*, p. 121.

22. *Ibid.*, p. 130.

23. F.J. Streng *op. cit.*, p. 130.

24. In PEW 26 (Jan. 1976): 21–32.

25. *Ibid.*, p. 21.

26. Joanna Macy, *Mutual Causality in Buddhism and General Systems Theory: The Dharma of Natural Systems.* (Albany, N.Y.: State University of New York Press, 1991).

27. kLong chen rab 'byams pa's *Ngal gso skor gsum*, tr. as *Kindly Bent to Ease Us* (*Part 2: Meditation*) by H.V. Guenther. Emeryville, Calif.: Dharma Pub., 1976. And the *Matrix of Mystery—Scientific and Humanistic Aspects of rDzogs-chen Thought.* (Boulder and London: Shambhala, 1984.)

28. S. Levi (ed.), *Mahāyānasūtrālaṁkāra* (Paris: 1911), p. 158.

29. K. Inada, *Nāgārjuna: A Translation of His* Mūlamadhya-makakārikā *with an Introductory Essay* (Tokyo: The Hokuseido Press, 1970), p. 114.

30. Such categorical breakdowns are made in divisions such as the twenty emptinesses (*śūnyatā*), ten stages (*bhūmi*), ten perfections (*pāramitā*), and thirty-seven factors of enlightenment (*bodhi-pakṣa*).

31. The *Abhisamayālaṁkāra* (*The Ornament of Realizations*) of Maitreya/Asaṅga is a more pronounced example of the extentional or discrete-state description of a transformational process.

32. The phrase "'molar' interpretation as contrasted with 'molecular' interpretation" is used and defined by Bertanlanffy, *op. cit.*, p. 238.

33. Streng, *op. cit.* p. 129.

34. *Ibid.* pp. 121 and 126.

35. A. Sloman, *The Computer Revolution in Philosophy: Philosophy, Science and Models of Mind* (Sussex: Harvester Press, 1978), p. 33.

36. SVW, p. 19.

37. ISP, p. 102.

38. ISP, p. 38.

39. See for example ISP, pp. 24 and 125, E. Laszlo, SVW, pp. 19 and 31–32.

40. ISP, pp. 47–53.

41. An environment is usually an enduring and relatively stable system within which function more dynamic flows are systems proper. These divisions, between systems, subsystems, and environments are clearly not fixed and to a degree arbitrary.

42. ISP, pp. 19–21.

43. ISP, p. 30. A more extensive definition is "a general property of ordered wholes of interdependent parts, governed by fixed internal constraints and exposed to externally introduced perturbations." ISP, p. 41.

44. ISP, p. 101.

45. ISP, p. 102.

46. ISP, p. 294.

47.   ISP, pp. 35 and 39 respectively.

48.   Mihram, *op. cit.*, pp. 69–70.

49.   Sloman, *op cit.,* p. 69.

50.   Mihram, *op. cit.*, p. 75.

51.   Sloman *op. cit.*, p. 7.

52.   *Idem.* p. 7.

53.   Mihram, *op. cit.*, p. 71.

54.   When Laszlo writes that "systems philosophy" seeks to unravel and solve basic philosophical problems (see ISP, pp. 12 and 15) there is no contradiction to the non-normative understanding here, for "systems philosophy" differs from both "systemic description" and "systems epistemology."

55.   The real versus ideational distinction made earlier does not cut across this for here, one only has a difference in regard to the physical versus mental status of a system, not a difference with respect to existence and non-existence. To reiterate, a real system has spatial location whereas an ideational one does not. An ideational system though not real is an aggregation of ideas none the less, and hence a natural system.

56.   ISP, p. 55.

57.   Contextuality bears peripherally on the criterion of "isomorphy" as the mapping of constructs to "natural systems" depends on methodological and procedural assumptions which may at least in part be contextually determined.

58.   A systems epistemology and epistemological criteria, as such, are not specified by Laszlo in a sustained and formal sense. A chapter in ISP titled "Cognition: Framework for an Epistemology" is essentially a statement of cognitive perspec-

tivism, and his observations must be extracted from some explicit statements and an implied position in the ISP.

59. See Robert Boguslaw, *The New Utopians: A Study of System Design and Social Change* (Englewood Cliffs, NJ: Prentice Hall, 1965).

60. Boguslaw has four system designs. The other two are ad hoc and operating unit.

61. Boguslaw, *op. cit.*, pp. 47–70.

62. *Ibid.*, pp. 71–98.

63. ISP, p. 55. This statement is specifically spoken of as scientific theory mapping, but it is general none the less.

64. Laszlo writes: "Economy of thought is an ever-present motivation of systemic theories, and systems philosophy is no exception." ISP, p. 159.

65. Streng, *op. cit.*, p. 121.

66. *Idem.*

67. Hence Laszlo clearly acknowledges an empirical content for systems philosophy. See ISP, pp. 3, 8, and in relation to cognitive systems, p. 144. Also Streng, *op. cit.*, pp. 120 and 130.

68. This is so when a natural system's constituents and relationships are readily perceivable and capable of precise definition, as one has for the most part in the physical and biological sciences when dealing with macro-objects. It becomes increasingly less true when one moves into areas where systemic constituents and relationships are opaque and difficult to define, as for example in theoretical physics, and some subject matters within sociology and psychology.

69. Some operational procedures for modifying and reducing some

of those problems are described in Fenner, Peter., "Asian Wisdom and Contemporary Psychology: A polymethodic approach to the study of meditation texts." In R.A. Hutch and P. Fenner (eds.) *Under the Shade of a Coolibah Tree—Australian Essays in Consciousness* (Lanham: University Press of America, 1984), pp. 163–186.

70. See ISP, pp. 3 and 197.

71. The empirical emphasis of Laszlo—a constant theme throughout his writings—is traceable to the biological base of his original subject matter.

72. ISP, p. 231. On this same page he writes that the "great schemes of metaphysical thought are relatively impervious to empirical confirmation or disconfirmation; the validity is largely determined by the appeal of their principles."

73. At all times his philosophy is empirical and *rational* (i.e., ordered and interpretative). See ISP, p. 8 and Macy, *op. cit.*, p. 22. With metaphysical systems he notes and concurs with "contemporary temper [...that] tends to seek connections between ultimate metaphysical principles and empirical experience." ISP, p. 291. Cognitive systems are in part known introspectively. ISP, p. 119.

CHAPTER TWO: *Analytical Meditation*

74. Middle Pathers are traditionally divided into two types— Middle Pathers who use paradoxes (*Prāsaṅgika Mādhyamikas*) and Middle Pathers who use their own independent arguments (*Svātantrika Mādhyamikas*). Throughout this study when we use the terms "Middle Path" and "Middle Pather," we are referring to Middle Pathers who rely on paradoxes. The study itself

is concerned with the structure and function of paradoxical analysis.

75. See PP on MK 18.7 (Sprung, p. 179).

76. Of the PP, Sprung, in the introduction to *Lucid Exposition of the Middle Way* (Boulder, Colorado: Prajñā Press, 1979), p.20, writes that "Beatitude—*nirvāṇa*—is understood in terms of two criteria: (1) the coming to rest of all ways of taking things (or of all ways of perceiving things); (2) the coming to rest of all named things [*prapañca*] (or of language as a naming activity). These two criteria are in Candrakīrti's application virtually one, though the second is the preferred formulation." A more elaborate account of what ceases (at PP: 25.24) are (Sprung, p. 20): "(1) assertive verbal statements, (2) discursive thought, (3) the basic afflictions, (4) innate modes of thought (*vāsanā*), (5) objects of knowledge, (6) knowing."

77. Robert A. F. Thurman, *Essence of True Eloquence: Reason and Enlightenment in the Central Philosophy of Tibet* (Princeton: Princeton University Press, 1983), p. 116.

78. From the viewpoint of Middle Pathers, all viewpoints or positions are self-refuting if they are examined with sufficient thoroughness.

It is important to bear in mind that the Middle Path arguments against intrinsic existence can also be applied to viewpoints that make non-intrinsic distinctions. In such cases the arguments would still be formally valid. However, the paradoxical consequences would be viewed as inconsequential for the entities occurring in such theses would be mere designations (*prajñāpti-mātra*) and so unrestricted with respect to their criteria of identification. That is to say, the entities in such theses would not be self-marked and so able to freely change their designation.

79.   Ashok Gangadean in his paper "Formal Ontology and the
       Dialectical Transformation of Consciousness," PEW 29.1 (Jan.
       1979), 21–48, has gone some way toward showing the struc-
       tural foundations that underpin Middle Path analysis using a
       classical Aristotelian model of interpretation, and some of the
       ideas in the first few sections are indebted to him. However,
       his explanation does not extend the explanation into a tempo-
       ral framework that attempts to relate "analytical activity" to the
       progressive insights that are gained by saints on a spiritual
       path. It is the integration of an analytical structure and the
       idea of "progress on a path" that we are attempting in this
       study.

80.   The term *prapañca* is often used to mean just verbal elabora-
       tion or even to denote elaboration, as in an exposition, yet
       clearly it must refer to mental or conceptual elaboration as
       well. The *Rab gsal me long* by Ge 'dun grub (Sikkim, Gangtok:
       Dondrup Lama, Deorali Chorten, 1978), f. 19a4, for example,
       glosses *spros pa* as *sgra rtog gi spros pa*. Also, were it just verbal
       elaboration, then people would absurdly gain nirvāṇa whenev-
       er they were silent.

81.   See Gangadean, *op. cit.*, p. 24 that "any well formed or signifi-
       cant thought may be analyzed into a relation between a logical
       subject and predicate."

82.   Paul M. Williams, "Some aspects of language and construction
       in the Madhyamaka," JIP, 8 (1980), pp. 24–25.

83.   The principle is recognized by Nāgārjuna, for example, MK,
       23.10–11 and Candrakīrti, PP, 220.
          In Taoism it is the deeply rooted principle of terminological
       reciprocity. See for example, chapter 2 of the *Tao Te Ching*.
       Their existence suggests non-existence, beauty-ugliness, good-
       ness-evil, short-long, etc. See Antonio S. Cua, "Opposites as

complements: Reflections on the significance of *Tao*," PEW, 31.2 (April 1981), 123–140.

There is an interesting book by Paul Roubiczek called *Thinking in Opposites: An Investigation of the Nature of Man as Revealed by the Nature of Thinking* (London: Routledge & Kegan Paul Ltd., 1952) that treats oppositional definitions lightly and in a non-rigorous way. Basically Roubiczek reduces various scientific, philosophical, and religious concepts to their existence in virtue of being defined through their conceptual opposites. Thoughts, percepts, and feelings, he shows, all arise through their opposites; e.g., good and bad (–good), light and dark (–light), inner and outer (–inner), pride and humility (–pride), pleasure and pain (–pleasure), etc. He also (pp. 170–171) indicates a spiritual efficacy in the practice of what he calls "interconnected opposites."

84.   Williams, *op. cit.*, p. 28.

85.   A logical opposite in this context, may be either a non-categorial (i.e., category unrestricted) negation or categorial (i.e., category restricted) negation. In both cases A and –A are *logically* and *reciprocally* dependent on each other.

86.   Williams, *op. cit.*, p. 27.

87.   L. Wittgenstein, *Philosophical Investigations*, tr. G.E.M. Anscombe, (Oxford: Basil Blackwell, 1974), p. 131. He elaborates that: "If I say I did *not* dream last night, still I must know where to look for a dream; that is, the proposition 'I dreamt,' applied to this actual situation, may be false, but mustn't be senseless." Does that mean, then, that you did, after all, feel something, as it were the hint of a dream, which made you aware of the place that a dream would have occupied?

88.   The notions of a position and opposite position are, of course, entirely relative, and the proposition that negates a

characteristic with respect to some subject may be advanced as a position, in which case Middle Pathers would claim to derive an *affirmative* or positive characterization rather than a negative one.

89.   Shohei Ichimuru, "A Study of the Mādhyamika Method of Refutation and its Influence on Buddhist Logic," JIABS, 4.1 (1981), p. 92.

90.   For example, MK, 8.7b (Streng, *Emptiness*, p. 193): "Foe indeed, how can 'real' and 'non-real,' which are mutually contradictory, occur in one place?"

91.   For example, MK, 7.30b, 25.11, and 25.14 (Streng, *Emptiness*, pp. 192 and 216 respectively).

92.   Ludvik Bass, "The mind of Wigner's friend," *Hermathena*, 112 (1971), p. 65.

93.   *Idem.* Bass himself has noted the soteriological import of absurdities in Nicholas Cusanus and made the interesting suggestion (p. 65) that "a persisting conflict of neural modes might itself exert an evolutionary pressure" and that it may be actually modified by mystics.

94.   D.M. Armstrong, *Belief Truth and Knowledge* (Cambridge: Cambridge University Press, 1973), pp. 104–106.

95.   *Ibid.*, p. 104.

96.   *Ibid.*, p. 105.

97.   For example, see bsTan pai nyi ma's (Fourth Panchen Lama) *gSung rab kun gyi snying po lam gyi gtso bo rnam pa gsum gyi khrid yig gzhan phan snying po* translated as *Instructions on the Three Principle Aspects of the Path* by Geshe L. Sopa and Jeffrey Hopkins in *Cutting Through Appearances* Ithaca: Snow Lion, 1989), pp. 38–39.

98.   This verse (Streng, *Emptiness*, p. 185) says: "What third [possibility] goes other than the 'goer' and 'non-goer'?"

99.   Candrakīrti also says [MABh: 100.12] that "there isn't an existent separate from the two (*gnyis ka dang bral ba yod pa … ma yin*) [of existence and non-existence]."

100.   See for example bsTan pai nyi ma *op. cit.*, p. 39.

101.   The fully fledged analysis of things in fact proceeds through four alternative ways in which things can be produced. These are that things can by produced from (1) themselves, (2) other things, (3) both themselves and other things, and (4) neither themselves nor other things.

However, the analysis of things (*bhāva*) through paradoxical consequences is fully accomplished—in the sense of gaining a full paradoxical proof for the openness of things—by refuting just the first two theses, that things are produced from themselves or others. This requires a little explanation. The third thesis in the tetralemma is that things are produced from a combination of self and other. In the *Introduction to the Middle Path* [MA] (6.98) this thesis is refuted by referring back to the earlier separate refutations of production from self and other. The assumption is that any mixture can be conceptually resolved into its constituents which are then refuted individually. In some instances this seems obvious, for example, in the case where production form self and other occurs serially, such as a sprout first being born from itself and then later from another. Or, where one thing is actually composed of two developmental continua (perhaps developing in unison), where one continuum is born from itself and the other from another. What does seem problematic, though, is the instance of one thing being produced from self and other simultaneously and with respect to identical aspects of the object. This last requirement is simply the definition of an object being singular, i.e.,

237

having just one defining facet. Middle Pathers obviously do not find this last case problematic and in so doing must be saying that there are no *real* mixtures, i.e., no compound processes that exist as a new mode of production outside of production from self and other. The problem is ameliorated, though, for in Middle Path philosophy the notion of production is mental imputation (as in Humean causation) and hence it is enough that any mixture can be *conceptually* resolved into the two modes of self- and other-production. Another way of seeing the Middle Path's position on this (and this applies to the next thesis of production without a cause as well) is that self- and other-production jointly exhaust the possible modes of production and so production from both (or from no cause) as *novel modes* are excluded on this count.

The fourth thesis, that things can arise from no cause is excluded not only on the grounds of a joint pervasion by the first two but through a category error. As I've explained, the class of things (*bhāva*) is identical with the class of products (*saṁskrti-dharma*), and so this last thesis in fact falls outside theses that explain the arising of things. That is to say it does not provide an alternative at all, for it denies that very concept of a thing=product that it purports to explain. Hence, this final thesis is improperly included. The third thesis, then, is resolved into the first two, and the fourth is wrongly included in the first place.

102.   See MA 6.14.

103.   In the more complete version of this analysis Candrakīrti specifies a total of seven ways in which the self and body-mind can be related. These are:

1. The self is not different from the body-mind.

2. The self is not the same as the body-mind.

3. The self does not possess or have the body-mind.

4. The self is not in or dependent on the body-mind.

5. The self is not such that the body-mind is in or dependent on it.

6. The self is not the collection of the body-mind.

7. The self is not the shape or form of the body-mind.

However, the last five relationships are structurally dependent for their refutation on the first two theses positing a sameness or difference (*tattvānyatva-pakṣa*) between the self and the body-mind. That is to say, the refutation of these additional relations hinges on the earlier refutations of the relations of identity and difference. As we explained earlier, the five additional relations are thought to be common ways in which the self and the body-mind may be related. The theses that the self is the collection or shape are analyzed in parallel fashion to the identity of the self and body-mind, and refuted on similar grounds, namely, that the collection (6.135) doesn't partake of the unitary characteristics of a self, nor (6.152a–c) the self of the plural character of a collection. Likewise, the self is not the shape (i.e., form constituent) due to similar contradictions based on the incommensurability between unitary and plural concepts. The two relations of containment and the relation of possession, on the other hand, are refuted on the basis that the relation of otherness is refutable. This is stated explicitly (6.142) for the two containment relations, and the relationship of possession is clearly dependent on the self and the body-mind being different.

In summary, if the self and body-mind are the same then the body-mind cannot be *in* the self, nor the self *in* the body-mind. Likewise, if the self and the body-mind are not the same then the self cannot *be* the collection or shape of the body-mind components. Hence, when the first two theses are refuted, *ipso facto* the other five theses lapse also (and any others specifying a relationship between the self and body-mind that could be conceived of).

The presuppositional role of the relationship of identity and difference, and derivative or subsidiary nature of the others is acknowledged by Candrakīrti in the *Clear Words* [PP: 194] where containment and possession are reduced to their presupposing a relation of difference, and is exemplified in the *Principal Stanzas on the Middle Path* [MK: 18.1] where the self is analyzed in terms of the two alternatives of identity and difference, according to Candrakīrti [PP: 166] for the sake of brevity. bsTan pai nyi ma in his meditative contextualization of Tsong kha pa's *Three Principal Aspects of the Path* (*Lam gyi gtso bo rnam pa gsum*) likewise ascertains the personal selflessness through a procedure based just on the first two of Candrakīrti's seven sections. Hence, the logical consequences required for precluding possible views about the mode of being of the person, and thus the demonstration of its openness, are completed within the first two theses.

Thus, with respect to the logical requirements of analysis (though apparently not for the psychological requirements) the five additional theses in the seven-section analysis are strictly unnecessary as are the two final lemmas of the tetralemma proof.

In summary, the last five final sections to the seven-section analysis of the person and the two final theses to the tetralemma proof of things *rely* on the first two sections of each analysis, and more significantly, that the analyses of the selflessness of persons and things can be *completed* within the first two theses of each of these sets of theses.

104.   This is perhaps the only theoretical requirement, for one can hazard a guess that for Buddhists anything other than the three types of *asamskrta dharmas* would in all likelihood not even be considered as unproduced. It would go without saying (and

without analysis) that a sprout, chair, etc. were not non-products and thus when the postulate of their being a product was ruled out the universe of discourse may be thought for practical purposes to have been exhausted.

105. Cf. MK, 5.4a (Streng, p. 188) that there is no object of characterization (*lakṣya*) in the absence of any functional characteristic.

106. A partitive analysis is non-paradoxical and involves ascertaining the non-existence of an *entity* through a failure to find it in and among its parts. In the case of a "partitive analysis of the self," a self is searched for *within* the body-mind dividing the constituents of the latter into coarse and then finer parts. Such forms of analysis establish that the self is not the latter but fail to exclude the possibility that the self is separate from the body-mind aggregation. They thus establish the non-phenomenality of the self but not its openness. See BCA, 9.58ff for this type of analysis.

107. For example, MK, 5.6: that if something *is* not at all of what will there be non-existence. Also 15.5 and 25.7. And BCA, 9.34.

108. The analyses at steps 3a and 3b is modeled after Nāgārjuna's analysis of movement in the second chapter of MK titled, "An Analysis of Coming and Going."

109. For a detailed discussion of the two types of negation see chapters six and seven of Anne Klein's *Knowledge and Liberation: Tibetan Buddhist Epistemology in Support of Transformative Religious Experience* (Ithaca, NY: Snow Lion, 1986).

110. See Sprung, *Lucid Exposition*, p. 36: that "this negation [of birth from self] is not intended to imply an affirmation."

111. Even so, perhaps the non-affirming character of Prāsaṅgika Mādhyamika negations is a formal condition for their logic as

it would seem that a logically generated non-affirming negation could only be derived through a paradox or *reductio ad absurdum* where the logical affirmation of the negation of a thesis could be derived through a syllogistic inference or what I've called a partitive analysis. Where both a thesis and contrapositive thesis are negated and their opposites affirmed through these affirming negations it is feasible that a coincidence of opposites, and hence demonstration of openness, could be gained through non-paradoxical analyses, which would go against Prāsaṅgika tenets. These are just some thoughts and I'm not sure whether there is a genuine distinction to be made here between the affirming character of paradoxical and partitive analyses.

112.   Perhaps there is a greater propensity to slide to an opposite viewpoint in the case of a self-conception given the janus-like nature of the self. In the case though of refuting say "birth from another" it seems that such a negation would in practice (as well as in theory) be non-affirming for it is unlikely that its refutation would result in the adoption of the "birth from self" thesis. This is born out by Jam dbyangs bzhad pa who says that of the four alternatives of production only the second need be refuted, presumably because all others are so unreasonable as not to be ascribed to in practice. (From a communication from Jeffrey Hopkins.) On the other hand, a slide couldn't be ruled out in the case of a refutation of the "birth from self" thesis, given the common-sense plausibility of the thesis of "birth from another."

113.   An example in translation is H.V. Guenther and L.S. Kawamura's *Mind in Buddhist Psychology* (tr. of Ye shes rgyal mtshan's *Sems dang sems byung gi tshul gsal par ston pa bol gsal mgul rgyan*) (Emeryville, Calif.: Dharma Publishing, 1975).

114.   AK, 4.1. Nāgārjuna defines it similarly in MK, 17.2–3.

242

CHAPTER THREE: *A Simulation Model of Middle Path Analysis*

115. Still, the issue of an instantaneous versus a gradual insight is much debated in Buddhist Mahāyāna literature. A comprehensive analysis of the topic (around the theme of the historical bSam yas debate) can be found in David Seyfort Ruegg, *Buddha-nature: Mind and the Problem of Gradualism in a Comparative Perspective.* (London: School of Oriental and African Studies, 1989.) Chinese approaches to this question can be approached through the essays in Peter N. Gregory (ed.) *Sudden and Gradual: Approaches to Enlightenment in Chinese Thought* (Studies in East Asian Buddhism 5). (Honolulu: University of Hawaii Press, 1987.)

116. According to Tibetan commentators, this text is written from the Svātantrika-Mādhyamika viewpoint.

117. See, for example, Karl Potter, *Presuppositions of Indian Philosophy* (Westport, Conn.: Greenwood Press, 1963), p. 236.

118. Ervin Laszlo, *System, Structure, and Experience: Toward a Scientific Theory of Mind* (New York: Gordon and Breach Science Publishers, 1969), p. 29.

119. *Ibid*, p. 50.

120. ISP, p. 30. A more extensive definition is "a general property of ordered wholes of interdependent parts, governed by fixed internal constraints and exposed to externally introduced perturbations." ISP, p. 41.

121. ISP, p. 101.

122. ISP, p. 294.

123. Laszlo writes (ISP, p. 35) that they are "applicable through the

range of phenomena of organized complexity that constitutes the terrestrial microhierarchy." In ISP he maps their appearance under qualitatively divergent transformations, most forcefully in natural and especially biological systems (from whence they derive). In *System, Structure, and Experience* these four are used to assist his description of the structures and patterns of human experience.

124. The four invariants are described in the *Systems View of the World*, pp. 27–75 and ISP, pp. 36–53.

125. To do otherwise is to let genuine behavioral properties of systems go undiscovered.

126. E. Laszlo, *The Systems View of the World*, p. 37.

127. *Ibid.*, p. 43.

128. ISP, pp. 127–8.

129. See L. Festinger, *A Theory of Cognitive Dissonance* (Stanford, Calif.: Stanford University Press, 1957).

130. ISP, pp. 128–34 and 190.

131. By and large Festinger and Kelley are seen to be presenting rival and opposed theories though, from a systems viewpoint, they are quite compatible within the one organism.

132. ISP, p. 48.

133. The final property of the systemic model, stochasticity, is questionably not an "invariant" given Laszlo's definitions (see *supra*, pp. 101–105, no. 4). Even so, stochasticity or random behavior is itself a non-randomly present feature in non-strictly-determinant systems. It is also a systemic parameter that is reciprocally related to organizational, stabilizing, and inter- and intra-systemic processes. Against its being an invariant, it may

be said that as "degrees of stochasticity" are determined by systemic constancies, stochasticity itself is not strictly an invariant. And that random behavior by itself, i.e., without the infusion of constancies, is unpatterned and hence without invariancies. In any event, it has an heuristic, interpretative, and rubrical function in this reconstruction and is so included and treated among the systemic invariancies. Furthermore, the model developed herein will not function fully without an element of stochasticity.

134.   Regularity, as we have noted before, does not preclude variation and modification.

135.   Environmental factors are here conditions rather than direct causes, for in Middle Path (*Mādhyamika*) psychology, misery—the avoidance of which is the motivation for systemic change—has its primary cause in the conception of intrinsic existence (*svabhāva*) which, though perceived to be a quality of phenomena, is, as a conception, really a part of the philosopher's interior landscape. In other words, the inputs causing change are primarily internal and only secondarily or cooperatively external ones. This is also the case where cognitive changes are induced by analysis that has been initiated by some other individual(s) for, whether or not an analysis is taken up would depend on an individual being internally predisposed to (a particular) analysis. It depends, in other words, ultimately on internal constraints. Neither of these two facts, though, alters the self-organizational characteristics of the liberative system for internal constraints are being modified. To think otherwise is to quibble unnecessarily over Buddhist distinctions between primary causes (*hetu*) and conditions (*pratyaya*).

136.   In an extreme case this results in a solitary peace or nonresidual nirvāṇa.

137.   ISP, pp. 43–44.

138.   The instantaneous theory seems to sever the notion of a *continuity* within an analyst's mental development and so to be open to the Middle Path critique of "birth from no cause."

139.   Dr. Manfred von Thun of La Trobe University has pointed out to me that this feature of the model has significant implications for its interpretation. An alternative model could be developed in which *magnitude*, which indicates the "degree of cathexis" is not modeled as a displacement within the field of consciousness. Such a model would behave differently from the one we have developed. My rationale for displaying the *magnitude* as a displacement within the field of consciousness is that cathexis, as a selective and focused deployment of alternative energy, serves to capture our awareness in such a way that we are precluded from being aware of objects that we haven't invested energy in. In other words, it displaces attention.

140.   See Eliot Deutsch, *Humanity and Divinity: An Essay in Comparative Metaphysics* (Honolulu: University of Hawaii Press, 1970), pp. 67–80 for an interesting discussion of the construction of habitual realities.

141.   E. Laszlo, *System, Structure, and Experience*, p. 60. Laszlo marginally qualifies this (pp. 60–61) by noting that a change in the one stimuli's intensity may change (in our denotation) the sign of an element. In other words at one intensity a stimulus may be pleasant and at another painful. The Buddhist spectrum of emotional reactions is contained in the list of *kleśas* tabulated in meta-psychological (*abhidharma*) texts.

142.   *Ibid.*, p. 61.

143.   The question of whether cathexis is attenuated with respect to all referents, including those unexperienced, relates to how

246

one conceives the states of liberation (*mokṣa, nirvāṇa*) and full evolution (*bodhi*). Clearly in the enlightened state all concepts must be affectively neutralised. In the case of liberating states either a constancy of experience must be ensured (perhaps through the effects of prior *karmas*) or cognitions must be such that new cognitive referents are unhesitatingly (automatically as it were) cognized without any accompanying effective reaction.

144. See Geshe Sopa, "Some Comments on Tsong khapa's *Lam rim chen mo* and Professor Wayman's *Calming the Mind and Discerning the Real*," JIABS, 3.1 (1980), p. 71. Tsong khapa's usage of these terms, according to Sopa, addresses itself primarily to Prāsaṅgikas who are less refined in their analyses.

145. Most of the Tibetan *sa lam* literature is based on the *Abhisamayālaṁkāra* and written from the Svātantrika Middle Path viewpoint which Tibetans say this text expresses. See E. Bastian, *Mahāyāna Buddhist Religious Practice and the Perfection of Wisdom According to the Abhisamayālaṁkāra and the Pañcaviṁśatisāhaśrikā-prajñāpāramitā* (unpub. Ph.D. diss., University of Madison–Wisconsin, 1980), pp. 328–332 for how the *Abhisamayālaṁkāra* accounts for the gradual removal of the *kleśas*. However, Middle Pathers who rely on paradoxes (*Prāsaṅgika Mādhyamikas*) also use this same explanation.

On this, I also mention that the Tibetan scholar Gyal tshab in his commentary to the ninth chapter of the *Bodhicaryāvatāra* talks of predisposition to understanding the emptiness of something (an illusory woman) as "weak and small and without the ability to overcome the holding as truly existent." See M.J. Sweet, *Śāntideva and the Middle Path*, p. 203. Such thoughts seem also to sanction that *svabhāva* can be conceived of in varying strengths.

146. See MA, 6.120.

147. R.S. Lazarus, J.R. Averill, and E.M. Opton Jr., "Towards a cognitive theory of emotion," in M.B. Arnold (ed.), *Feelings and Emotions: The Loyola Symposium* (New York: Academic Press, 1970).

148. One idea that occurs to me is that the removal of *tṛṣṇā* may be productive of *śamatha* and the perfection of meditation (*dhyāna*) while the removal of *avidyā* may result in the actualisation of *vipaśyanā* in the perfection of insight (*prajñā*).

149. E. Deutsch. *op. cit.*, p. 71.

150. It is not possible to lucidly display a continuous change in two dimensions for the concepts, as they are depicted, would be snaking under and over each other.

151. Perhaps this exaggerates the situation a little, and it is the case that a meditator is mostly aware of a pair of logically opposed concepts, but that there is no recognition of the ontological dependency between the concepts.

152. As the concepts at the top of the display represents the concept at the extreme periphery of awareness (due to the attention gradient progressively dropping off as the displacement from the horizontal axis increases) it is appropriate to consider that the concepts of an opposite sign to those which are only present singly in the display exist somewhere *above* the line of concepts at the top of the display, which define the limits of awareness.

153. *Supra*, pp. 40–41 and 50–51.

154. Two input parameters govern the random movement. One parameter controls the *probability* for the concepts to undergo some displacement from one profile to the next. The other controls the average displacement or *degree of change* between two profiles.

248

155.   *Supra*, pp. 44–46.

156.   Streng, *Emptiness*, p. 156.

157.   See Peter Fenner, *The Ontology of the Middle Way*, p. 54.

158.   In other words, there will definitely be a path of greatest efficiency. Interestingly, in the model a final statis is achieved most quickly if the objects are analyzed in order of decreasing cathexis.

159.   *Catuḥśatakaśāstrakārikā*. Tib. tr. as *bstan bcos bzhi brgya pa zhes bya bai tshig le'ur byas pa* in D.T. Suzuki (ed.) *Tibetan Tripitaka*, (Tokyo–Kyoto: Suzuki Research Foundation), 1955, v. 98, p. 136, f.3, l.3.

160.   Quoted in *Madhyamakāvatāra-bhasya*, p. 200.

161.   The lists of two, sixteen, and twenty kinds of emptiness (see, for example, MA: 6.181–223) would simply be a scholastic categorization.

162.   *Supra*, pp. 119, 223.

163.   MA: 6.113 and MABh: 344–5.

164.   *Supra*, pp. 86–8.

165.   What happens in this case is that a factor called *inducement* that is responsible for drawing affirmations and negations together increases or decreases in direct proportion to increases in the sum of the magnitudes.

166.   V. Bhattachārya, *op. cit.*, p. 193.

167.   Laszlo, *System, Structure, and Experience*, p. 8.

168.   See Jeffrey Hopkins, *Meditation on Emptiness*, p. 109.

CHAPTER FOUR: *A Therapeutic Application of Middle Path Analysis*

169. See Padmasiri de Silva, *Twin Peaks: Compassion and Insight.* (Singapore:Buddhist Research Society, 1991), Ch. 3, "Theoretical Persopectives on Emotions in Buddhism" for a discussion of various frameworks for understanding emotions in Buddhism including "cognitive frameworks."

170. A. Ellis, "Rational and Emotive Therapy 1." In R. Corsini (ed.), *Current Psychotherapies* (Itasca, Illinois: 1973), p. 170.

171. R. S. Lazarus, "Thoughts on the relations between emotion and cognition," *American Psychologist,* 37.9 (1982), pp. 1019–1024.

172. Other scholars have suggested English equivalents, such as afflictions, defilements, affects, and passions.

173. Vasubandhu, [AK]. Trans. by Louis de la Vallee Poussin. Bruxelles, Melanges Chinois at Bouddhiques (reprint), 1980, vol. 4, p.2.

174. *Ibid.,* vol. 4, p. 74.

175. *Ibid..,* vol. 4, p. 80.

176. *Ibid.,* vol. 4. p. 88ff. Other Buddhist Abhidharmas list the six emotional predispositions (*anuśaya*) as the six root *kleśas* and expand the list of subsidiary *kleśas*. The *Collection on Phenomenology* [AK] itself, expands the list of defiling mental events in chapter 2.

177. *Ibid.,* vol. 4, p. 74.

178. H.V. Guenther and L.S. Kawamura, *Mind in Buddhist Psychology: A Translation of Ye shes rgyal mtshan's "The Necklace*

of Clear Understanding." (Emeryville, California: Dharma Publishing, 1975).

179. B. K. Matilal, "Ignorance or misconception?—a note on avidyā in Buddhism." In S. Balasooriya, et al., (eds.), *Buddhist Studies in Honour of Walpola Rahula* (London: Gordon Frazer, 1980), p. 162.

180. *Ibid.*, p. 163

181. Śāntideva, *Bodhicaryāvatāra.* V. Bhattacharya (ed.). (Calcutta: The Asiatic Society [Bibliotheca Indica Series]), 1960, p. 221.

182. MABL, 234.

183. R. Lazarus, *op. cit*., p. 1019.

184. *Idem.*

185. *Idem.*

186. *Ibid.*, p. 1021.

187. *Ibid.*, p. 1023.

188. *Ibid.*, p.1022.

189. *Ibid.*, p. 1022.

190. *Ibid.*, p. 1019.

191. *Ibid.*, p. 1019.

192. *Ibid.*, p. 1022.

193. A. Ellis, *op. cit.*, p. 167.

194. *Ibid.*, pp. 74 and 81.

195. *Ibid.*, p. 167.

196. *Ibid.*, p. 173.

197. R. Lazarus, *op. cit.*, p. 1022.

198. A. T. Beck, *Cognitive Therapy and the Emotional Disorders* (New York: International Universities Press, 1976), pp. 76ff.

199. A. Ellis, "Rejoinder: elegant and inelegant RET," *Counseling Psychologist*, 7.1 (1977), p. 78.

200. A. Ellis, *op. cit.*, p. 78.

201. *Idem.*

202. Vasubandhu, *op. cit.*, vol. 1, p. 165ff.

203. *Idem.*

204. A. Adler, *Understanding Human Nature* (New York: Greenberg, 1927) and *The Science of Living* (New York: Greenberg, 1929).

205. G. A. Kelly, *The Psychology of Personal Constructs* (New York: Norton, 1955).

206. A. Ellis, "Rational Emotive Therapy 1" and *Reason and Emotion in Psychotherapy* (New Jersey: Citadel Press, 1979).

207. V. Raimy, *Misunderstanding of the Self* (San Francisco: Jossey-Bass, 1975).

208. E. G. Williamson, *How to Counsel Students: A Manual of Techniques for Clinical Counselors* (New York: McGraw-Hill, 1939).

209. A. T. Beck, *op. cit.*

210. D. Meichenbaum, *Cognitive-behavior Modification* (New York: Plenum, 1977).

211. A. Ellis, "Elegant and inelegant RET," *op. cit.*, p. 74.

212. *Idem.*

213. *Ibid.*, p. 75.

214. Vasubandhu, *op. cit.*, vol. 4, p. 9. Definitions vol. 4, p. 15.

215. Streng, *op. cit.*

216. *Ibid.*, chap. 12.

217. *Ibid.*, 1967, p. 197.

218. Middle Path scholars may note that Nāgārjuna's analysis in the "Collection Chapter (*samagripariksa*)" of the *Fundamental Stanzas on the Middle Way* [MK] is a temporal analysis. While it analyses the ability of a cause and conditions (*hetu-pratyaya*) to produce an effect, it is not, as the title of the chapter might suggest, an analysis of how an assemblage or collection of causes and conditions is no better able to produce an effect than the causes and conditions considered separately. To be sure, one could very well use a temporarily structured analysis in a clinical context. It would be initiated by a series of questions related to the temporal relationships between the cause-conditions and their effects. One would be asking: Does the effect arise after the cause or simultaneously with it? One would then adduce logical paradoxes (*prasaṅga*) for these two alternatives. Candrakīrti's analysis is chosen here, however, as I believe it proceeds along a more *natural* and intellectually compatible basis. In other words, I think it can be more effective in a clinical setting. In fact, of course, the greater an analyst's repertoire of analytical formats the more flexible and effective he or she can be.

INDEX

255

non-contradiction, 46–48, 54,
56–57, 82
the reciprocal dependence, 76
principles of thought, 45
production
from self, 58–59, 62, 69, 98
from another, 60, 62, 69, 96, 98
from no cause, 97
modes of, 58
psychoanalysis, 183
psychology, 168
psychological analysis, xvii
psychological principles, 46
psychotherapy, xx, 183–184
psychotherapeutic practice, xviii
pudgala, 55
Putting the Cycle of the Philosophy in
Motion Sermon (Dhammacakkap-
pavattanasutta), 179

rāga, 169, 189
rage, 164
Raimy, V., 183
ramification, 105, 109, 155, 156
randomness, 105, 110
rate of concentration, 135
Rational Emotive Therapy (RET),
xix, 167–168, 176–181, 184–185,
188–189, 197, 206
reactive emotions, 119, 149, 168,
171–172, 182–183
realism, 118, 123, 188
reality, 31, 106
Reality Therapy, xix
reciprocal dependence, 74
recognition, 34
reconstruction, 5, 6, 11, 14, 24
reductio ad absurdum, 49, 93, 242
regret, 182

relational origination, 36, 39, 109,
155, 171
release, 9
resentment, 169
residues, 9
Roubiczek, P., 235
Ruegg, D. S., 243
rūpaskandha, 64

sahaja, 37, 86, 153, 174
sahakāripratiyaya, 176
saintly truths, 122
samādhi, 56, 106, 163–164, 166, 195
śamatha, 56, 106, 165, 166, 195, 248
samjñā, 34, 35
saṃskāra, 9, 189
Śāntarakṣita, 227
Śāntideva, 6, 30–31, 53, 88, 172, 226
satkayādṛṣṭi, 86, 121, 168, 172, 190
Saussure, F., 35
scholasticism, 113
self-acceptance, 186
self-control, 186
self-defined, 35
self-development, 164
self-organization, 102, 107
self-maintenance, 104
self-stabilization, 102–103, 107
sensory process, 101
serenity, 56, 160, 165
meditation, 106, 163, 165, 195
Schrodinger, E., xvi
siddhānta, 6
sign, 115, 117
simplicity, 25
simulation
model, xv, 20
modeling, 7
skandha, 71

ABOUT THE AUTHOR

PETER FENNER, PH.D.

PETER FENNER is a senior lecturer in Philosophy and Religious Studies at Deakin University in Australia. He has lectured in Buddhism and East-West Psychology at universities in Australia and the United States. His books include *The Ontology of the Middle Way* (Kluwer Publishers, 1990) and *Intrinsic Freedom*, with Penny Fenner (Millennium Press, 1994). He was a Buddhist monk in the Tibetan tradition for nine years and is presently offering innovative courses in Australia and the United States based on the perspective of the Middle Path (Mādhyamika) and Complete Fulfillment (rDzogs chen).

WISDOM PUBLICATIONS

Wisdom Publications is a non-profit publisher of books on Buddhism, Tibet, and related East-West themes. Our titles are published in appreciation of Buddhism as a living philosophy and with the special commitment to preserve and transmit important works from all the major Buddhist traditions.

If you would like more information or a copy of our mail order catalogue, and to be kept informed about future publications, please write to us at: 361 Newbury Street, Boston, Massachusetts, 02115, USA.

THE WISDOM TRUST

As a non-profit publisher, Wisdom is dedicated to the publication of fine Dharma books for the benefit of all sentient beings. We depend upon sponsors in order to publish books like the one you are holding in your hand.

If you would like to make a donation to the Wisdom Trust Fund to help us continue our Dharma work or to receive information about opportunities for planned giving, please write to our Boston office.

Thank you so much.

Wisdom is a non-profit, charitable 501(c)(3) organization and a part of the Foundation for the Preservation of the Mahayana Tradition (FPMT).

ALSO BY WISDOM PUBLICATIONS

MINDSCIENCE
An East-West Dialogue
The Dalai Lama, Herbert Benson, Robert A. F. Thurman,
Howard E. Gardner, Daniel Goleman, and participants in the
Harvard Mind Science Symposium

What is the subtle relationship between mind and body? What can today's
scientists learn about this relationship from masters of Buddhist thought?
MindScience explores these and other questions. Based on a day-long Harvard
Medical School symposium in which the Dalai Lama and other Indo-Tibetan
scholars met with leading authorities from the fields of medicine, psychiatry,
psychology, psychobiology, neurobiology, and education, *MindScience* offers
important new insights into the workings of perception, cognition, and the
mind/body concept.

$12.50, 152 pp.

JUNG'S PSYCHOLOGY AND TIBETAN BUDDHISM
Western and Eastern Paths to the Heart
Radmila Moacanin

Radmila Moacanin reconciles an ancient Eastern spiritual discipline with a
contemporary Western psychological system. She touches on many of the
ideas and methods of each and finds that, although there are fundamental
differences, both are vitally concerned with what Jung called "the tremendous
experiment of becoming conscious," successfully bridging the gap between our
deepest yearnings for spiritual fulfillment and the demands of our mundane life.

$12.95, 144 pp.